A Critical American

A Critical American

The Politics of
DWIGHT
MACDONALD

Stephen J. Whitfield

ARCHON BOOKS
1984

Composition by The Publishing Nexus Incorporated
1200 Boston Post Road, Guilford, Connecticut 06437

Printed in the United States of America

The paper in this book meets the guidelines
for permanence and durability of the
Committee on Production Guidelines for Book Longevity
of the Council on Library Resources

Frontis courtesy of Dwight Macdonald Papers, Yale University Library

Library of Congress Cataloging in Publication Data

Whitfield, Stephen J., 1942–
A critical American

Bibliography: p.
Includes index.
1. Macdonald, Dwight. 2. Intellectuals—United
States—Biography. I. Title.
E748.M147W48 1984   973.9'092'4[B]   84-16764
ISBN 0-208-02007-1

For Erica and Ben,
whose future will be shaped
by past politics

Tzu-lu said, "The ruler of Wei is waiting for
you to serve in his administration. What will be your
first measure?" Confucius said, "It will
certainly concern the rectification of names. . . . With
regard to what he does not know, the superior
man should maintain an attitude of reserve. If names are
not rectified, then language will not be in
accord with truth. If language is not in accord with
truth, then things cannot be accomplished. If
things cannot be accomplished, then ceremonies and
music will not flourish. If ceremonies and
music do not flourish, then punishment will not be just.
If punishments are not just, then the people will
not know how to move hand or foot. Therefore the
superior man will give only names that can be
described in speech and say only what can be carried out
in practice. With regard to his speech, the
superior man does not take it lightly. That is all."

Wing-Tsit Chan,
A Sourcebook in
Chinese Philosophy

Contents

Acknowledgments

Intellectual debts are difficult to tabulate and virtually impossible to repay, but at least the following persons may be cheered to learn that they are absolved of any responsibility for the judgments expressed in this book and for other errors it may perpetrate.

David Axeen was the first to draw my attention, while we were both graduate students, to the intellectual pleasures of reading Dwight Macdonald. I salute him— now Dean Axeen—across chasms of time and space. Francis and Bette Cole reinforced my interest and enthusiasm, and Richard King has given me the benefit of his own formidable knowledge and insight.

Special mention should be made of John P. Roche, who supervised an earlier draft of this work. Himself a reader of Macdonald's *Politics* during the Second World War, Roche never permitted his own subsequent deviationism to discourage me in any way from reaching my own conclusions. The pungency and shrewdness of his own politics were nevertheless bound to exert some sort of influence upon the pages that follow, both in remedying my ignorance and in enhancing my skepticism.

An undergraduate seminar I have taught on American political thought from the 1940s through the 1960s helped me to clarify some of the issues that Macdonald raised. Colleagues at Brandeis University, especially Lawrence Fuchs and Jacob Cohen, have always been available to talk about politics; and Grace Short has been decisive in creating an atmosphere conducive to work and thought.

After the basic research for this book was completed, Yale University Library made accessible Macdonald's papers—stretching across seventy-three feet, packed into 170 archival boxes. I am very grateful to the Yale University Library, and particularly to Judith A. Schiff, for permission to draw upon and quote from this archive, which has enriched my understanding of Macdonald's work and his place in our intellectual history.

For permission to reprint and adapt some earlier musings on Macdonald, I wish to thank the editors of *Journalism History* and the *Yale Review*.

Obligations of a personal nature are owed to Lee Hall; to Joan Whitfield; and to Ron and Deena Whitfield, whose children are celebrated on the dedicatory page.

These acknowledgments end on a bittersweet note. Dwight Macdonald read an earlier draft of this book and offered a unique critical perspective upon it, at once harsh and supportive, disputatious and genial. We met only once—but it consumed over six hours of an evening that he considered "exhaustive—and exhausting." I cherish the memory not only of the formal hospitality that he and Gloria Macdonald provided but also the mental hospitality he exhibited to the reconsideration of his own views. When he died almost a year ago, the nation's intellectual life was diminished; for no one was quite like him in the keenness, vitality, passion, and wit that characterized his responses to modern politics and culture. It is saddening that this book kicked too long in its womb for him to read it—and object exuberantly to it. But the sense of a far wider deprivation is tempered by the comfort of the example he set, the standards he maintained, and the glimpse he provided of a free and honest man.

I
Introduction

"Dwight Macdonald is not a snob, but a bit stupid," Leon Trotsky observed shortly before his assassination.[1] Since then the usual judgments have been the reverse. Educated at Phillips Exeter and Yale, Macdonald became a scourge of mass culture, a dissenter from popular taste and middlebrow acceptability, and therefore a target for those suspicious of "elitism." The caliber of his mind earned him a secure niche among the American intelligentsia. For over four decades he was intimately affiliated with its New York contingent, and in 1970 one poll included him among the nation's ten most eminent intellectuals.[2] Already by the 1940s he could be recognized in the satires of Mary McCarthy, helping to stimulate her "Portrait of the Intellectual as a Yale Man" and serving as the model for her character Macdougal Macdermott in *The Oasis*. So fully had Macdonald come to personify the American intellectual that, in Woody Allen's "The Whore of Mensa," the eponymous heroine offers to provide a private investigator with "photographs of Dwight Macdonald reading."[3]

There is nevertheless something problematic about his reputation, an unease that must be confronted by any scholar, such as myself, who intends to argue for Macdonald's intellectual importance and political pertinence. Especially in the era when his influence was greatest, from the end of the 1930s until the beginning of the 1950s, he was often reproached for the inconstancy of his ideology and the playfulness of his temperament.

Macdonald struck some of his contemporaries as a thinker-on-the-run, specializing in the hop, skip, and jump as he switched from Luce to Trotsky to Gandhi without breaking stride. He himself accepted the designation of "a systematically unsystematic thinker," quickly dissatisfied with any theoretical lens through which to perceive the data of experience. He was thus "always being surprised"; and the price he paid for his receptivity to change, as he once told Paul Goodman, was that he "couldn't remember anything more than three months back."[4] This fickle tendency—what Irving Howe once called his "table-hopping mind"—led others to assume that Macdonald was not fundamentally serious. An acquaintance from the 1940s, Freda Utley, later recalled that, "despite his intelligence and compassion, Dwight's lack of personal experience of men and politics in action, or of the trials, tribulations and sufferings of the greater part of mankind, stunted his political growth."[5] Macdonald himself acknowledged characteristically that he was "always ready to trade a formulation for a good wisecrack or for a bit of data that is logically superfluous but dramatically conclusive."[6]

This book is an attempt to rebut those charges by placing Dwight Macdonald's politics within a historical context, and may be interpreted as an extension of William Phillips' reminder that "to understand Macdonald one has to understand the way he reflected or reacted to the ideas around him and to the people who held them." It is then a study not only of ideas but also of intellectuals, in particular the left intelligentsia of New York. Especially in the period which began with Auden's "low, dishonest decade" of the 1930s and ended after the onset of the Cold War, Macdonald's politics were shaped, altered, and transmuted. He never learned to "write a book in cold blood."[7] Instead he practiced a journalism that was invariably lively and often inspired, which is why, in this study of his career, polemic looms larger than philosophy.

And Macdonald never lacked opponents. A liberal in the employ of Time, Inc., a cultivated democrat among the epigoni of Leon Trotsky, an opponent of World War II despite the bombings of Pearl Harbor and Rotterdam, an anarchist living in the welfare state, he was a maverick whose mind was inherently critical and skeptical and whose prose had a whiplash sting. His dissents thus illuminate the ambience in which he lived, just as the most constant element of his politics was his vigilant criticism of the Communists for having devastated so many dreams and of the liberals trapped in their own illusions.

Until the end of the 1940s his anti-Communism was accompanied by the quest for an alternative social vision and for viable tactics of institutional change. This key to his politics ceased to fit after the 1940s, although the emergence of the New Left in the 1960s revived his own expectations, at least briefly and more tentatively than two decades earlier. Macdonald never ceased to feel estranged from the dominant policies and values that guided American society, but that estrangement did not persistently form itself into political radicalism. He never became a conservative; and if he occasionally supported and voted for liberal candidates, such as Eugene McCarthy in 1968 and George McGovern in 1972, it was because of his opposition to American military intervention in Vietnam, not because he was sympathetic to the general aims of the Democratic party.

Nevertheless it must be acknowledged that Macdonald's career was not noteworthy for its consistency. If his politics exhibited more positions than the *Kama Sutra*, it must be added that there is nothing admirable about mental rigidity; and some flexibility and openness to experience are surely signs of a mature and serious intelligence, a mind aware of its own fallibility and limitations and of the need for growth and tolerance. There is no a priori reason to assume that the world will make sense at the age of fifty or seventy the way it did at the age of thirty, in large part because—as Macdonald himself pointed out in copping this particular plea—the world itself has changed so astonishingly. "Experience should change one," he told an interviewer late in his life.[8] Macdonald's transformations are not only explicable in the light of events and personalities, as this book attempts to demonstrate. Nor were his hairpin turns unique; and several intellectuals with whom Macdonald was to lock antlers, such as Archibald MacLeish and James Burnham, proved to be at least as flexible in their responses to world events. It might be added that half a dozen books have been devoted to the political philosophy of Walter Lippmann, whose incompatible views, as articulated in his major works, did not disqualify him from being taken seriously.

Trotsky's charge that Macdonald was "a bit stupid" has occasionally beeen repeated; one young critic, for example, referred to Macdonald's "usual amiable obtuseness."[9] Macdonald was certainly no theorist, no purveyor of overarching visions, no schematic thinker. But because he did not pretend to be able to swing for the fences does not mean that he need not have been played deep. His wit misled some of his readers into believing that his essays could be dismissed as jeux d'esprit, his cleverness invited condescension, and his remarkably engaging and lucid style denied to its author the indulgence granted to clumsier writers, who are often beneficiaries of the belief that behind that impenetrable prose they must be thinking. He practiced that sort of political and cultural criticism that flowed from his own taste. "One kind [of art] I like very much," he told an interviewer, "is something that seems to be light and worldly, and even frivolous, and yet really is quite profound. I mean Mozart's music, Jane Austen's novels, Tiepolo's painting, *The Importance of Being Earnest*—that kind of thing, as against Beethoven and Wagner—not that they're not great, too, in their own heavy way."[10] Macdonald's own apparent effortlessness should not inhibit appreciation of writings that, in their independence of judgment and incisiveness of voice, are among the finest that the past half-century of intellectual journalism has bequeathed.

For the pungency of some of his ideas has preserved his work as effectively as the salt of his style. Though he reminded a British critic of "the sort of mad professor who used to appear . . . years ago in boys' comics with a butterfly net and an air of poetic absent-mindedness,"[11] his one-man magazine *Politics* demonstrated not absent-minded madness but present-minded sanity. Admittedly he lacked the experience of some of the authors he printed: he never fought in Spain, he never faced martyrdom at Dachau, he never hammered out editorials from a Resistance basement, he rarely even bothered interviewing American politicians. But his elucidation of the modern predicament was a grim one, and his own gritty integrity helped account for the force of his criticism of the "free world" and of Communism.

For over four decades he tried to define no less than the condition of being an American. When a British journal introduced one of his pieces with a pious disclaimer—"We would not publish Mr. Dwight Macdonald's spirited and witty comment on American life were not Mr. Macdonald himself a good American"—the author was quick to take offense. "How do you know I *am* 'a good American'?" he demanded of the editor. "Patriotism has never been my strong point, and I don't know as I'd call myself A Good American. I'm certainly A Critical American" with a cultural and moral preference for England. Then, forgetting his own disregard of, say, native Stalinist objections to American policies, Macdonald concluded: "A Bad American, cynical and traitorous, might still make perfectly sound criticisms of his country. And if they were sound, it would be your editorial duty to print them."[12]

Sporting a goatee and loud shirts and ties, speaking with "the voice of a North American screech owl,"[13] virtually restricting his professional life to the borough of Manhattan, gracing an occupation noted for the obsolescence of its legacy, Dwight Macdonald nevertheless located the scars inflicted by totalitarianism, war, racism, and technology. He thus created a body of work which compels attention and admiration.

2
From *Fortune* to *Partisan Review*

Macdonald was born on 24 March 1906 in New York City, the descendant of several generations of Americans. His father was an attorney, but not a prosperous one, except while working for Triangle Films during the era of the Great War. Though Macdonald recalled being "hard up" from his midadolescence, his family was successful enough for him to attend Phillips Exeter from 1920 until 1924. There he formed a club whose other members also sported purple batik ties, monocles, and canes; their motto was "*Pour Épater les Bourgeois.*"[1] From 1924 until his graduation four years later, Macdonald attended Yale College. In a class record compiled four decades later, he remembered the college as a "stagnant backwater. . . . All my education was gotten by myself, from writing for all the publications going . . . [and] from a dozen or so friends who were as isolated as I was from the general spirit (philistine, barbaric) of our classmates and profs and the whole damn place (except the Elizabethan Club), and so we stuck together and educated each other." Among those friends was Fred Dupee, who recalled, "We were in search, very vaguely, of order and orthodoxy"; as F. W. Dupee, he was to become an English professor at Columbia University.[2] In 1927 Macdonald received a letter from a Phillips Exeter student, an aspiring writer who professed admiration for Macdonald's contributions to the *Yale Lit* and to the campus *Monthly*. James Agee would become one of Macdonald's closest and most cherished friends, no doubt because—as Agee observed at the age of seventeen—"we evidently write and think remarkably alike . . . Our likes and dislikes are the same," especially in a shared enthusiasm for movies.[3]

Macdonald's father had died in 1926; and after graduation, the necktie counter at Macy's beckoned. He went through a six-month executive training course but seemed bereft of aggressively mercantile skill. Alfred Kazin, who did not know Macdonald at that time, has alluded to a "personal restlessness" that drove Macdonald and Dupee toward radicalism in the 1930s; but the evidence is conjectural. How far Macdonald remained from the radicalism that would characterize his career could be measured by the eagerness with which he seized the chance to write for a new monthly magazine designed to celebrate the triumphs of American business. The year was 1929.[4]

The stock market crashed shortly before the first issue of *Fortune* appeared on the newsstands and soon after—with greater obscurity— the John Reed clubs were born elsewhere in Manhattan to encourage the creation of radical literature. The very commitment to capitalism of Henry Luce's second magazine forced its writers to probe the workings of the "free enterprise" system; and many of the gifted and curious journalists—Agee, John Kenneth Galbraith, Louis Kronenberger—did not like what they discovered. Macdonald, who had jeered at the earnestness of Yale's Liberal Club, observed that "*Fortune* breeds liberals, perhaps through the workings of the dialectical principle." As the liberals on the staff gradually enlarged their numbers and influence, and as their employer was himself racked between his own adherence to the business credo and his journalist's sense that Franklin Roosevelt was a bigger newsmaker than the Stock Exchange's Richard Whitney, *Fortune* drifted to the left.[5]

Archibald MacLeish, whom Macdonald called "the most valuable member of the writing staff," engineered the drift; Macdonald himself continued to drift. In 1935 he read Karl Marx for the first time and experienced "contradictory sensations of familiarity . . . and shocked discovery . . . Marx stripped the intellectual veil from capitalism," and a stylish disdain for business materialism could now be girded not with satire but with the fragments of a system. Engels, Luxemburg, Lenin, Trotsky, Hilferding, John Strachey's *Coming Struggle for Power*, and R. Palme Dutt's *Fascism and Social Revolution* accelerated the radicalization that Macdonald shared with so many of New York's intellectuals.[6]

Two sets of statistics indicate the severity of the crisis. Early in 1933 the New York Public Library announced that it would purchase only 50,000 books that year instead of the normal 250,000 volumes; and in 1935 the *New Masses* proclaimed that its distribution of International Publishers literature had skyrocketed from 50,000 pieces in 1929 to

600,000 in 1934. [7] The relationship here is of course not direct but rather emblematic of the meaning of the Depression. Farmers could puncture tires and spill milk cans on highways and then participate in AAA allotments; businessmen could engage in price-fixing so long as they slapped the blue eagle decal on their windows; workers lucky enough to get jobs might even join labor unions to ensure their survival in a competitive society. But how could intellectuals, especially those who had not met Jerome Frank or studied under Professor Frankfurter, confront the challenge that soup kitchens and slaughtered piglets so starkly represented?

When Roosevelt made fun of H. L. Mencken at a banquet, the New Deal critic vowed: "I'll get the son of a bitch."[8] Mencken's failure to do so was symptomatic. For by the late 1930s, flinging satiric darts at the booboisie seemed inadequate: the task was to expropriate the ruling class. Art could no longer be a refuge against the Babbitts: it had to be forged into a class weapon against them. Education could not be worn as a badge of superiority: it had to be utilized for agitprop. The historical task was to represent the proletariat, to speak for the silent ones; and when the capitalists retaliate, don't mourn, organize. Afraid to work with the Southern Tenant Farmers Union because its leaders are beaten and shot and driven off the land? Then help pay for Norman Thomas's trip down to Arkansas. Unwilling to risk imprisonment for criminal syndicalism in Harlan County, Kentucky? Then work for Theodore Dreiser's National Committee for the Defense of Political Prisoners instead. Afraid of passing out copies of the *New Republic* in Birmingham after what happened to Jack Conroy and Nelson Algren? Then contribute to those new magazines like *Anvil*, *Blast*, *Partisan Review*, and *Dynamo*.

For many writers picket lines were becoming as important as deadlines, but Macdonald tried to record his radicalism in the pages of *Fortune*. In 1936 he wrote a series of three articles on the United States Steel Corporation, attacking the company's ugly treatment of labor as well as its business inefficiency. Macdonald ignored managing editor Ralph Ingersoll's suggestion that the irrefutable blemishes be attributed to the late Elbert Gary. (The legendary former chairman of the board had conveniently died in 1927 when, or so it was said, he saw a blast furnace for the first time.) Macdonald prefaced his climactic final article with a quotation from Lenin's *Imperialism*, which was like waving a red flag in front of a bull like Thomas W. Lamont of J. P. Morgan and Company, the bankers of U.S. Steel. Before the presses finished rolling, Lamont convinced Ingersoll to rewrite the offensive article. An unflattering portrait of Gary's successor, Myron C. Taylor, was replaced with a more attractive one; and the deterministic prediction that monopolistic capitalism would give way to socialism was scuttled. Ingersoll himself considered Macdonald's views "informed and intelligent" and proposed the solution of granting Macdonald a byline. But Macdonald later admitted that, bored by *Fortune*'s brand of journalism, he "was looking for trouble and got it."[9]

Macdonald was then earning a handsome $10,000 a year, which he needed in part to support his mother. Despite his own tilt to the left, he got along well with Henry Luce himself. Indeed, when Macdonald married Nancy Rodman in 1934, Luce and his first wife were invited to the wedding; "and they came and it was nice and natural . . . I respected him because he was a man, a *mensch*, not a stuffed shirt or a hypocrite." Luce listened well, Macdonald added, and "was curious and alive . . . interesting and sympathetic." But their political disagreements were formidable. By 1936 the employee had learned all he could from the sort of journalism that Time, Inc. had largely invented. Buttressed by his own accumulated savings and by his wife's income from a trust fund, Macdonald resigned in protest in June.[10]

The next year he showed his appreciation by contributing to the *Nation* another three-part series, in this instance about Time, Inc. The valedictory note to his seven-year labor for *Fortune* was founded upon economic determinism. Macdonald explained that 1932 to 1936 was "the N.E.P. period in *Fortune*'s history, when it was necessary, in order to exist, to retreat temporarily from capitalism"—an odd metaphor, since the N.E.P. period in Soviet history was of course a retreat *to* capitalism. But, Macdonald noted, "as the depression lifted, Luce . . . began reminding his writers that *Fortune* was, after all, a business magazine."[11]

The former employee insisted that such a magazine could "flourish only within a healthy, self-confident capitalistic culture," because its editors' preoccupation with balance sheets and machinery was predicated upon the existence of a viable social order. For them, "how a corporation makes its money is the point, not how it functions as a social organism." But Macdonald assumed that the facts of an economy in disarray would increasingly threaten the plutocracy and that Time, Inc., "itself so deeply intrenched in the industrial-financial plutocracy," would impose "some super-rationale [sic] principle" like fascism upon "the stubborn, unwelcome facts." Although he unjustly called his recent employer "Il Luce," he conceded that it would be "premature to call Time, Inc. fascist. Proto-fascist would be more accurate." (Neither term was fair, or true.) Certain that capitalism could not heal its own self-inflicted wounds, Macdonald could not have realized that, according to one leading C.I.O. official, the truncated U.S. Steel series had so tarnished the reputation of the corporation that Taylor was forced to concede a major organizing victory to John L. Lewis in March 1937. Macdonald nevertheless repudiated "a commercial philosophy which regards money-making as the prime end of man" and hoped for the demise of a "vulgar and stupid" plutocracy.[12]

That same spring the editorial offices of the *New Republic* received a hefty tome entitled *The Case of the Anti-Soviet Center: A Verbatim Report Published by the People's Commissariat of Justice of the USSR*. This tran-script of the second of the great purge trials was reviewed in the April 7 issue by Malcolm Cowley, who had replaced Edmund Wilson on the editorial staff. Cowley had been shaken by his visit to Harlan County and, though he never joined the Communist party, frequently apolo-gized for its behavior.[13]

He conceded at the outset of his review that Leon Trotsky was both temperamentally uncongenial (for Cowley "never liked the big-city intellectuals of his type") and intellectually unappealing (for he "never liked Trotsky's books"). But what especially bothered Cowley was the exiled Bolshevik's unfortunate obsession with Stalin which, combined with the doctrine of "permanent revolution," might gravely weaken "socialism in one country" in a period of fascist peril. Because a Soviet defeat "would be a catastrophe from which I very much doubt that our present civilization would recover," and because a fanatic like Trotsky might stoop to an alliance with Hitler or Hirohito, the editor of the liberal weekly gave the Stalinist case against the "shirkers and traitors" the benefit of the doubt. Accepting "the scrupulousness and good faith of the Soviet authorities," Cowley noted that the trial record nevertheless revealed "a great deal of disaffection among the higher Soviet officials," which he attributed to the excessive zeal of the police, the oligarchic nature of the Soviet state, and an inept agricultural program in which "Russian peasants were collectivized too rapidly." He nevertheless urged friends of the Soviet experiment to remain loyal, even though visitors may suffer inconveniences like "bedbugs in the new hotel, ugly furniture, a telegram to Stalin that has to be written obsequiously."[14] As the

Bolshevik regime was consigning millions to torture, enslavement, and death in the Gulag Archipelago, Cowley was calling for patience. Macdonald was not one to write obsequiously to either Stalin or to the cultural custodians of the Popular Front, and he fired off a five-page letter to the *New Republic*. The magazine sliced it to one-third its original size, despite the author's protests, and printed it 19 May 1937. Macdonald, who suspected merely that Trotsky's rights had been infringed, did not deny the possibility of a conspiracy. He considered the trials an alibi for Soviet economic failures because the transcript "proves too much. No one could be as consistently malevolent as the Trotsky of these confessions. Word for word, the testimony dovetails into Stalin's foreign and domestic policy." He heatedly denied Cowley's implication that Trotskyism leads logically—in Communist parlance, "objectively"—to fascism, and he flaunted his own membership on the American Committee for the Defense of Leon Trotsky. Noting Cowley's objections to the resident of Coyoacan, Mexico, Macdonald confessed to his own "deep-seated prejudice in Trotsky's favor. It's hardly necessary to give my reasons. They are about the same as Mr. Cowley's."[15] Touché.

Mid-1937 thus marked Macdonald's debut into the politics of the left intelligentsia. Not only had he attempted to puncture *New Republic* illusions, but he had joined a committee whose purpose was "to safeguard Trotsky's right to asylum" and "to further the organization of an impartial commission of inquiry." Most of its members were not Trotskyists but social democrats and liberals, and a few—James Burnham, Sidney Hook, and Mary McCarthy— would cross Macdonald's path again.[16]

At this time Dupee, a former editor of the *New Masses* who had become disenchanted with Communism, introduced his old Yale friend to William Phillips. Phillips bore virtually all the stigmata of the radical New York intellectual; for he was the son of Jewish immigrants, the recipient of a B.A. from City College, an instructor of literature at New York University, and a former secretary of the city's John Reed Club. When the club had decided to sponsor a literary journal, Phillips had joined another young critic, Philip Rahv, an immigrant whose formal education ceased after high school, in editing *Partisan Review*. The John Reed clubs became a victim of the shift to the Popular Front; Granville Hicks sniped at the journal from the pages of the rival *New Masses*; and by the spring of 1937 Rahv and Phillips suspended *Partisan Review* for the second time.[17]

Without a magazine or a clearly defined relationship to the Communist party, Phillips invited Macdonald to his home one Sunday—Phillips' wife grandiloquently termed it "bloody Sunday"—when Rahv was also present. Macdonald was then leaning toward a confused brand of fellow-travelling Communism, and Phillips later reminisced: "We argued all day long, from morning to night. I had his back up against the wall. . . . My wife was yelling, 'Leave him alone, leave him alone, leave him alone, let him breathe'. . . . At the end of the day Dwight Macdonald finally gave in. Then we became practical and decided to put out *Partisan Review* again," without affiliation to any political party.[18] Less than a year after leaving *Fortune*, Macdonald decided to cast his lot with *Partisan Reveiw*.

Another friend from Yale, George L. K. Morris, also agreed to become an editor and was in fact the chief financial angel of the magazine from 1937 to 1943. Morris had founded the American Abstract Artists Group in 1936; apolitical, he was far more influenced by Arp than by Marx. Along with Dupee came a sixth editor, Mary McCarthy, who continued to contribute frequently, especially as theater critic, after resigning her position following the third issue. She was not especially interested in politics; but with her "wholly destructive mind," she made young Alfred Kazin "realize that it would now be possible to be a radical without any idealism whatsoever."[19] McCarthy felt contempt for the Communists because of "their lack of humor, their fanaticism, and the slow drip of cant that thickened their utterance like a nasal catarrh"; and she and Macdonald persuaded Phillips, Rahv, Dupee, and Eleanor French to attend the Second American Writers' Congress in early June.[20]

The earlier congress had been held in 1935 at the Mecca Temple, where chief speakers Malcolm Cowley, Granville Hicks, and Earl Browder argued the case for "Prolet-cult." But the 1937 convocation demonstrated the Communist party's new respectability: in Carnegie Hall Browder shared the speaker's platform with Archibald MacLeish and Ernest Hemingway, and class war was ignored in the attempt to bring decent and progressive writers together in an antifascist coalition. Granville Hicks, a party member since the Popular Front was inaugurated in 1935, was to preside over the craft session on criticism. Macdonald was not supposed to have attended since he had not joined the League of American Writers. But he and Mary McCarthy, who told Cowley that "we're just wreckers," convinced the others affiliated with *Partisan Review* to make Hicks's session the focus of their attack.[21]

Confrontationist tactics worked, for the notes from the session show that none of the proposed topics was discussed. Hicks was led so far astray from the agenda that when Joseph Freeman asked him, "Can I say one word about criticism?" Hicks replied, "No, Joe, that's one thing we can't discuss." Perhaps because Macdonald announced his support "for Trotsky," Hicks erroneously concluded that both Macdonald and McCarthy were merely agents of the anti-Soviet center who had dragged the other dissidents "into their [Trotskyist] net."[22] In fact they disrupted Hicks's session in order to repudiate the middlebrow tastes which awarded prizes to Carl Sandburg's *The People, Yes* and John Howard Lawson's *Marching Song*. They also came to protest the policy which, while a revolution was again eating its children, echoed Brecht's "*Erst kommt das Fressen, dann kommt die Moral.*"

Having had little real effect upon the congress, Macdonald then complained in a letter to the *Nation* that attacks upon the anti-Stalinist left were hardly a propitious tactic against fascism. He considered the congress "one long 'pep talk,' reminiscent of the rallies I used to attend at Phillips Exeter Academy on the eve of the annual football game with Andover. In this case, Andover was replaced by fascism [and] . . . as to the strategy—that was entirely up to Quarterback Stalin. Anyone who criticized his tactics was a Trotskyite wrecker and assassin (read: 'lacking in school spirit')." Henry Hart, who edited the published proceedings of the American Writers' Congress, predicted the following week that within a couple of years the League of American Writers would become the first "cultural organization, with its roots in the masses, that will actually have meaning and power." But Hart evaded Macdonald's charges of Communist domination and of extirpation of dissent from the left.[23]

A stronger counterattack was launched a few months later. Beneath the headline, "Trotsky Schemes Exposed," the October 19 edition of the *Daily Worker* announced that Rahv and Dupee had been "expelled from the Communist Party for their collaboration with 'known Trotskyites' at the June Writers' Congress."[24] Hicks continued to suppress his own "private doubts" about the party he joined in order not to hamper its "great struggle agianst evil"; and in the December *New Masses*, he criticized the *Nation* for being soft on Trotskyism. Hicks's form of revenge against the half-dozen "troublemakers, nuisances, obstacles in the way of people like myself . . . trying to fight Fascism" was to urge readers of the *Nation* to demand censorship of the "little clique of anti-Communists" who reviewed books and contributed articles to the liberal weekly.[25]

Though the *New Masses* included Macdonald as an advocate of "sterile, destructive and reactionary" Trotskyism, Hicks concentrated his attack upon a "particular turncoat" named Rahv, whom he accused of "general incompetence as a literary critic and . . . peculiar unfitness to review books on the Soviet Union."[26] That month *Partisan Review* was resurrected, and Rahv miraculously survived the disapproval of the *New Masses* to personify, if anyone did, the deracinated modern intellectual. Born in the Ukraine, he had changed his name from Greenberg to the Hebrew word for "teacher." He learned English well enough to write essays of exquisite beauty and force, and yet it is unlikely that he felt himself fully at home in a country whose polity and general culture he deplored. Toward the end of his life, Rahv wistfully remarked that he should have settled in Palestine. Instead he became the "Doctor Johnson of his small group of radical intellectuals." Alfred Kazin considered him "naturally a talker rather than a writer, a pamphleteer, a polemicist, an intellectual master of ceremonies and dominator who just escaped being entirely absorbed in parties, gossip and talk by his genuine absorption in issues and ideas. . . . To listen to Rahv talk with so much passion and scorn, the syllables crunching in his speech with biting Russian sincerity, was to realize that radicalism was Rahv's destiny." Indeed, by the time of his death four decades later, his Marxism had barely abated.[27]

With only 10,000 subscribers even in its heyday, *Partisan Review* was a small magazine, but there were those who loved it. Admittedly its editors and New York contributors possessed a rather low McLandress dimension, which a later social scientist defined as the number of seconds a person can concentrate on any subject other than himself.[28] Kazin once heard Rahv inquire "Who's in it?" of an author who handed him a short story. But another contributor, Leslie Fiedler, detected in *Partisan Review* a certain kind of bad manners, traditional in the Marxist movement . . . [a] strange mingling of malicious gossip and disinterested argument about ideas, which characterizes a social evening in New York. What the café is for Europe, such parties are for America." The special attributes that Irving Howe once assigned to the New York intellectuals were particularly true of their house organ—"a flair for polemic, a taste for the grand generalization, an impatience with what they regarded (often parochially) as parochial scholarship, an internationalist perspective, and a tacit belief in the unity . . . of intellectual work."[29]

Partisan Review attempted to restore that belief despite pressures toward disunity which had lasted for a generation. The satirists and muckrakers who had worked for the old *Masses* had sensed no disjunction between radical politics and avant-garde art: the Paterson pageant and the Armory show had seemed part of the same human epic; the capitalist and the philistine were virtually indistinguishable. But by the 1930s it was no longer possible to determine the ministers of the forthcoming revolutionary government from the guest list of a Mabel Dodge Luhan soiree, and *Partisan Review* grappled with this disjunction by mixing Marxist political analysis with poetry and fiction to which no political tests were applied. The radical manifesto "Toward a Free Revolutionary Art," signed by André Breton, Diego Rivera, and Leon Trotsky, was the exception; praise of Rosa Luxemburg following poetry by an Anglican monarchist named T. S. Eliot was more common. The magazine rejected not only "socialism in one country" but also culture in one country, and the Boulevard St.-Michel seemed more familiar than Sunset Boulevard. Hostile to the Comintern, scornful of bourgeois government, and comtemptuous of the vapid culture of the masses, *Partisan Review* helped make alienation (a term omitted as late as 1935 from the *Encyclopedia of the Social Sciences*) the most important noun in the esperanto of the intelligentsia.[30]

Addressing itself to estranged intellectuals rather than two-fisted proletarians, *Partisan Review* glided increasingly into predominantly cultural concerns. Phillips had never been primarily interested in politics, and Rahv gradually forsook political criticism without ignoring the social context of artistic creation. It was therefore quite misleading for Macdonald to have informed Trotsky that an editorial board that included Phillips, Mary McCarthy, and George Morris was "committed to a Leninist program of action," and quite natural for Trotsky to have considered the politics of the magazine "a little too vague." Writing to Macdonald early in 1938, Trotsky praised the intelligence and talent of the editors. But the heresiarch added that *Partisan Review* was "based on political, cultural, and esthetic disorientation." Its editors "have nothing to say," defending themselves against the Stalinists "like well-behaved young ladies whom street rowdies insult."[31]

Macdonald left the most telltale Marxist fingerprints upon his pieces, as in his description of the *New Yorker*'s urbane humor as "an accurate expression of a decaying social order." No doubt as a sacrifice upon the altar of journalistic responsibility, he even ventured south of the Hudson River to report his impressions of Washington, D.C. There he found that senatorial speeches were "entirely for the sake of form, a veneer over the crudity of the actual processes of government"; and he noticed the fasces on walls of "fortresses, and the enemy is the life of the people."[32] But trips to the capital of the class enemy could not satisfy Macdonald's hunger to edit a politically engaged journal; and his influence over the other editors can be gauged by Cowley's complaint that *Partisan Review*, far from adhering to its December 1937 declaration of nonpartisanship, had promoted "a grand anti-Russian campaign under the infra-red banner of the Fourth International." Cowley's attack on "their opinions solidified into hatreds" impelled Edmund Wilson to write his successor on the *New Republic*: "You're a great guy to talk about the value of a non-partisan literary review after the way you've been plugging the damned old Stalinist line, which gets more and more cockeyed by the minute."[33]

In the summer of 1939 Macdonald organized and served as acting secretary of the short-lived League of Cultural Freedom and Socialism. Its statement in the *Partisan Review* not only denounced the totalitarian cultural repression in Germany, Italy, and the Soviet Union, but also protested the abdication of critical independence among American intellectuals. "The deification of Hitler and Mussolini" was to be challenged not by "the deification of Stalin, the unqualified support of Roosevelt," but by a "socialist democracy." Otherwise, the league's statement asserted, the coming war would lead inevitably "to military dictatorship and to forms of intellectual repression far more violent than those evoked by the last war."[34]

At the same time a rival group of intellectuals, organized by Sidney Hook and nominally headed by John Dewey, appeared. The Committee for Cultural Freedom was officially as unimpressed by the merits of socialism as was the Dewey Commission on the Moscow Trials. Unlike Macdonald's league, it confined itself to criticism of foreign totalitarianism and its local offshoots like the German-American Bundists and the American Communists. Provoked by the Macdonald and Dewey groupings, four hundred friends of the Soviet Union expressed their conviction in the *Nation* that "Soviet and fascist policies are diametrically opposed" rather than linked by a common totalitarianism. The letter, which called the Soviet Union "a bulwark against war and aggression," unfortunately appeared a scant three days after the strains of "*Deutschland über Alles*" welcomed German Foreign Minister Joachim von Ribbentrop to the Moscow airport.[35] As Poland was carved up in a mutually acceptable fashion, and as secret police representatives planned to exchange their political prisoners across the Brest-Litovsk bridge, fascism was downgraded from Litvinov's "enemy of all progressive forces" to what Molotov reputedly called a "question of taste." The collapse of the Popular Front in America became quite palpable, and led Macdonald to smirk: "The liberal weeklies have indignantly flounced out of bed; such great minds as Granville Hicks and Heywood Broun . . . have ventured to express their suspicions of the Kremlin in public. . . . But all is not lost! Stalin still has Corliss Lamont."[36] The blitzkrieg the following spring drove Macdonald and his wife to organize a *Partisan Review* Fund for European Writers and Artists endangered by advancing German troops. Among those rescued was Victor Serge, a revolutionary intellectual then in Gascony, who recorded in his *Memoirs*: "Among us a squalid battle is beginning for places in the last lifeboat from the sinking ship. However, from Switzerland and America breathtaking replies reach us. These letters, from the poet J.-P. Samson and from Dwight Macdonald—two men I have never seen in my life— seem to clasp my hands in the dark. I can hardly believe it. So then, let us hold on."[37]

But for countless others, hands in the dark did not reach out in time. Macdonald himself could not foresee the possibility of effective aid without a prior social revolution and was appalled by the willingness of others to fight fascism under the existing bourgeois governments. With the liberal weeklies calling for active support of the Allies, and with the other editors on *Partisan Review* taking refuge in literary pursuits, Macdonald concluded that manifestoes were not enough. Only one political party seemed committed both to revolution at home and to anti- totalitarianism abroad, and in the fall of 1939 he joined the Socialist Workers party.

3
The Only Really Moral People

Expelled from the Politburo, then from the Bolshevik Party, and finally from the Soviet Union itself, hounded from Turkey to France to Norway to Mexico, revered by inmates of Stalinist labor camps who were executed with the "Internationale" on their lips, Leon Trotsky felt as reluctant to establish an alternative revolutionary organization as Milton's Lucifer might have felt to "reign in hell." But both fallen angels responded to exile with defiance; and in September 1938 the Fourth International was born in a village near Paris. Max Shachtman, a Warsaw-born founder of the American Communist party whose Trotskyist deviationism had resulted in his expulsion from the Comintern in 1928, presided over the one-day conference; and the American section of the movement soon established itself as the most influential wing of Trotskyism.[1]

Allen Ginsberg once took pardonable poetic license to wonder: "America[,] when will you be angelic?/ When will you be worthy of your million Trotskyites?" In fact membership in the Socialist Workers party usually hovered closer to a thousand. Having completed the "French turn," by which Trotskyists attached themselves to the Socialist party of America only to seek its destruction, they formed a new theoretical organ, the New International, under the joint editorship of Shachtman and James Burnham.[2]

Despite the minuscule size of the sect, the two editors could scarcely have differed more. "In Shachtman's appearance," Irving Howe has reminisced, "there was nothing impressive.... His was a face you'd expect to find in a bazaar or a diamond center: swarthy, expressive, shrewd." An ironist, Shachtman would have been a suitable writer and speaker within a larger movement, for "he was a superb though cruel debater; but in the cramped quarters of the sect he seemed uneasy as ideologue and leader." Shachtman himself remembered Burnham as "very scholarly . . . very urbane," with "a reputation for impersonality, impartiality, fairness, and logical thought." Burnham had been born into a wealthy Catholic family in Chicago, finished first in his class at Princeton, earned an M.A. at Balliol College, Oxford in English literature, and went on to teach medieval and Thomistic philosophy at N.Y.U. With such an exalted background, the dry and cultivated Burnham lent the Socialist Workers party a touch of class.[3]

Burnham had combined with his colleague in the N.Y.U. department of philosophy, Sidney Hook, and with a wiry labor organizer named A. J. Muste in heading an earlier version of the Socialist Workers party. But on his way home from a pilgrimage to Trotsky's house in Norway, Muste visited the Cathedral of Saint-Sulpice in Paris, where he saw a vision of Christ and renounced revolutary socialism in favor of Christian pacifism and a dose of Gandhian satyagraha. Hook's repudiation of revolutionary Marxism was less dramatic but nevertheless quite apparent.[4] By the summer of 1938 Burnham, scouting for new talent, persuaded Macdonald to contribute articles to the New International, which for awhile boasted a higher circulation than Partisan Review.[5]

Macdonald later recalled the attractive pull of the movement he joined in the fall of 1939: "It was the most revolutionary of the sizable left-wing groups. . . . There had been the moral shock of the Moscow Trials. . . . And above all . . . it was led by Trotsky, whose career showed that intellectuals, too, could make history." Yet intellectuals in a putative workers' party were not above suspicion; and the dominant figure in the organization, James P. Cannon, allegedly suggested that Macdonald might have been "happier as a sympathizer than as a member." The seriousness of Macdonald's commitment to revolution can be gauged from his choice of a party name: "James Joyce."[6]

This underground pseudonym was tinged with irony, for in his own twenty-minute colloquy with the real James Joyce in Paris in 1932, the author of Ulysses uttered little more than monosyllabic grunts.[7] Although a novice revolutionary, Macdonald hurled himself into sectarian controversy with intense speeches, prolific articles on party organization and strategy, and theoretical speculations. A colleague remembered him as a whirling dervish during the seemingly interminable debates, "spluttering angrily when he had objections to express," undeterred by Trotsky's acerbic remark from Mexico that "everyone has the right to be stupid, but Comrade Macdonald abuses the privilege." Resplendent in wool tweeds that draped his blue workshirt,[8] Macdonald made his debut in party circles with what must be considered a classic example of chutzpah: he told Leon Trotsky how to make a revolution.

How the Bolsheviks had gone astray had been a puzzling historical issue for the anti-Stalinist left. In 1937 and 1938, participants in this debate included Anton Ciliga, a former member of the Yugoslav Politburo; Max Eastman, Trotsky's translator and in Stalin's opinion a "gangster of the pen"; Victor Serge, the former editor of the Comintern's monthly; and Boris Souvarine, an early biographer of Stalin. All had suggested that the crooked road had veered toward Kronstadt, the port where the Bolsheviks had crushed an uprising of sailors and anarchists in 1921. As Serge himself noted, the Bolsheviks were committing mass executions there months after the revolt was over. Trotsky himself denied his own personal responsibility in the affair but defended the Politburo decision—in which he had concurred—as necessary to avoid counter-revolution. Almost two decades later Trotsky remained inflexible on the subject of Kronstadt: "I am ready to admit that civil war is not a school of humane behaviour. Idealists and pacifists have always blamed revolutions for 'excesses.' The crux of the matter is that the 'excesses' spring from the very nature of revolution, which is in itself an 'excess' of history."[9]

Coming in near the end of the debate, Macdonald called Trotsky's defense "disappointing and embarrassing." In effect he accused the embodiment of the Fourth International of not being a revisionist: "He seems to be more interested in defending Leninism than in learning from its mistakes." Macdonald further accused Trotsky of not being a liberal: "This refusal to consider aims, programs, theories, anything except the objective fact of opposition—this cast of mind seems to me dangerous." Trotsky well understood Macdonald's impulses and later commented, "He discovers that I am 'in reality' . . . a Macdonaldist." Meanwhile Shachtman and Burnham explained patiently that Macdonald had missed the main point: the October Revolution must not be discredited.[10]

For Macdonald to make his debut as a dissident in so sectarian a party was, he later reflected, "either high-minded or arrogant or naive or just plain schitzy, maybe a bit of each. It was also characteristic." The editors of the New International nevertheless printed his direct criticism of Trotsky's apologia, though it was to prove an early warning signal of Macdonald's refractory unsuitability as a revolutionist.[11]

The editors could not have known that, shortly thereafter, the Soviet secret police defector Walter Krivitsky met with Whittaker Chambers, who was struggling to break free himself. Immediately after agreeing that the Soviet regime had become "*faschistische*," Krivitsky made the gnomic remark the "*Kronstadt war der Wendepunkt*"— Kronstadt was the turning point. Soon thereafter Krivitsky was murdered, presumably by the G.P.U.[12] What did the vast scale of such crimes, stretching from the Arctic wastes of the Gulag, to the naval base in the Gulf of Finland, to the Soviet defector's hotel room in Washington, D.C., reveal about the character of the Soviet regime? What had it become? And should it be defended in case of aggression?

Trotsky classified the Soviet Union as a degenerated workers' state which still represented the progressive forces of history. Bolshevism had, after all, abolished private property; it had crushed the power of the Russian aristocracy and bourgeoisie. Its social system still reverberated with the echoes of the ten days that shook the world. (Never mind that, at the moment, the Russian regime was more interested in crushing "Trotskyism" than in subverting either fascism or capitalism.) Unwilling to confront the bleak possibility that there had been an irremediable *Wendepunkt* in the history of Bolshevism, the "Old Man" insisted from Mexico that Russia had to be defended—even by its victims. A small band of his ostensible disciples, including the poet Harry Roskolenko and Max Eastman's son, Dan, disagreed. This faction openly challenged Trotsky's position around the time Macdonald joined the party; and a movement founded by excommunicants resolved to cast out as heretics some of its own members.[13]

Sitting upon the dais were the eleven leaders of the party, each with a milk container in front. Ulcers were the occupational disease of the Trotskyists, though some of them mixed milk with rye to survive the week of sixteen-hour-a-day sessions. Roskolenko recalled, "As they talked, belched, coughed and spit, it looked more like a hospital for assorted disorders than a national convention for a future world order." Looming behind stacks of Internal Bulletins which were designed for members' consumption only, Shachtman raised his index finger as he intoned: "There are those who say that Stalinism is the result of the one-party rule. Like [Nicholai] Bukharin, I believe in multiple parties—one party in power, the others in jail!" Perhaps with inadvertent tactlessness, Shachtman had mentioned the name of one of the most famous victims of the *Yezhovschina*; and the hall echoed with cries of "Shame!"[14]

Then Cannon arose. The man who had been expelled with Shachtman from the Comintern denounced Burnham for his theory that the Soviet Union had ceased to be essentially a workers' state. Cannon had been the hero of the triumphant truck drivers' strike in Minneapolis in 1934; Burnham was really a tory fallen among Trotskyists, a theater-goer who wore hundred-dollar suits. And when Cannon, sipping the obligatory milk, threatened Burnham with expulsion "as a dangerous mongrel from our ranks," the philosophy professor caved in. In the spirit of the occasion, Cannon thereupon picked the Oxford-honed professor to deliver the expulsion speech against the Roskolenko-Eastman group which refused to come to the defense of the Soviet Union.[15]

That winter war came to the socialist motherland, not in the form of fascist invasion, but as an attack upon Finland. Macdonald was outraged at Trotsky's insistence that the strategic needs of the Soviet Union were more important than the independence of its neighbor. Harboring such sentiments, Macdonald had no more business being in the Socialist Workers party than Shachtman and Burnham, who in fact took Macdonald along with them when they led the "minority" faction out of the party in the spring of 1940. As a founding father of the Soviet Union, Trotsky had a deep personal stake in its survival; and Cannon agreed that even when in the clutches of a Stalin, the workers' state had to be supported. But to the "minority" the attack on Finland made Russia an imperialist aggressor and therefore made opposition obligatory, though Macdonald later noted: "'Support' and 'oppose' had no practical meaning, of course; the Cannonites didn't volunteer for the Red Army (which would have shot them); nor did the Shachtmanites go to Finland to fight under Baron Mannerheim." The Shachtmanites did however form the Workers party, taking the *New International* with them. Burnham compounded the confusion by resigning a month after helping found the new party, and he exited stage right—so far, in fact, that he later testified in court in support of the Department of Justice effort to declare the party subversive.[16]

In a revolution the goal is presumably to seize a citadel, if only symbolic, like the Bastille or the Winter Palace. But in the slapstick world of 116 University Place, the citadel was the room which contained the printing press. Thus in its first issue, *Fourth International*, the theoretical organ of the Socialist Workers party, blasted the Workers party "turncoats" for "stealing the name and the mailing rights of the [Cannonites'] magazine." The "revisionist and anti-Trotskyist" perpetrators of the "foul attack on the Marxist doctrine" were considered little better than common criminals: "Obviously, we are dealing here, not with an ideological dispute but a case of petty larceny."[17]

Macdonald's pen remained in the service of the cause, and he even wrote an anonymous leaflet which began as follows: "FOR A SOCIALIST DEFENSE AGAINST HITLERISM! People of the Bronx! Take the First Step! Elect Shachtman to Congress!" Though he was an editor of probably the most prestigious cultural journal in the Western hemisphere, the articles he submitted for publication in the Internal Bulletin were rejected with monotonous regularity. Macdonald was particularly admired by the members and fellow-travellers of the Trotskyist youth movement, a remarkable school for sharpening intellectuals' skills. From that school came graduates who were to make an impact on social science, literary criticism, and journalism: Howe, Martin Diamond, Leslie Fiedler, Irving Kristol, Melvin Lasky, Seymour Martin Lipset, Marvin Meyers, Isaac Rosenfeld, Milton Sacks, and Philip Selznick. Even Bernard Cornfeld, the future "Midas of mutual funds," was a fledgling Trotskyist. It was a heady experience for the young. "Never before, and surely never since," Howe wrote in his memoir, "have I lived at so high, so intense, a pitch, or been so absorbed in ideas beyond the smallness of self. It began to seem as if the very shape of reality could be molded by our will."[18]

Macdonald's greatest influence within the movement was probably as a regular contributor to the New International. His economics articles, replete with graphs and standard Marxist patois, have sunk of their own weight into oblivion. But the verve of his writing at its best often bubbled to the surface of "Reading from Left to Right," the columns in which he mordantly analyzed his fellow journalists. He wrote that Westbrook Pegler, for example, "has played shrewdly on the common American suspicion that ignorance is a guarantee of impartiality." He noted of Walter Lippmann, Dorothy Thompson, and a few others that "the apathy with which the columnists view the sufferings of the unemployed vanishes when they see the skillful use the New Deal is making of this misery." Turning book reviewer he thumbed through Earl Browder's The 1940 Elections: How the People Can Win, "in the hope that he would explain how 'the people' can lose an election which is decided by the majority of their votes."[19]

Yet Macdonald's political journalism in this phase of his career has proven quite perishable, because he could not turn his own ambivalence to advantage. His reasons for becoming a Trotskyist were primarily moral, yet he was unnaturally led to subscribe to an ideological framework which facilitated merely mechanical applications of doctrine to the effluvia of history. Such a course was unnecessary. Moralists like Randolph Bourne, Arthur Koestler, and Albert Camus have provided succeeding generations of readers with eminently salvageable pieces of political journalism, as have ideologists like Marx, Engels, and Trotsky; but Macdonald lacked the courage of his own Marxist convictions or the perceptions of a genuinely independent analysis. The residue of what his revolutionary colleagues considered bourgeois morality kept getting in the way.

Although he considered Roosevelt "a responsible bourgeois statesman" rather than "personally inhumane or villainous," he continually argued that Roosevelt and the liberals were not redeeming their own promises, a form of condemnation that Marxists would consider sufficient only for purposes of proselytization. Perhaps Macdonald was attempting to do no more than convince the unconverted ("I was a highly exoteric writer"),[20] but the suspicion nags that he could not have become a successful esoteric writer even had he so desired. Having become a revolutionist partially because he advocated the drastic redistribution of wealth and power, he kept complaining that those who had not followed his example refused to share their wealth and power.

Yet Macdonald imbibed just enough Marxism to make serious errors of political judgment. No longer a pragmatist forced to pick locks by trial and error, he now possessed a key to history; and the dialectic seemed to reveal the weaknesses of capitalist democracy but not its strengths. He was certain that an America which entered the war would have to become fascist, that only the monopoly capitalists could derive economic benefit from war, and that U.S. ruling circles after the war could not be other than "'Bonapartist' totalitarians." He observed abject apathy among the masses, but no signs of resiliency, no doughty willingness to fight for objectives that were more prosaic than Woodrow Wilson's "soap bubble vision of a League of Nations."[21]

Yet immersion in Marxism did not assuage his growing doubt of its curative powers. By the summer of 1940 Macdonald asserted that the failure to predict either Soviet imperialism or Nazi military strength was merely the "failure . . . to correctly apply Marxism."[22] But his own attempt to apply Marxism not only embroiled him in sectarian disputation but also challenged his capacity to accept the intellectual legacy of the movement. The necessity to understand totalitarianism eventually forced him into a more independent political analysis and deepened and extended his anti-Communism. But because Macdonald at first kept within intellectual furrows that had already been plowed, the origins of the debate over the postrevolutionary state must at least be fleetingly mentioned.

For orthodox Marxist-Leninists the question of the postrevolution-ary regime was not exigent until 1917; Engels's prediction, in his *Anti-Dühring*, that the state would simply "wither away" had presumably settled the matter. In 1917 Lenin felt confident that the workers could perform whatever administrative tasks would be necessary; and the new Commissar of Foreign Affairs, Leon Trotsky, exaggerated to make a point when he announced: "I will issue a few revolutionary proclamations to the peoples of the world, and then close up shop."[23] But manifestoes could not save the revolutions in Berlin, Bavaria, and Hungary; the capitalist states were predictably belligerent; the Politburo saw no reason to preside over the dissolution of the Czarist empire; "socialism in one country" meant the consolidation of one country's one-party govern-ment; and then the "dictatorship of the proletariat" ceased to resemble a temporary expedient.

Perhaps, then, Kronstadt had come earlier, at the very dawn of the twentieth century, when Lev Bronstein had discovered a pseudonymous, illegal pamphlet called *The Evolution of Social Democracy*. Its actual author was also in exile in Siberia; there Bronstein read Waclaw Machaj-ski's warning that intellectuals might make a revolution in the name of the proletariat but would actually use the workers' struggle to establish their own new class of privileged technicians, professionals, and officials. This startling notion, Trotsky later recalled, "gave me a powerful innoculation against anarchism." But despite the Bolsheviks' prohibition against the republication of Machajski's books, and despite *Pravda's* denunciations when he died in 1926 and again at the height of the purges in 1938, the idea refused to die.[24]

It reappeared in 1939 in Bruno Rizzi's *La Bureaucratisation du Monde*: "In Soviet society the exploiters do not appropriate surplus value directly, as the capitalist does when he pockets the dividends of his enterprise; they do it indirectly, through the state, which cashes in the sum total of the national surplus value and then distributes it among its own officials." Rizzi, a mysterious figure with sympathies for Italian Fascism, called this new form of society "bureaucratic collectivism" and considered it the prototype of less perfectly realized forms of political economy, such as the Nazis' *Gleichschaltung* as well as the New Deal.[25]

In his rebuttal Trotsky insisted upon the qualitative difference between the Soviet Union and other states; so long as capitalism had been eliminated, Russia even under Stalin was historically progressive. Trotsky continued to assume that the bureaucratic apparatus that had betrayed the revolution—and which was to organize his impending assassination—was "only an *episodic* relapse" in the healthy growth of the revolutionary struggle. To believe otherwise, Trotsky feared, was to conclude that the working class had been the victim of a vast deception, that Marxism was simply a species of "false consciousness" which continued to impede the leap from necessity to freedom. Naturally unwilling to shake the foundations upon which five decades of his life had been built, Trotsky nurtured the hope that the Second World War would bring social revolution in its wake. Otherwise, he conceded, faith in the proletariat as the heroic agent of history was indeed fraudulent.[26]

Neither Shachtman nor Burnham had quite the same stake in the notion of the degenerated workers' state as Trotsky, and their repudiation of that definition of the Soviet Union became the theoretical underpinning of the "minority" faction and of the Workers party. Rizzi had argued that a managed, planned economy was an improvement over laissez-faire capitalism, that even fascism could be judged as economically progressive.[27] This complacent tone Macdonald also detected in *The Managerial Revolution*, the book Burnham completed in 1941. Macdonald acknowledged general "agreement with Burnham on the emergence of a new non-capitalist and non-socialist form of society," but he considered Burnham's book "of small value" primarily because of its sloppy methodology. Macdonald nevertheless added that collectivism had to be considered regressive and that politicians rather than technicians wielded actual power in the totalitarian states.[28]

Unlike Burnham, he advocated social revolution as the only meaningful alternative to bureaucratic collectivism; unlike Trotsky, Macdonald realized that in fact bureaucratic collectivism had undermined dialectical materialism itself. As early as 1940 Macdonald was therefore groping toward a radicalism unencumbered by Marxist rigidity, toward a more intellectually supple critique of the leviathan state.

His deviationism was becoming serious enough to compel Trotsky himself to respond in August 1940. The "Old Man," then sixty years old, spent several days dictating an article critical of Macdonald's views.

Shortly thereafter a G.P.U. agent, Ramon Mercador, murdered him, the blood spattering on pages of Trotsky's manuscript on Stalin. In Howe's summation, "None of the great Marxist figures lived so dramatic a life . . . , none with so tragic a conclusion." Macdonald, who had never met Trotsky, was arrested after the assassination by New York City policemen while picketing the Soviet consulate.[29]

The reasons for remaining a Trotskyist were becoming shakier, as the movement itself struggled with factionalism promoted by its failure to anticipate or comprehend the sweep of events. Macdonald had understood Marxist doctrine to require only two kinds of social systems, so that if socialism did not triumph, capitalism would not decline. But in the America of Franklin Roosevelt, capitalism was proving remarkably resilient; in the Germany of Adolf Hitler, a totalitarianism was emerging that the dialectic had not accounted for; and in the Russia of Joseph Stalin, the socialism that had emerged was a desolate and malignant travesty of progressive dreams. When Macdonald attempted to analyze the Nazi economy from the perspective of bureaucratic collectivism, the *New International* chopped his article to one-sixth its original length. Its indignant author realized that heterodoxy rather than stylistic ineptitude was the cause of the problem; and in March 1941 he fired off an 8,000-word letter condemning the bureaucratic calcification of the Workers party itself and insisting upon publication of another 4,000 words of his piece on the German economy.[30]

Even though Shachtman could also be placed on the line running from Machajski to Rizzi to Burnham and Macdonald, and over a decade later to Milovan Djilas, and even though the Workers party did not consider the Soviet Union a workers' state, the sect could not repress its horror of deviationism. Shachtman warned Macdonald that "all our political activities must be carried on in consultation with the Party, and under its supervision"—including his editorial responsibilities for *Partisan Review*. Macdonald resented what he took to be a new and undemocratic policy. He found himself unable to share the conviction that Trotsky had voiced in 1924: "In the last instance the Party is always right."[31]

Angry with the *New International*'s refusal to disseminate his views of the German economy, and disenchanted with the "undemocratic organization" of the Workers party, Macdonald resigned that spring.[32] He wisely disregarded Shachtman's advice that resignation would be "a tragic blunder. . . . Outside the movement, you and your talents are as nothing." Distancing himself from such "metapolitics"—what Daniel Bell more correctly labeled "micropolitics"[33]—proved to be invaluable in the formation of Macdonald's unique intellectual journalism, and inconceivable had he remained a sectarian.

Withdrawal did not make Macdonald inconspicuous; by Trotskyist standards he was merely transformed from a dissident into a renegade. Drawn into a controversy in the *New International*, he wrote a letter that included a salutation which provoked the fury of editor Albert Gates: "We are ready to forgive Macdonald his failure to understand Marxism, economics, history or politics. But we cannot forgive his impudence. In addressing us as 'Dear Ex-Comrades' he again reveals his bad taste." Gates explained that Macdonald quit the Workers party because it "rejected his ideas, his ill-digested theories. . . . He wasn't greatly interested in the practical work that party was doing because in his opinion it was a waste of time and effort, since it didn't conform to his 'theories'. . . . It gave far more time to him as an individual than was warranted."[34]

Macdonald disagreed. He pinpointed the extirpation of dissent as the most offensive aspect of Trotskyism. Intolerance, he charged, was a reflex of the desperate attempt to demonstrate seriousness, just as cannibalism practiced on other radical sects created a sense of accomplishment and a feeling of importance. Hence Macdonald detected delusions of grandeur, which he labelled "political pathology." For example, a Trotskyist youth leader, riding a Fifth Avenue bus, once pointed to the skyscrapers and commented, "Some day that will all belong to us . . . "[35] Macdonald concluded that Trotskyism was merely "a variant of Stalinism" rather than its only potentially effective opponent: "The question of party organization and party democracy is as important as that of program," and ethics as well as the dialectic had to be reconsidered.[36]

The thrust of his criticism was best revealed in the aftermath of a perverse application of the Smith Act. In 1941 Troskyists were falsely accused and convicted of conspiring to advocate the violent overthrow of the American government in behalf of a foreign government that loathed and killed their comrades. Cannon, other leaders of the Socialist Workers party, and key members of Minneapolis Teamsters Local 544 were then confined to a federal penitentiary. Though Macdonald had split from the Shachtmanites three years earlier and the Cannonites four years earlier, he not only excoriated the "monstrous frame-up by the Roosevelt

Administration" but asserted that, except for their support of the Soviet Union, he agreed with very much of the victims' political program.[37]

Yet Macdonald, reading Joseph Hansen's account in *Fourth International* of Cannon's journey to Sandstone Prison, was struck by the political pathology of Trotskyism. Hansen had concluded from Cannon's conversation that future historians would ransack the back files of the Socialist Workers party newspaper, the *Militant*, in preference to archival backwaters like Hyde Park; and Macdonald then imagined what such a history of his own era would resemble. The temptation to quote him is irresistible:

CHAPTER IX: 1929 DEPRESSION BEGINS, JAMES P. CANNON AND MAX SHACHTMAN LEAVE COMMU- NIST PARTY. CHAPTER XII; CIO LAUNCHED, LITTLE STEEL STRIKE, JAMES P. CANNON AND MAX SHACHTMAN LEAVE SOCIALIST PARTY. CHAP- TER XV: NAZI-SOVIET PACT, WORLD WAR II BEGINS, JAMES P. CANNON AND MAX SHACHTMAN LEAVE EACH OTHER.[38]

But what especially bothered Macdonald was Cannon's allegation that John Dewey had improperly injected his own antisocialist politics into the independent investigation of the charges against Trotsky. Cannon had informed Hansen: "When the history of this epoch is writ- ten . . . they'll discover that the only really moral people were the Trotskyists." To which Macdonald replied: "From what I know of Can- non and his followers, which is considerable, and from what I know of Dewey's public behavior, which is less but sufficient, it is not Cannon who has the right to talk about morality."[39]

Cannon knew of Macdonald's article and responded in a series of letters to his wife; the tone of his remarks suggests a posturing directed at party comrades if not at posterity. Cannon tried hard to be generous: "I am ready to admit . . . that Macdonald is not motivated by personal malice or jealousy . . . for I believe that he is sincerely stupid and is only guilty, at the most, of indulging his cultivated knack for misunderstand- ing things and his faunlike impulse to play pranks on inappropriate occasions."[40] Cannon reserved judgment on the question of whether his own name would be accorded more space in history books than Roos- evelt's, and he questioned Macdonald's credentials as a supporter of much of the Trotskyist program: "Such people are not worth very much. Their 'convictions' are on the side of the proletarian revolution but all their deep-rooted instincts, feelings and spontaneous reactions—their heart and soul—are in the other camp." Finally he reiterated his conviction that Trotskyists were morally superior to "other conscious political elements" and advised "petty-bourgeois critics" like "Macdonald and his ilk" to restrict "their moralistic sweatings to eternal abstractions."[41]

The salvos ceased a year later, with agreement of sorts. Cannon blasted certain dilettantes of revolution and named Macdonald "the archtype [sic] of these political Alices in Wonderland," and Macdonald approved the choice of metaphor: "Alice is presented in Carroll's book as a normal and reasonable person who is constantly being amused, bewildered or distressed by the fantastic behavior and logic of the inhabitants of Wonderland. . . . [In] the Trotskyist movement, I must confess I often felt like Alice."[42]

4
Farewell to *Partisan Review*

Unlike James P. Cannon, Irving Howe of the Workers party had become an authentic and adept polemicist, already by the age of twenty-two. Imitating Macdonald's own proclivity to examine the latest trends in journalism, the young contributor to the *New International* turned his attention to *Partisan Review* early in 1942 and detected the fissures that would soon widen into irreconcilable editorial differences. He deplored the magazine's increasing preoccupation with literature and branded Macdonald, who opposed the war of rival imperialisms, "intellectually dishonest" for accepting "a rotten compromise with Rahv and other pro-war editors." Yet Howe faulted Macdonald not only for collaborationism with the class enemy but also for his increasingly daring attempts to break the intellectual mold of Marxism: "As Macdonald brings up the rear guard of the left intellectuals drawing away from revolutionary Marxism . . . the magazine—to the degree that it notices politics at all—is concerned less and less with its former task of smiting those ex-radicals who jump onto the war bandwagon." *Partisan Review*, Howe added rather haughtily, is "more and more involved with Macdonald's personal 'theoretical' predilections—his fatal desire to criticize what he has failed to study and understand sufficiently: Marxism."[1]

Macdonald conceded differences with Phillips and Rahv but could not share a characteristically sectarian demand for monolithic unity: "I've never believed this was a sensible way to organize a political party which hopes to achieve democratic social ends. And I'm even more sure, as a professional journalist, that it's not the way to produce a good magazine of ideas." Yet he was clearly troubled by Howe's insistence that *Partisan Review* take a stand against the war; he simply could not effectuate such a stance. As a critic of American entry in the Second World War, Macdonald was outnumbered on the editorial staff. He also feared that more vigorous opposition to the imperialist war would invite government repression of *Partisan Review*. Nor could he see value in his resignation, since it would abruptly cut off whatever dialogue then existed among the editors, whatever hope could be nourished for a more critical editorial line against the war. Troubled by the accuracy of Howe's attack, Macdonald lamely accepted the recent editorial definition of the journal as "primarily a cultural magazine" and saw at that time no alternative to his awkward position.[2]

Macdonald, Rahv, and Phillips worked in harness so long as the defense of high culture was at stake. *Partisan Review* had been reborn in order to free culture from political constraints, to defend the modernism of James, Eliot, Kafka, Proust, and Joyce from the flaccid "progressive" standards of the League of American Writers. Macdonald was particularly sensitive to what he considered the American brand of *Kulturbolschewismus*, the condemnation of literature for its politically harmful consequences.

In 1935 Archibald MacLeish had informed the *Modern Monthly* that he would oppose participation in the next war "under *any* circumstances. There is only one possible position against the menace of militarism: absolute hostility." He further predicted that "the propaganda machinery [would] whirl up the dust of its own choosing" without any connection to real aims of a future conflict. But in 1940 the poet began to promote a liberal definition of war aims and, as Librarian of Congress, attacked the "irresponsibles" of the 1920s whose literary expression of disillusionment did "more to disarm democracy in the face of fascism than any other single influence."[3]

Both Edmund Wilson and Macdonald found MacLeish's remarks obnoxious. Wilson mounted the attack with greater precision: (1) MacLeish had not read the fiction of the 1920s very carefully, since novelists like Hemingway had hardly challenged the virtues of courage and gallantry; (2) MacLeish "might be trying to prepare us for a new set of political slogans . . . from the same sort of sources as those that launched the publicity of World War I. . . . It is not very assuring, at this moment of strain and excitement, to find the Librarian of Congress making a fuss about 'dangerous' books"; and (3) if antiwar novelists like Erich Maria Remarque had been so influential in Germany, as MacLeish implied, then the *Wehrmacht* would not have taken Paris. "If this school of writers in general had the importance which Mr. MacLeish assigns to them," Wilson concluded, "we should have had no second World War."[4]

Macdonald considered MacLeish's speech to the American Association for Adult Education a sign of "the drift toward totalitarianism"; but he leveled his attack primarily at Van Wyck Brooks, whose "Primary Literature and Coterie Literature" vilified not merely pacifist literature but the very modernist tradition which *Partisan Review* had been committed to defend. Characteristically ignoring the logicians' injunction that an ad hominem argument is invalid, Macdonald charged: "Up to 1920 he urged American writers to be more critical of bourgeois society; in the twenties they followed his advice, found society rotten, said so; today, although (or perhaps because) society is incomparably more rotten, Brooks wants the verdict reversed." Proust, far from being a "spoiled child" unable to cope with "the common life," and Joyce, far from being "the ash-end of a burnt-out cigar," had demonstrated "the over-mastering reality of our age: the decomposition of the bourgeois synthesis." Macdonald saw through Brooks's need to psychologize rather than analyze the architects of the modern imagination: "The official critic, since he is attempting to defend what is historically indefensible, is forced at every turn to attribute petty and base motives to the serious writers of his day."[5]

Macdonald's warning against American versions of Goebbels's *Kulturbolschewismus* was frenzied by contrast to the response of other intellectuals to the MacLeish and Brooks speeches. *Partisan Review* conducted a symposium based on Macdonald's article, and William Carlos Williams's reaction was typical. He considered Brooks' address so "ludicrous" that he had trouble "taking it seriously. But you may be right, such things should be noticed, as when a locomotive goes off a track. . . . I prefer to drive by." Lionel Trilling agreed with Macdonald's literary judgments but doubted that Americans would "willingly enter the moral stuffiness that Brooks desires. And I do not share Macdonald's assumption that socialism promises a moral and literary regeneration."[6]

Edmund Wilson, who had completed the journey that had taken him from Axel's castle to Petrograd's Finland station, offered to write Brooks a letter of reprimand. But Macdonald was dissatisfied: "The responsibility of writers on *our* side of the fence [is] to stick their necks out now, to speak publically [sic] against this sort of thing. Personal letters don't do the job at all. (You'll recall we had the same disagreement at the time Cowley made his smear attack on P.R. in the New Republic—and I still think the personal letter you wrote him at the time . . . was the wrong tactic.)" Wilson, who remained adamantly opposed to the Second World War even after Pearl Harbor and who joined the *New Yorker* eight years ahead of Macdonald, saved a lampoon of Brooks for a short story, "The Milhollands and Their Damned Soul," which appeared in 1946 in *Memoirs of Hecate County.*[7]

Other writers enlisted in the campaign. The Trotskyist James T. Farrell classified Brooks and MacLeish as "ideological policemen" in the "league of frightened Philistines," and H. L. Mencken wrote Farrell that he regretted not being twenty years younger, so that he could tackle "Brooks and company and give them something to think of." The Stalinist V. J. Jerome condemned—in 1940, of course—a certain Librarian of Congress as well as other prowar authors who "fawn when their imperialist masters crack the whip."[8] But if Irving Howe is correct that New York's radical intelligentsia in this period not only "helped destroy . . . Stalinism as a force in our intellectual life" but also cast "the kinds of rhetoric once associated with Archibald MacLeish and Van Wyck Brooks . . . into permanent disrepute,"[9] then Macdonald deserves some of the credit.

Immediately after the challenge seemingly posed by Brooks and MacLeish had passed, Leslie Fiedler wrote that an "atmosphere of . . . self-congratulation" hovered around the offices of *Partisan Review.*[10] But as its learned editors should have known from *La Chanson de Roland*, blowing one's own horn can be a sign of trouble. As the threat to culture became less exigent, the politics of war tore the editorial staff asunder.

Commentary editor Elliot Cohen once told his successor, "The main difference between *Partisan Review* and *Commentary* is that we admit to being a Jewish magazine and they don't."[11] Four of the six founding editors of *Partisan Review* in 1937 were Gentiles. But it was surely no accident—to borrow a favorite Communist phrase—that *Partisan Review* had a cosmopolitan flavor uncommon in literary journals, that its definition of politics could not be encompassed by the quadrennial transactions of Republicans and Democrats, and that it helped make "alienation" a main entry in the lexicon of the contemporary intelligentsia. Nor was it mystifying that as Hitler's legions extended the destruction of life and culture already begun in central Europe, Rahv and Phillips virtually ceased their criticism of American society and supported the attempt to crush the Nazi juggernaut. The radicalism which

Kazin considered Rahv's destiny was redefined as the mere publication of T. S. Eliot, a subtle and anguished poet who in the new Dark Ages submitted two of his *Four Quartets* to the magazine.[12]

By contrast Macdonald was more consistent—an attribute whose value he often doubted. He could not suppress his contempt for the New Deal, nor keep his socialism in abeyance until the collapse of the Third Reich. Until 6 August 1945 he opposed the Second World War, not because he was a pacifist, but because he was a revolutionist convinced that war would mean fascism for America unless his comrades were in charge of its conduct. Macdonald vilified the bourgeois governments not because he wished their fascist enemies to triumph but because he believed that only proletarian governments could eliminate Hitler and Mussolini.[13]

The British poet Stephen Spender considered Macdonald unrealistic and, given the improbability of socialist revolution, guilty of "excessive fatalism." Spender's good sense deserves to be repeated: "The implication is that the world is going to be punished, and very severely, because it will not follow the policy of *Partisan Review*. I admire the generosity of mind which has already presented the British Empire to Hitler before he himself has taken it, and which promises him the Americas, unless the democratic powers adopt the correct attitude in an argument."[14]

Luftwaffe bombs were then exploding around the *Horizon* offices in London; but Macdonald remained undeterred, still insisting that only his program could defeat Nazism. He advocated the overthrow of Winston Churchill, who differed from Neville Chamberlain "only in being more energetic, able, and more realistically aware of the threat offered by Hitler to British imperialism." This revolutionary goal could be achieved only through "a bitter armed struggle"; and Macdonald suggested, while the battle of Britain was still raging, "organizing strikes in munitions plants" as a starter. Macdonald was unwilling, however, to help inaugurate a similar program in his own country, with its thousand Trotskyists: "I see no prospect of socialism in America. But I do see, both here and abroad, in the coming years the probability of more than one 'revolutionary situation.'"[15] In 1940, with the apparent success of the blitzkrieg, with all quiet on the eastern front, Macdonald assumed that the only political alternatives were fascism or revolutionary socialism. He had committed the fallacy of the excluded middle.

During that bleak summer Macdonald argued the "case for

socialism" in the starkest terms: "The choice . . . is not between victory under Willkie-Roosevelt or defeat by Hitler, but rather between defeat under Willkie-Roosevelt or victory under a native fascist regime (perhaps led by one of those individuals)." To this dismal prospect Macdonald contrasted the vision of a streamlined socialist economy which would sensibly dispense with "the antiquated mummery of profits, interest, gold reserves, etc." He predicted far less repression under socialism, since only "the former ruling class—a small minority" could possibly raise objections. Readers of *Partisan Review* were assured that fifth columns would emerge more readily in Nazi-occupied territory because their "class brothers" would rule America. Woodrow Wilson might well have been envious of Macdonald's confident appeal for "a crusade which would take the *offensive* for a positive social good, for a form of society which is historically progressive, which does not conflict with but carries further industrial progress, and which for the great mass of people represents a giant stride towards a better kind of life." Macdonald's article was an embarrassing manifestation of the dualism of heart and head. Several paragraphs later he admitted that "the revolutionary movement has suffered an unbroken series of major disasters in the last twenty years, and we must examine again, with a cold and sceptical eye, the most basic premises of Marxism."[16]

A year later, with England bloodied but intact, and with Churchill speculating about "a favorable reference to the devil in the House of Commons" in favoring aid to the new Soviet ally against Germany, Macdonald could not transcend the either/or of his earlier analysis. He brought Clement Greenberg, who was not a Trotskyist but a rather apolitical art critic, onto the editorial staff of *Partisan Review*, and then persuaded him to coauthor "Ten Propositions on the War."[17]

Max Eastman jibed that the "Ten Propositions" had "as much to do with the realities around us as a virgin birth of Christ made blissful by the twilight sleep,"[18] and no wonder. What is one to make of an article which assures its readers that "social revolution in England or America . . . would most probably be short and relatively peaceful and lead to an immediate intensification of the war effort"? Which claims that the New Deal is "so discredited by its military incapacity," and the Churchill government "so demoralized by its own mistakes," that they would "surprise everybody with the suddenness and completeness" of their disintegration? Which blandly assumes that the counterrevolutionaries, being such inept chaps, such plodding organizers, would allow the socialists enough time to wage war effectively against the German General Staff? Whose authors cannot find "organized leadership for such a revolutionary policy as we advocate," but nevertheless assert that "while this is a serious lack, it is not a fatal one"? Pundits and prophets are entitled to a share of mistakes, but how would the soldiers who learned new and awful geography lessons at Omaha Beach and the Ardennes have reacted to the assertion that "the democracies cannot defeat Hitler by force. They cannot get close enough to slug it out"?[19]

The most sustained criticism of the "Ten Propositions" came from a fellow editor, Philip Rahv. A Marxist purist, he shared a hatred of Stalin, a fear of postwar imperialism, and a preference for socialism over capitalism. But the Nazi threat was paramount, and he therefore endorsed Arthur Koestler's epigram as a summation of his own attitude toward the Second World War: "We are fighting against a total lie in the name of a half-truth."[20] Recognizing that Macdonald and Greenberg represented "no movement, no party, certainly not . . . the working class, nor even . . . any influential group of intellectuals," Rahv asserted that their propositions were an echo of Lenin's "revolutionary defeatism." Yet even Lenin's strategy assumed "the approximate identity of the social system in all the belligerent states and . . . that the defeat of a country would not result in the loss of its national independence, in its being swallowed up by the victor."[21]

Insinuating that Rahv "apparently takes seriously Roosevelt's fireside chats," Macdonald and Greenberg compounded the confusion over the imminence of revolution as a viable alternative to blood, tears, toil, and sweat. "The *objective* factors for socialism have matured," the authors of the "Ten Propositions" claimed, but unfortunately the American workers were not "*subjectively* in a revolutionary mood." Therefore "politically minded writers, including Rahv" were obligated to quicken the revolutionary consciousness of the masses rather than accept "the shabby hypocrisy of the present British and American war aims." Their imputation to Rahv of a Macbeth-like desire "to profit by the crime without committing it,"[22] to defeat fascism and create socialism without doing anything effective toward those ends, was surely at least as applicable to those who withheld support of the Allies. "Ten Propositions" was documentary evidence for the doctrine of revolutionary socialism in one editorial office: the objective factors for revolution were absent, but two editors were subjectively in a revolutionary mood.

By 1942 Macdonald was backpedalling. While denying that

Churchill and Roosevelt could fight the Axis effectively, he conceded the possibility of "a purely military victory," but added that the social and political struggles were important too.[23] He had asked the poet Karl Shapiro to tell the readers of *Partisan Review* how undemocratic the United States Army was, but oddly enough Shapiro could find "no undue patriotic and political pressures, unfair treatment of Negroes, or poor relations between officers and men."[24] Macdonald's Marxist prognostication had been skewed: the New Deal at war was "not fascistic, or even developing with any speed in that direction: like the Churchill government, it finds its chief mass base in the labor movement; civil liberties have been preserved to a remarkable degree."[25]

But what continued to haunt Macdonald was the ambiguity of war aims, the apparent slaughter wthout any purpose except the sinister greed of monopoly capitalism. Roosevelt had not articulated coherent war aims, and had sought instead to depoliticize the conflict. Into the vacuum stepped the people Macdonald loved to call "liblabs"—he claimed the term was of British provenance— who supplied the humanitarian rhetoric to mask the designs of predatory capitalism. Sixteenth-century France had been racked with the War of the Three Henrys; the twentieth century, Macdonald feared, might suffer the consequences of the War of the Two Henrys, Henry Luce and Henry Wallace.

In 1941 *Life* had published a lot of Luce talk about the United States as both "the dynamic leader of world trade" and as the legatee "of all the great principles of Western civilization—above all Justice, the love of Truth, the ideal of Charity." The Time, Inc. publisher predicted the coming of "the American Century," in which the United States would become "the powerhouse from which the ideals spread throughout the world." The following year vice president Henry Wallace contrasted this vision of the American Century with a vague formulation of his own: "I say that the century on which we are entering—the century which will come out of this war—can be and must be the century of the common man." But Wallace never managed to explain how the expansionist capitalism he championed could be harnassed to the worldwide social revolution with which he sympathized. Macdonald was suspicious of both visions. If Henry of Navarre could consider Paris worth a Mass, then the publisher of *Fortune* had adopted the creed of humanitarian internationalism in order to secure Asian markets. In Macdonald's eyes the American Century blurred with the century of the Common Man, and liberal imperialism took shape as the most plausible product of a United States victory.[26]

Here Macdonald showed himself an attentive reader, for he could not have known then about the letter Luce sent to Wallace, wondering how the American Century of Time, Inc. differed from the vice president's Century of the Common Man. Wallace admitted that he could recall nothing substantial in the publisher's essay "of which I disapprove."[27]

But Macdonald could console himself only with increasingly far-fetched hopes of revolutionary change. Rahv and Phillips, however, felt the need for some alternative to revolutionary defeatism and by early 1943 had found a counterweight to Macdonald—Sidney Hook. When Kazin called the N.Y.U. philosophy professor "the most devastating logician the world would ever see," he seems to have overlooked, for starters, Aristotle, St. Anselm, St. Thomas, Duns Scotus, Mill, and Russell. Yet it may well have been true that "when it came to close argument, Hook was unbeatable; one saw that he could not imagine himself defeated in argument." Few figures in American academic life were more valiant; his early opposition to Stalinism caused the young instructor to be hissed by students as he walked through Washington Square in the 1930s. And no philosopher was ever more feisty. "I've had a wonderful week," Hook once told a friend, "I've had a fight every day."[28]

When he inaugurated *Partisan Review*'s "New Failure of Nerve" series in the January-February issue, Hook had not contributed any political articles to the magazine in two years; but like Macdonald, he was appalled by the political and intellectual impoverishment of American radicalism. He did not have in mind the Communists, whom he dismissed as "little more than the American section of the G.P.U."; and he saw no further need to thrash "obscurantists" like MacLeish. Hook would have liked to analyze the policies of the Socialist Party "if its declarations were sufficiently clear."[29] The party wanted an Allied victory and a German defeat; but as one Socialist evangel put it, "it was not our job to say so." To keep its remnants together, the party ignored or left ambiguous its foreign policy positions and concentrated on domestic injustices.

But Hook did criticize "romantic revolutionists," or rather "Bohemian revolutionists, since outside of Dwight Macdonald's lively pages in *Partisan Review*, the view is proclaimed mainly by half-sober blusterers at cocktail parties." Hook unleashed his scorn at "theoreticians without practical or theoretical responsibility . . . [who] say that a socialist government has the best chance to defeat a Fascist enemy and then conclude illogically that a democratic capitalist government which hasn't the same good chance, has none at all, and that whatever chance it has cannot be increased by the activity and agitation of socialists who give *critical* support to the war." Apparently denying a distinction between critical and open approval, he added: "The struggle for democracy, whatever *else* it requires of those who still believe in socialism, at least demands open support of the war against Hitlerism."[30]

While Macdonald spoke vaguely of revolution, Hook outlined a program, which he termed a "'Clemenceau thesis' from the left." Unlike the liblabs, for whom "Roosevelt has taken the place of a program," an independent bloc "should insist that *in the very interest of a complete military victory over Hitler* all the submerged interest of the nation be given a greater stake in that victory. . . . By preserving its independence, by giving critical political support to the war against Hitler without accepting entire political responsibility for its conduct, the labor movement will be in a much stronger position to influence its course, and to take the lead in domestic reconstruction when post-war reaction sets in."[31] Hook's version of the "Clemenceau thesis" was no more effectively realized than Macdonald's appeal, but the synthesizer of Marx and Dewey had at least presented a persuasive case for a radical alternative to both revolutionary defeatism and the liblab abdication of criticism.

Rahv shared Hook's conviction that Roosevelt at least ought to be forced to pay a price for labor's support; Macdonald feared that doing business with the president would further corrupt the proletariat. Both Hook and Macdonald wanted to keep socialist ideals alive; both feared that "when Hitler is finally defeated and the workingclass movement gets its famous 'breathing spell,' it may have quietly expired from holding its breath so long." But Macdonald refused to accept the "lesser evil" until an Allied victory, and he later noted ruefully that those who advocated "critical support" of the war effort found little, if anything, to criticize.[32]

In his own contribution to "The New Failure of Nerve" series, Macdonald declined to abandon his faith in proletarian-based collectivism merely because economic determinism had been invalidated. Though he expressed alarm that "the state is becoming an end in itself, subjugating the human being as the Church did in the Middle Ages," he could not conceive of communitarian anarchism as an effective obstacle to governmental encroachment. Writing as though still handcuffed to the ghost of Leon Trotsky, Macdonald rejected a political philosophy which found its ethical locus in the individual. Since human nature is "a historical, not a psychological, phenomenon" and since "man is shaped by his institutions," only "workingclass socialist collectivism" could serve as an antidote to bureaucratic collectivism. Though Macdonald rejected the doctrine of inevitability and admitted that "in general means must be related more closely to ends," he asserted that Marxism itself ought to be implemented rather than discarded.[33]

That summer *Partisan Review* ran out of money, and his contribution to "The New Failure of Nerve" proved to be his last article as editor. Greenberg, the coauthor of "Ten Propositions," had recently been drafted into the Army; and in June Macdonald had proposed to Rahv the death of *Partisan Review* and its rebirth in a politicized form under the editorship of Dwight Macdonald. Rahv demurred; and Macdonald agreed to resign if money could be found to keep *Partisan Review*, with its cultural preoccupations, intact. Rahv and Phillips secured financial respiration, and Macdonald quit.[34]

He was, however, able to pick his own successor, Delmore Schwartz, who had published his short story, "In Dreams Begin Responsibilities," in the first issue of a reborn *Partisan Review*. It catapulted him to fame; but his relations with the various editors, as with everyone in his life, were to be tumultuous and problematic. The poet, critic, and short-story writer was privately against the American war effort, asking himself in his notebook in 1942: "Why is Edmund Wilson silent? And why does [Allen] Tate apply for a commission to defend finance-capitalism, the order he has so often attacked?" But Schwartz also refused to take a public stance of opposition, which provoked Macdonald to write his friend late in 1942: "Why don't you ever have the guts to speak out in print on anything? As I told you a long time ago . . . you're ruining your career (not to speak of your moral being as a man) by trimming your sails to prevailing winds." Schwartz was therefore a congenial editor in the politically cautious atmosphere of the magazine's office; and though he was then a promising and even prodigious talent rather than the poète maudit he would sadly become, he proved an administratively irresponsible editor.[35]

Macdonald's withdrawal inevitably produced an exchange of letters in its wake. The former editor expressed regret that he no longer felt much of "the *esprit de corps* necessary to put out a 'little' magazine" and announced that he would invade "the thorny field of politics" with his own magazine later in the fall. In a less graceful farewell, Rahv and Phillips proclaimed the discovery of sinister motives in Macdonald's conception of *Partisan Review*. His desire to politicize the journal was deemed "a familiar strategy of left-wing politicians," "the use of literature as bait." Rahv and Phillips objected to his politics as "basically Trotskyite—plus a few personal variations, or heresies. . . . The more evident it became that the old revolutionary movement is in a state of decline, the more he wanted P.R. to take over its functions." In a private letter Rahv explained to Macdonald that the reply to the letter of resignation "was pretty sharp, but you left us no alternative. Your own letter was an attack on the magazine—in effect advice to readers to stop taking the *Partisan*." Rahv also hinted that "there are a thousand and one ways of slipping political discussions into the magazine—reviews, ripostes, etc."[36] But that was a private reassurance.

In the journal itself the remaining editors upheld the independence of culture from politics, especially from "a sectarian political line" which ran the danger of "self-righteousness, academic revolutionism, and the incessant repetition of a few choice though all-too-elementary notions." Later that fall Burnham expressed to Rahv an attitude of good riddance, and George Orwell assured him that his "Letter from London" would not be sent to any address other than *Partisan Review*.[37] William Barrett, an N.Y.U. philosopher who soon helped edit *Partisan Review*, later observed that Macdonald's "effectiveness was sorely missed. He was a journalist of superb and facile talents, ready at a moment . . . to bat out a sparkling polemic. Now that he was gone there was no one to take his place."[38]

Legend has it that early in the century, a miner stalked into a magazine office and demanded that the editors embark on another muckraking crusade. He was told, "Well, you certainly are a progressive, aren't you?" To which the visitor replied: "Progressive! Progressive! I tell you I'm a full-fledged insurgent. Why, man, I subscribe to thirteen magazines."[39]

Beginning early in 1944 other full-fledged insurgents would be able to read another—but quite unique— magazine.

5
Politics: An Evaluation

Macdonald spent the fall of 1943 planning the magazine of which he became "sole owner, publisher, editor and, putting it mildly, the most prolific contributor." The capital came from several sources: (1) the residue of his *Fortune* paychecks (perhaps as much as $20,000 had been saved), (2) business manager Nancy Macdonald's trust funds (her grandfather had been president of the New York Stock Exchange), and (3) the generosity of anarchist Carlo Tresca's widow, Margaret De Silver, "the first person one went to for help if the project was not very sensible." Upon the suggestion of an offbeat University of Maryland sociologist named C. Wright Mills, Macdonald rejected fancier titles (such as *The Radical Review*) and settled upon a journal that would be named simply, *Politics*.[1]

The February 1944 issue sold about 2,000 copies; the circulation eventually climbed to 5,000. There it remained until its transformation from monthly to bimonthly to quarterly unmistakably signaled the death of the magazine five years later. The typical *Politics* reader was male, college-educated, urban, under thirty-five, and a middle-class professional. He was also politically unaffiliated, though he was probably a Socialist if he belonged to any party. Curiously enough, slightly more of the readers were Republicans than Trotskyists. One-fourth of the subscribers were students; and another one-fourth were in the armed forces, where *Politics* was sometimes passed from hand to hand.[2]

Politics was antiwar and antimilitarist, but no censorship legally barred it from army camps any more than from civilian homes; nor did the publisher-editor learn of informal military interference with the reading habits of *Politics* subscribers. Though Macdonald's attitude toward the war was at least as much influenced by Randolph Bourne as by Vladimir Lenin, differing fates befell American journalism during the two world wars. The appeal for intellectual integrity and nay-saying, the repudiation of liberal idealism, the quest for a "trans-national" culture, the increasingly fervent opposition to the state, the hunger for a revitalized ethic with which to measure the devastations of war—these Bourne and Macdonald held in common.[3] But Bourne's articles helped bring on the downfall of *Seven Arts* and produced "some fuss on *The Dial*,"[4] while governmental and vigilante repression poisoned and killed the *Masses* as well as less vibrant representatives of socialist journalism. Freedom of expression was largely unimpaired in the Second World War: after Pearl Harbor virtually no antiwar constituency formed, and those who read *Politics* were more likely to write poetry or letters to the editor than leaflets urging "revolution." Although Milton Konvitz, a constitutional lawyer, warned Macdonald that his criticism of the Second World War was "not less 'seditious' than the statements in the court record" of the Smith Act prosecution of the Trotskyists, Konvitz's "friendly advice" proved to be unwarranted; *Politics* was left undisturbed.[5]

Macdonald himself wrote against the war for a longer period of time while he was an editor of *Partisan Review* than when he was the editor of *Politics*, a magazine which appeared during the final year and a half of the conflict. And Macdonald did not apply rigid ideological tests to his contributors, many of whom fought in and supported the Second World War. In short, *Politics* was not a completely accurate reflection of his own politics, for his "editorial style was to have none." He "tried to judge manuscripts not by whether their politics agreed with mine but how well they made their points: the quality of the style, logic and research."[6]

Politics maintained the *Partisan Review* tradition of insisting upon the internationalization of culture, and it thus avoided the vague aura of incest that hovers over a "little magazine" as much as the steamy set of a Tennessee Williams play. With the possible exception of Macdonald's own essay, "The Root Is Man," the three most discussed articles in *Politics* were written by Europeans: Bruno Bettelheim's "Behavior in Extreme Situations," Albert Camus's "Neither Victims nor Executioners," and Simone Weil's "The Iliad, or the Poem of Force." The shock of totalitarianism and modern warfare also explains why nearly all the most fertile contributors were Europeans: Andrea Caffi, a Russian-Italian; Nicola Chiaromonte, an Italian; Lewis Coser, a German Jew who later credited Macdonald with being his "first guide to the American intellectual scene"; Peter Gutman, a Czech Jew; Victor Serge, the Belgian-Russian whom Macdonald had helped bring to Mexico; Niccola Tucci, an Italian; and George Woodcock, an Englishman.[7]

Apart from Macdonald himself, the only American to contribute as frequently as the Europeans was Paul Goodman. Veterans of the American left generally avoided *Politics* due to "mutual suspicions," but Goodman was a major exception. But then Goodman, who had served for a spell as *Partisan Review*'s movie critic, was an exception to virtually every rule. Among New York's radical intelligentsia he was considered "a member in bad standing because of anarchist deviations," and unlike nearly all Jews he refused to support the war. "When they tried to draft me," he recalled, "I made such a pain of myself they rejected me as not military material—'a stinker case'. . . . Although I do not criticize those who stopped an immediate evil, I believed you had to be a pacifist in order to prevent the next war."[8] *Politics* also made a few necessary introductions, printing the work of unknowns whose intellectual influence would be felt in the succeeding decades. Subscribers read Bettelheim when the survivor of Buchenwald and Dachau had just begun to work at Chicago's Orthogenic Institute. They read Camus within a year of the translation of his short novel, *L'Étranger*, into English. Simone Weil had died in 1943, after refusing to consume more than the rations allowed in occupied France; only after her death and several articles in *Politics* did she achieve her reputation for spiritual pertinence.

Macdonald's magazine also introduced readers to younger writers closer to home. *Politics* printed C. Wright Mills when virtually no subscribers had heard of him; it printed reviews by a couple of the titans of postwar historiography, Richard Hofstadter and Oscar Handlin; it printed Milton Mayer when he was listed on the publicity staff of the University of Chicago; it printed Irving Kristol after he had left an obscure dissident Trotskyist journal; it printed Macdonald's close friend James Agee after *Let Us Now Praise Famous Men* had flopped and when he still toiled anonymously for *Time*; it printed Nathan Glazer when he was a graduate student at the University of Pennsylvania; it printed Marshall McLuhan before he became Marshall McLuhan. The precocity of such talented contributors is as remarkable as their variety.

These contributors, and particularly the editor and publisher, helped to fulfill a rather chronic need for independent radical criticism. In the very month that *Politics* first appeared, Edmund Wilson complained that "the exponents of the various traditions of radical and liberal writing have mostly been stunned or flattened out by Hitler's bombs and tanks. The socialists are now for the most part simply patriots . . . the Communists are Russian nationalists who would not recognize a thought of Lenin's if they happened by some mistake to see one; the liberal weeklies are . . . false phantoms whose noncandescence is partly due to an alien mixture of the gases of propaganda injected by the Stalinists and the British."[9]

From England Orwell reported the "Stalin seems to be becoming a figure rather similar to what Franco used to be"—exempted from criticism. But by June, Orwell was able to "recommend anyone who has a friend in New York to try and cadge a copy of *Politics,* the new monthly magazine, edited by the Marxist literary critic, Dwight Macdonald." Orwell continued to write for *Partisan Review* despite its wartime suspension of anti-Stalinism; as for *Politics,* he could not "agree with the policy of this paper, which is anti-war (not from a pacifist angle), but I admire its combination of highbrow political analysis with intelligent literary criticism."[10] Only in retrospect has it become clearer that Macdonald's skepticism and candor, his polemical verve, his unpretentious sensibility, and his facility for writing equally well about both politics and culture made Macdonald the American journalist who most resembled George Orwell himself.[11]

Partisan Review's defense of modernist literature and its erstwhile anti-Stalinist radicalism lingered strongly in the pages of *Politics,* but Macdonald added a few twists of his own which made his journal as unique as a signature. Freda Utley asserted that her friend's "individualistic temperament . . . rendered him incapable of collaborating for any length of time with anyone"; and having kept that temperament "more or less under wraps" as a Trotskyist and *Partisan Review* editor, Macdonald discovered that he "could finally come out as I felt only when I had my own magazine."[12]

The "highbrow political analysis" which Orwell immediately recognized and admired was enmeshed in paradox. Macdonald was irresponsible in the largest sense, for the train schedules for Auschwitz were not to be delayed or canceled pending the outcome of a socialist revolution. He nevertheless developed valuable insights forfeited by intellectuals whose advocacy of the war was more open than critical. The eccentric "Ten Propositions" remained a part of his attitude, but they were soon buried alive by his energetic muckraking. Rahv and Hook, for example, knew that socialist revolution could not assault *Festung Europa* no matter how many copies of *Partisan Review* were sold; and they reached the appropriate, if unpleasant, conclusion that bourgeois governments had bigger battalions than the Shachtmanites. But Macdonald, who could not accede to a war on such terms, became as a consequence more sensitive to its cost and more alert to its implications. He was more loyal to the vocation of the critical intellectual than to the duty of the citizen who must sometimes decide between two evils. Macdonald's rejection of the war undoubtedly had no more effect than Rahv and Hook's acceptance of it. *Politics* can thus be judged in terms of intellectual coherence more than its political consequences.

Within those terms Macdonald succeeded admirably; he became not only the Bourne but also the Mencken of the period. He was both thoughtful and sardonic, half-hoping and cynical, independent and curious, painful and funny. As his Marxist faith collapsed, he no longer hoarsely echoed Lenin's cry to convert an imperialist war into a class war; and he reached more tentative conclusions from the evidence of concrete facts. His expository powers enlarged; he fashioned some short articles which were as hard and bright as diamonds. Fanciful position papers like the "Ten Propositions" were scrapped in favor of political analysis that was often indistinguishable from textual analysis; and even when he removed ugly globs of fatty tissue from the rhetoric of General Patton or Marshal Stalin, the skill of such excisions was often dazzling. He resembled the surgeon who once explained his choice of profession: "I like to cut." Mac the Knife.

Macdonald had to study politicians' speeches and *The New York Times* closely, because he enjoyed almost "no contact with congressmen or government officials or businessmen or labor leaders."[13] The editor of *Politics* did not claim this political isolation as a virtue; he simply learned to read very, very carefully and to view language as a prism which refracted when it did not illuminate modern politics. "The chief defect of his writing, in fact, is perhaps an excessive energy and ingenuity of expression, so that the style sometimes obscures the development of the thought. . . . But whether obscured or not, the structure is usually there; the most casual of . . . [his] articles are distinguished from most products of leftwing journalism in that they are equipped with a beginning, a middle and an end. . . . As a polemicist . . . he usually maintains an easy, witty, even genial, tone; there is more of Voltaire about him than of Jeremiah. A certain gaiety is indeed a feature of his style."[14] That is Macdonald on Trotsky, but it might as easily be Macdonald on Macdonald.

Daniel Bell, a *Politics* contributor, would have disagreed with this description. For he accused Macdonald of being "completely cocksure of his position and unmerciful to an opponent . . . [and] in the next historical moment . . . often as dogmatic in the new stance as in the old." Bell exaggerated Macdonald's dogmatism. Even the Marxism of "James Joyce" had been conditional, and his adherence to later creeds was not steadfast to the ideology upon which he initially founded *Politics*. Macdonald's anarchism was more a symptom of his dread of the nation-state than a deeply felt and fully articulated philosophy that pervaded his writings, much less his life. His pacifism, which he also recognized as "*faute de mieux*," did not survive the imposition of the Berlin blockade.[15] Macdonald was strikingly openminded, and he threw open the pages of his magazine to others similarly disinherited.

As dialectical materialism ceased to make sense to him, Macdonald relied increasingly upon a psychological approach to politics. His articles in *Politics* abounded with psychological and psychiatric terminology, whether analyzing the "political pathology" of left sectarians or the "psychology of killing" which the Second World War required. He stressed the bland impersonality stamped upon the crew of the *Enola Gay*, which bombed Hiroshima, and upon the residents of American cities as well. Macdonald's use of psychoanalytic insights was more evocative than fastidious or intensive, but it was usually appropriate and lent to his writing considerable poignancy and resonance. Bell in fact considered the theme of *Politics* to be "depersonalization,"[16] a theme which therefore served as a wry tribute to an editor who rather successfully resisted the process.

Politics received many tributes. Mills told Macdonald that he "enjoyed" the first issue "immensely; it's lively and it has the discernible air of free and hard-hitting truth seeking." A quondam Trotskyist studying Canadian socialism, Seymour Martin Lipset, wrote from Regina: "Whether you realize it or not, you are editing the best magazine the Left has ever had." Lipset was nevertheless troubled by the magazine's failure to develop "constructive alternatives" to the regnant order. Still a Trotskyist in the 1940s, Howe remembered *Politics* as "sharp and amusing, feckless and irritating, [but] . . . the liveliest magazine the American Left had seen for decades," "the one significant effort during the late 40's to return to radicalism."[17] Paul Goodman also called *Politics* "the best magazine in my adult memory." A special tribute was provided by Mary McCarthy, who in 1961 recommended two possible editors for an American equivalent of the British *Observer* and *Sunday Times*, then under consideration. She suggested Robert Silvers, who would begin editing the *New York Review of Books* two years later, and Dwight Macdonald, "by far the most inspired and cordial editor I've ever had anything to do with. . . . The proof of this, for me, is that he used to succeed in getting me to write for nothing. . . . People who read *Politics* still talk about it and hold onto their yellowed files of it. . . . Incidentally, he's an extremely nice man, kind-hearted and genially eccentric."[18]

Even those whose persuasion was quite distant from the anarchism and pacifism the magazine came to champion were impressed. From the *New Yorker*, Richard Rovere hailed *Politics* as "the best thing that has happened in left-wing journalism—or for that matter in any sort of political journalism—in this country since I've been able to read." He wrote Macdonald that he lacked sympathy with the magazine's perspective, but he praised its honesty. Rovere went even further two years later: "*Politics*, is, I imagine, the best political magazine this country has ever had." From Notre Dame the editor of the *Review of Politics*, Waldemar Gurian, recorded the "great interest" with which he read Macdonald's magazine, "though as you know I do not agree with your basic views. . . . I think some of the articles of *Politics* are impressive proofs against secularism and pure humanism."[19]

Gurian's friend Hannah Arendt became Macdonald's friend as well, and an admirer of—though not a contributor to—*Politics*. She had immigrated on an emergency visa in 1941, and three years later Bell was writing Macdonald: "I'm sending under separate cover a remarkable article by Hannah Arendt, which appeared in the *Jewish Social Studies*, called 'The Jew as Pariah.' . . . It's very well done." Bell, who was then helping to edit the *New Leader*, added: "Possibly you could ask this Hannah Arendt (she is a Zionist and a writer on Jewish historical studies) for some pieces for *Politics*." A year later Macdonald acknowledged her brilliance in an article on totalitarianism he did for his magazine. Two decades later Arendt herself, whose politics were quite different from those of Macdonald, praised the magazine's "relevance for contemporary political matters." She traced that quality to Macdonald's "extraordinary flair for significant fact and significant thought."[20]

Much more surprising were the responses of Malcolm Cowley and Granville Hicks, whose Popular Front politics had so angered Macdonald. Writing in the *New Republic* in 1947, Cowley acknowledged disagreeing with most of Macdonald's conclusions. "But at least they are reached by the almost forgotten process of thinking them out for himself;

and I admire his custom of stating them simply and without much regard for personal or party expediency." Cowley praised the prose style of the magazine, which was also why Granville Hicks wrote Macdonald that *Politics* "is the most readable magazine I see."[21] These reactions may reflect upon the generosity of spirit of Cowley and Hicks, or upon their capacity for formulating literary judgments independently of their political views, or upon Macdonald's own flair for engaging in sharp polemics without leaving too much personal bitterness in his wake.

But the special place which *Politics* filled for the radical intelligentsia can be marked by comparison to its stepmother, *Partisan Review.* The anti-Stalinism which Phillips and Rahv downplayed during the struggle against Germany returned in full force after the war, accompanied by a certain impatience with the ideological squabbles of the 1930s and an assessment of world politics which smacked far more of realpolitik than of revolution. Along with a preoccupation with the psychology of the artist and intellectual emerged a more complacent attitude toward the society that often inflicted the sense of estrangement.[22] When Arthur Schlesinger, Jr., confided that his contribution to a 1947 symposium on socialism had been read in the State Department, Rahv replied, apparently without tongue in cheek: "One thing that one could say about *Partisan Review* is that the pieces in it do get read by the right people."[23]

The right people were not reading *Politics*, and the criticism which *Partisan Review* directed at it provides a revealing glimpse into the postwar mood which Macdonald so stubbornly resisted. Some of the criticism was packaged in the form of frozen invective, as when associate editor William Barrett blasted *Politics* for its "crackerbox bluster, wide-eyed idealism and ingènue dogmatism," a magazine deemed so unsophisticated and inconsequential that it "might just as well be put out at some tiny whistle-stop in Oklahoma." Burnham, who was to join *Partisan Review*'s advisory board in 1948, accused Macdonald of adopting "a program of revolution in one psyche. . . . It provides Macdonald himself with that glow of self-righteousness which seems to be his most compelling need." Calling him "ignorant" and "a joke," Burnham announced that Macdonald derived all of his ideas either from "the commonplaces of the radical tradition" or from James Burnham.[24]

Criticism from the two editors of *Partisan Review* was more cogent and intelligible, however. In fact they deftly turned the Macdonald of 1943 on his head, accusing him of taking refuge in "moral rectitude and passivity," terms he had once used in denouncing their own return to the womb of literary criticism. As he had considered their acceptance of the war as conducive to fascism, Rahv and Phillips wrote in 1946 that what Macdonald's "position comes down to—in objective terms— is a complete surrender to Stalin. With a truly oriental passivity, Yogi Macdonald prostrates himself beneath the wheels of the advancing juggernaut." Communism should be combatted with "every available means," they wrote, and that did not include pacifism.[25]

Reflecting postwar disenchantment and the recognition of limited choices, Phillips raised a familiar objection: "Macdonald's position is more of a moral stance than the result of a political analysis. . . . When the left is reeling from defeats and confusions, it seems to me to be politically irresponsible to substitute revolutionary pep-talks, as Macdonald does, for the task of reconciling the great promise of the socialist movement with its uninterrupted failure."[26] Macdonald in fact lost his faith in revolution soon thereafter. He too began to stumble in a desert of shattered dreams, becoming like Eliot's *Gerontion,* "an old man in a dry month . . . waiting for rain."

But when replenishment seemed to come in the form of communitarian experimentation, Rahv accused him of seeing mirages. Rahv had been struck by Max Weber's writings on bureaucratic rationalization and was unable to conceive of anarchism in an industrial age. He once asked Macdonald's friend Chiaromonte how trains could operate without crashing and confusion were anarchism instituted. He was startled by Chiaromonte's reply that, were anarchism adopted, trains would not be necessary.[27] Rahv admonished Macdonald for being "far more open to the romantic lure of extreme ideologies . . . than to the appeal of rational analysis." In order to combat Soviet Communism, the *Partisan Review* editor advocated "a strategic alliance . . . with the bourgeoisie as a class"—a formulation that betrayed Rahv's own addiction to the romance of "extreme ideologies." He added that flirtation with anarchism and nonviolent resistance showed Macdonald to be "a writer of engaging personality," but with "a marked deficiency of political intelligence."[28]

Macdonald eventually came to accept the justice of much of Rahv's criticism as well as Phillips's, and to recognize the claims of political realism. Indeed, for all his idiosyncrasies, the *Politics* editor never strayed too far from the rarified and intense atmosphere of the New York intellectuals, especially the home office. "He would occasionally barge into one of our informal sessions at William Phillips' house," Barrett recalled, "and plunge into argument with everyone. Outnumbered and outgunned in such arguments, Macdonald nevertheless seemed to be in his element and thoroughly enjoying himself, unmindful of the barbs." Barrett in retrospect "admired his courage and openness, and his willingness to put himself on the line." Eileen Simpson, who was then married to the poet John Berryman, has drawn a sharp portrait of Macdonald in those days, "gesturing with his head, arms and shoulders like a giant bird . . . wearing eyeglasses and a goatee, [Dwight] looked the way a radical should look."[29] In his capacity to subjugate engaged emotions to civility of temper, he was also a model of how anyone should behave.

The story of *Politics* is largely the record of one man's search for a principled radicalism which could transcend smugness and disillusionment, for the means with which to disavow the present without foreclosing a more humane future. Macdonald knew that something disastrous had happened in his lifetime. The concentration camp had become the representative institution as the Gothic cathedral had been of an earlier century, and America too was implicated in crimes against humanity. And for the five-year history of *Politics*, he sought to impose intellectual order and to invoke a viable ethic against what he feared was the imminence of apocalypse.

6
The Responsibility of Peoples

Because Roosevelt had stripped the war of political meaning, Macdonald wrote, the purpose of his new magazine would be to provide a political interpretation of the slaughter. Because the call for "national unity" disguised a policy supporting the status quo, Macdonald hoped "to create a center of consciousness on the Left," whose "predominant intellectual approach will be Marxist." But he proclaimed not the dialectical materialism of *Capital* but the humanism of the 1844 *Manuscripts*: "To be radical is to grasp the matter by the root. Now the root for mankind is man himself."[1]

The first issue was suffused with a more conventional Marxism, however, a set of attitudes that had lingered from his Trotskyist career. He affirmed the "Ten Propositions"; he defined the fascist enemy as "bureaucratic collectivist"; he called for the creation of "a potential new *human* culture, in Trotsky's phrase, which for the first time in history has a chance of superseding the *class* cultures of the present and past." But his Marxism also blended into his incipient anarchism, as when he feared that "by one of those dialectical turns so common in history, the more the antipolitical concept of 'national unity' gains, the wider the power of the State can be extended and the more thoroughly can all of society become politicalized [sic]" and thus contaminated with totalitarianism.[2]

When Roosevelt suggested that the political slogan "New Deal" be replaced by the less controversial "Win the War," Macdonald noticed that both Republicans and liberals sniffed danger, though for reasons quite different from the "anarcho-cynicalist" *Politics*. The G.O.P. "denounced the President's attempt to evade responsibility for the horrors of his first two terms. 'Can the leopard change his spots?' asked the

Republican National Chairman—a little nervously, one suspects, for if spots *can* be changed, Roosevelt is the leopard to do it." But Macdonald had nothing but scorn for liberals who hoped that the internationalization of the New Deal might result from the Teheran conference. They had "proceeded to give Roosevelt one of those lessons in *realpolitik* with which liberal editors are constantly favoring the shrewdest and most amoral political strategist of our day. . . . Roosevelt and Stalin were present at Teheran—and the editors of the *New Republic* weren't."[3]

Neither of course was Macdonald; but from a speech which Churchill delivered in May, Macdonald sensed the future arms race, which would lead the United States alone to spend a trillion dollars on weaponry in the next twenty-five years. In 1944, he wrote, no other journalists took notice of Churchill's opinion that the Big Three would be "'obligated to keep within certain minimum standards of armaments.' The word one would expect there is 'maximum,' that is, a limitation of armaments. . . . The more they exceed the minimum, the greater will be, presumably, their contribution to international peace and harmony." Macdonald was amazed that the editors of the *New Republic* "were disturbed to find in the speech 'several hints' that Churchill thinks more in terms of power politics than of liberal ideals. . . . 'This will not do, Mr. Churchill,' warn Bruce Bliven, Malcolm Cowley, George Soule, Michael Straight and Stark Young in one thunderous squeak. . . . He can't say he hasn't been warned."[4]

Tone-deaf to the seductive harmonies of the two-party system, Macdonald spotted a shift in the liblabs' position after they had helped to elect Roosevelt in November: "As near as I can work out the new line, it is that it was necessary to re-elect Roosevelt in order to continue to have a chance to put pressure on him from the left."[5] The incumbent, who once remarked that the one American book Russians should read was a Sears, Roebuck catalog,[6] was deemed no different than Thomas E. Dewey; and Macdonald believed that the subsequent reorganization of the State Department proved his point. All its new leading officials were conservatives except for his onetime *Fortune* colleague, Archibald MacLeish, whom he dismissed as "an empty-headed rhetorician." Macdonald warned that "foreign policy is today the crucial sphere of American capitalism."[7]

Capitalist apologetics received the same treatment as the *New Republic*. He seized upon Eric Johnston's *Reader's Digest* article entitled "Three Kinds of Capitalism: Which Offers the Poor Boy the Best

Chance?"—the sort of unimprovable title which is unfair to satirists. Macdonald quoted the Chamber of Commerce president's remark that "only America . . . can light the world toward an ultimate capitalism of *everybody*," and clucked: "So we now have a 'people's capitalism' as a fitting companion to the 'people's war' and the 'people's century.' I suppose next we shall be hearing about 'people's cartels' and 'the imperialism of the common man.'" Macdonald made the moral of the story psychoanalytic: "The compensatory mechanism is obvious: the more monopolistic industry becomes, the more the State intervenes into capitalism, the more the middle classes are squeezed out of the control-sector of the economy, the more all this happens, the more powerful the compulsion to believe in the possibility of a future reversal of these tendencies."[8]

Macdonald insisted that capitalism was no less predatory when termed "people's capitalism" or when coated with liblab rhetoric. However horrified he felt at the prospect of an Axis victory, he warned that a United Nations peace would mean "postwar reaction on a world scale, [and] the redivision of Europe and the colonial regions between the three dominant imperialisms."[9] He questioned the Allies' commitment to self-determination and democracy when they favored Admiral Darlan over General Giraud, and Giraud over the recalcitrant General DeGaulle, when they preferred Marshall Badoglio to Count Sforza, and Sforza to socialists who lacked "a proper flexibility of the spine." Though Macdonald called attention to Roosevelt and Churchill's desire to abort socialist revolution, he censured the Communists as "the worst stumbling-block to any popular revolutionary movement," because they merely exploited the hopes for progress and falsely connected the ambitions of the Soviet Union with the interests of the proletariat. The prospects for popular uprising in Europe, Macdonald lamented, were bleak indeed.[10]

As early as May 1944, he discerned the origins of what Herbert Bayard Swope would be the first to call the Cold War; and *Politics* affixed a war guilt clause to one nation: "Russia has a much more aggressive and definite foreign policy than either of her war partners. This . . . is the basic fact about world politics today. . . . Since Teheran the Kremlin has taken a whole series of unilateral actions, without consulting her partners, which have shattered whatever unity and confidence once existed among the Big Three."[11] His dire interpretation of Soviet behavior was confirmed that fall when the Red Army patiently watched the *Wehrmacht* crush the Warsaw uprising and thus eliminate the rivals of the Polish Communists. Macdonald's article, one of his most emotionally charged, concluded with the following description of the Kremlin: "This butcher of popular insurrection, this double-crosser of its own allies, this factory of lies and slander, this world center of counterrevolution can have nothing in common with socialism. We cannot compromise with it if we would achieve our aims as socialists. Our slogan must be, once more: *Écrasez l'infame!*"[12]

Macdonald's indomitable anti-Communism was bound to ruffle the Old Believers. In 1943 he had helped spearhead a campaign to protest Warner Brothers' version of Joseph Davies's bestseller, *Mission to Moscow*. The film was faithful to the former ambassador's belief in the validity of the purge trials and in the political correctness of Stalin's elimination of a potential fifth column. The American Trotskyists were the first to protest such blatant propaganda and disregard of the findings of the Dewey Commission, and Macdonald was fairly successful in uniting intellectuals who objected to Hollywood's tarting up of Stalin's reputation for foresight and wisdom. Always on red alert, Macdonald even tangled with his dear friend, the *Nation's* film critic, James Agee, who labeled *Mission to Moscow* virtually the first Soviet film ever produced in a Hollywood studio, but who was not—according to Macdonald—sufficiently distressed by its historical distortions.[13] He also detected a shift in the nature of the intellectuals' apparently endless debate over the Soviet Union: "Up to about 1939, arguments about Russia revolved mostly around matters of fact; both sides accepted—verbally, at least—the same general criteria of good and evil." But by 1944 its apologists had almost ceased "denying the facts alleged by the critics. . . . Combining economic determinism with Original Sin, they argue that Russia is as close to socialism as the historical circumstances and the imperfections of human nature will permit, and hence that, 'for all practical purposes' it *is* socialist."[14] For Macdonald, who founded his politics upon the rectification of names, the definition had to fit the facts, not obscure them.

Macdonald's penetrating vision into Soviet conduct was enhanced by the removal of the mote of the Atlantic Charter beloved by the "liblabs." Asserting that "one doesn't have to be a Karl Marx to see there are many serious discrepancies between [the progressive New York newspaper] *PM's* war and the actual war," he assumed the thankless but necessary task of criticizing American policy and behavior as well.[15] Macdonald quickly grasped a fundamental fact of technological warfare—that remoteness facilitated the remorseless decimation of the inhabitants of a city, that populations could be consigned to extinction without emotion and without meaning. Liberal propaganda could not be connected to the depersonalized absurdity of the Second World War, whose essence was "the domination of modern man by his own creations, his involvement in processes beyond his control and contrary to his desires, the contrast in our society between noble ends and ignoble means, the dissolution of ends into means, so that the Marines fight for the honor of the Marines" and for little else.[16]

Encouraged by the extent of neuropsychiatric disorders among inductees and servicemen, Macdonald inquired: "May we not assume that a good proportion of them were simply too sane to fit into the lunatic pattern of total war?"[17] He may have been generous in his estimate of the number of soldiers who resembled Yossarian, the protagonist of Joseph Heller's later novel, *Catch-22*; but Macdonald found solace in the existence of a paladin who fit very neatly into the war's lunatic pattern, George S. Patton. Macdonald called him "my favorite general," but it was a left-handed salute: Patton's outrageous utterances ought to have made "militarism . . . a dead issue in this country." Not even Patton was that effective, despite Macdonald's lengthy quotations from his speeches, followed by his terse summary: "At once flat and theatrical, brutal and hysterical, coarse and affected, violent and empty—in these fatal antinomies the nature of World War II reveals itself: the maximum of physical devastation accompanied by the minimum of human meaning." When some soldiers defended their favorite general in letters to *Politics*, Macdonald replied: "Far from the justness of the war excusing Patton's barbarism, Patton's barbarism calls into question the justness of the war. There is something suspect about an end which calls for such means."[18]

Patton's belief that "this Nazi thing is just like a Democratic and Republican election fight"[19] also called into question the army's opposition to racism, and early issues of *Politics* were sometimes devoted to what was then—rather quaintly—called "Negroism." Macdonald publicized a suit which attorney Conrad Lynn had brought on behalf of his brother, who had been drafted into a Jim Crow army. However, the American Civil Liberties Union whittled down Lynn's attempt to attack racial discrimination as inherently unconstitutional. As its counsel, Arthur Garfield Hays, explained in a letter to *Politics*: one step at a time appeared most feasible. But Macdonald denounced Hays's "Mandarin-like legalistic quibbling" and found something sinister in the A.C.L.U. tactic:

"Lynn's original brief . . . brought right out into the open the realities of the American Jimcrow system. Even an adverse decision on the basis of the brief would have been a politically educational document. Granting to the colored people in words what is later taken back in deeds has been standard practice in this country since the Fourteenth Amendment. . . . But it is precisely this kind of education that liberals like Arthur Garfield Hays are anxious not to promote."[20]

Despite the technically narrow grounds upon which the A.C.L.U. appeal was filed, the Supreme Court refused to hear the case, and Macdonald concluded bitterly: "The Trotskyites go to jail, the colored draftees continue to be jimcrowed. No fuss, no complications, and, above all, nothing on the record. Who says the New Deal has no future?"[21] "Free and Equal," which was supposed to be a regular department of the magazine, usually got lost in the shuffle of other editorial interests and global concerns. Macdonald did cite letters from servicemen in integrated situations to confirm his belief that "human beings can get on with each other if they are not set at loggerheads by customs and institutions. . . . Whether in uniform or in mufti, Jim Crow is a most useful servant of the present social order in America."[22]

In the spring of 1945 *Politics* published Macdonald's most substantial article about the war, "The Responsibility of Peoples." The title came from a phrase by Chiaromonte, and there was a deeper intellectual debt to two other refugees, Arendt and Bettelheim. *Jewish Frontier* had published Arendt's "Organized Guilt and Universal Responsibility" that January, and Macdonald's essay can be understood as his meditation upon her argument. For Arendt had claimed that "systematic mass murder— the true consequence of all race theories and other modern ideologies which preach that might is right—strains not only the imagination of human beings, but also the framework and categories of our political thought and action."[23]

In reprinting Bettelheim's "Behavior in Extreme Situations" from the *Journal of Abnormal and Social Psychology*, Macdonald wrote to the psychiatrist early in 1944 how "moving and illuminating" the article was. Bettelheim had provided "a glimpse into a new world. Nothing I've read has given me such a sense of the horror of the Nazi concentration camps." Bettelheim, already a subscriber to *Politics*, thanked Macdonald for his encouragement and interest "in my evaluation of the training the Gestapo provided for me."[24] In realizing the importance of the writing of Arendt and Bettelheim before the war in Europe was over, Macdonald

became among the first writers to grapple with the meaning of genocide.[25] Neither a survivor of a camp nor a refugee, not even a Jew, he
was nevertheless prescient in daring to confront the horror of what
became generally labeled, nearly two decades later, as the Holocaust.
Macdonald described the character of Nazism much as Arendt was
later to do: though Hitler's movement "learned much from mass production, from modern business organization," those means were directed
toward ends which were irrational and "gratuitous" by any ethical code
other than the Nazis' own. Their worst atrocity, the so-called solution of
the Jewish problem, was "not a means to any end one can accept as even
plausibly rational. . . . The Jews of Europe were murdered to gratify a
paranoic hatred . . . but for no reason of policy or advantage that I can
see." Macdonald later recalled that "this statement provoked much
dissent at the time"[26]—but historical research and interpretation have
vindicated his sensitivity to the nature of the Second World War. It was
not simply another addition to the annals of slaughter, raised to the nth
power by the awful ingenuity of technology; the camps had made the
conflict qualitatively different.

And as a rationalist Macdonald could not believe that more than a
small minority of the German people could be implicated in the Nazis'
crimes. He noted the various kinds of resistance which numerous Germans summoned against Nazism, and he relied upon Bettelheim's article
in *Politics* to demonstrate the necessity of conditioning Germans to
pursue anti-Semitism to its "logical" conclusion: "It would seem probable
that the kind of extreme *behavior* required of mass-executioners and
torturers can only be psychologically conditioned by extreme *situations* . . . involving either complete physical control of the individual in a
prison camp or else his willing cooperation in a lengthy and rigorous
training process." Macdonald did not dispute the impact of Nazism upon
Germany, but he doubted that the S.S. had been given enough time to
create such extreme situations for masses of Germans.[27]

Many *Bürger* did not protest the extermination of the Jews, Macdonald conceded. He ascribed this failure not to malice or ignorance,
though the S.S. went to some lengths to keep the extermination camps a
"terrible secret." Instead he blamed the depersonalization of modern
society: "Few people have the imagination or the moral sensitivity to get
very excited about actions which they don't participate in themselves. . . . The scale and complexity of modern government organization, and the concentration of political power at the top, are such that

the vast majority of people are excluded from this participation." He cited examples of Allied atrocities for which he assumed no personal responsibility: the saturation bombings; the incarceration of Japanese-Americans; racist brutality and immigration quotas; the starvation of "liberated" areas; the betrayal of General Bor's Warsaw rebels; the deportations to Siberia; and the imperialist throttling of India. "I and most of the people I know are vigorously opposed to such policies and have made our disapproval constantly felt in the pages of the *Nation* and on the speaker's platform of the Union for Democratic Action. . . . [But] the Germans could say the same thing."[28]

Yet the "organic" theory of the state connected citizens to the atrocities of their leaders; the theory made the common citizen the accomplice of madmen and served to justify the Allied doctrine of unconditional surrender. This policy, and the saturation bombing used to enforce it, made no sense to Macdonald: "The common peoples of the world are coming to have less and less control over the policies of 'their' governments, while at the same time they are being more and more closely identified with those governments. . . . As the common man's *moral* responsibility diminishes (assuming agreement that the degree of moral responsibility is in direct proportion to the degree of freedom of choice), his *practical* responsibility increases."[29]

The "responsibility of peoples" was pregnant with several meanings. Allied bombers held citizens of Cologne accountable for the horrors inflicted by the Nazis, yet Macdonald denied the validity of such accountability. He did not expect much resistance to unjust government under modern conditions; but he was groping toward a new and special definition of the responsibility of peoples, in which resistance, though impractical, would nevertheless be essential for free men and women. In a striking passage he wrote that "it is not the law-breaker we must fear today so much as he who obeys the law. . . . One of the most hopeful auguries for the future of this country, with the Permanent War Economy taking shape, is that we Americans have a long and honorable tradition of lawlessness and disrespect for authority."[30] Yet his essay was too brief to articulate some standards and conditions to justify lawlessness, other than in "extreme situations."

"What have I done?" cried a former death camp functionary who was told he would probably be executed; and Macdonald believed that "the worthy paymaster—imagine the civilization that has produced the job of paymaster in a death camp!—is sincerely outraged by the proposal to hang him for his part in killing several million human beings."[31] In satirizing this response, Macdonald invoked no ethic certifying the execution of the paymaster. Perhaps the perennial skeptic was credulous here. After the war, when Danes were asked why they had *en masse* rescued nearly all Jews living in their country, they did not reply "What have I done?" or "What could I do?" but "What *else* could I do?" In his outrage against Allied bombing policy, Macdonald not only exaggerated German aloofness from the Third Reich but also ignored national differences and conditions. Although the Danish demonstration of non-violent resistance might be explicable in terms of the intimate bonds between subjects and a king who expressed willingness to wear the yellow star, Macdonald's theory of depersonalization would not explain why the Bulgarians resisted German anti-Semitism and the Rumanians did not, or why the Polish underground heroically fought the Germans but refused to assist a similarly desperate uprising which began at Mila 18.[32] He asserted that over half the German people voted against Hitler in their last free election. He did not attach significance to the converse—that nearly half the voters supported Hitler when his Brown Shirts openly anticipated the day, as they sang in the streets, when Jewish blood would spurt from the knife. Macdonald cited rare instances of German resistance to Nazi crimes; he ignored patent evidence of Hitler's popularity—so long as the *Führer's* policies appeared to be successful.

In his climb to the chancellery, Hitler had frequently played upon the myth of the *Dolchstoss*, by which treachery behind the lines had defeated otherwise invincible German arms in 1918. Macdonald showed no understanding that Allied bombing policy and the demand for an unconditional surrender were at least partially an attempt to avoid such an error again. Because Macdonald's opposition to the war itself exempted him from the obligation to pass judgment on particular dilemmas which government officials faced, he did not bother to suggest an alternative to Allied strategy. In the autumn of 1944, Heinrich Himmler suspended the gassing of Jews in the crackpot belief that the Allies might negotiate with the S.S. commander as a "moderate."[33] Had Macdonald known of the offer, would he have suggested negotiations? And what should have been on the agenda? If the German people were not in some sense responsible for the government's policies, how could a Himmler represent Germany at a conference table?

Macdonald compounded the confusion when he agreed with the French novelist Jean Malaquais's revision of his thesis: "A 'people' is itself always socially heterogeneous, politically confused, and morally nonexistent. . . . Social classes, since they have specific interests and pursue definite aims, may be expected to be politically conscious and thus may be held responsible. There is a politics and a morality of classes, not of peoples."[34] There was indeed a politics of classes: early in the previous decade, Stalin based his agricultural policy upon the desire to "liquidate the *kulaks as a class*."[35] (My emphasis.) But in the sense that Malaquais meant class politics, workers under totalitarianism behaved no more heroically or independently than anyone else. Macdonald claimed that if all are guilty, none is guilty; but nearly all classes and class organizations after the inauguration of the *Gleichschaltung* and the first Five-Year Plan implemented the policies of the Nazi and Bolshevik rulers against the leftist traitors and *Untermenschen* and against the *kulaks* and Trotskyist wreckers. Macdonald's agreement with Malaquais is therefore puzzling.

But he was hardly the first or the last writer to fumble the enormously complicated question of the proper relation of the individual to the state. Macdonald's rejection of the organic theory opened the possibility of useful discriminations, but he never revealed by which ethical code or by which legal rules guilt for crimes against humanity could be ascertained. The chilling novelty and extent of the evil were located, but the problem of punishment was fudged. He later sneered at the Nuremberg Trial of the surviving Nazi leaders: "If aggressive warfare is a crime, then may we expect a Leningrad Trial in which the leaders of Russia's attack on Finland in 1939–1940 will be duly tried and executed?"[36] But if Goering and the other defendants in the dock at Nuremberg were not "responsible," was anyone? Macdonald's apparent belief in crimes without criminals—except for "ruling classes" of indeterminate membership—made his description of depersonalization more emphatic but made the conumdrum of jurisprudence even more difficult.

Macdonald was certainly correct to note the effect of "unconditional surrender" in blurring the distinction between the Nazis and the rest of the German population. In promoting the unification of Germany behind its Nazi leadership, Roosevelt's policy may well have prolonged the war. But Macdonald failed to suggest an alternative; and given his grisly insight into the nature of totalitarianism, he could not have been happy with a peace treaty negotiated with the Nazi leaders. His moral outrage at the Allied terror bombing led him to ignore a perhaps more effective argument—that it did not work. The military defeat of the Third Reich might well have been dramatically accelerated had Allied bombers skipped the raids on civilian centers and instead consistently attacked the oil refineries. In his memoirs, the former armaments minister, Albert Speer, recalled how vulnerable the indispensable ball bearings factories were, and speculated that a different Allied bombing strategy would have been decisive as early as 1943.[37]

Whatever the ambiguities and omissions in "The Responsibility of Peoples," Macdonald's article was favorably received, and rightly so. The sociologist Robert MacIver called Macdonald's thesis "entirely realistic . . . balanced and statesmanlike"; and Reinhold Niebuhr termed the article "one of the sanest and profoundest analyses of the problem of individual and collective guilt which I have read." Lewis Coser called the article "by far the best thing I have seen on this problem anywhere"— though he noted Macdonald's failure to account for the historical causes allowing a civilized nation to fall into the grip of psychotics. Even in 1951 the eccentric conservative Willmoore Kendall could not recall "when I've learned so much from an article as I have from 'Responsibility of Peoples.' Certainly not since way before the war."[38]

Five months after Macdonald had protested vainly against the aerial devastation of Germany, an atomic bomb was discharged from a B-29. President Truman boasted to the crew of the USS *Augusta*, "This is the greatest thing in history"; and it hastened the end of a war that had begun, almost six years earlier, with an invasion of Poland resisted by cavalry. To Macdonald Hiroshima was an atrocity which beggared description. He could only urge the readers of *Politics* to " 'get' the national *State before it 'gets' us*. Every individual who wants to save his humanity— and indeed his skin—had better begin thinking 'dangerous thoughts' about sabotage, resistance, rebellion, and the fraternity of all men everywhere."[39]

Macdonald suggested that the dangerous thoughts be founded upon "negativism," but the dawn of the atomic age also shattered his Marxism and branded him a pacifist. The discovery of fire thousands of years earlier had resulted in death at Hiroshima from the flash of a thousand suns. To Macdonald the hopeful pride of science had become obscene. He rejected a socialism which had been "the great crown of scientific progress," and he expressed agreement with Simone Weil that war in the age of technological mayhem corrupted any political ends. The obliteration of Hiroshima deepened his pessimism and sense of futility: "Since . . . [most] Americans did not even know what was being done in our name—let alone have the slightest possibility of stopping it—The

Bomb becomes the most dramatic illustration to date of the fallacy of 'The Responsibility of Peoples.'" His was a pacifism rooted not in faith in human possibilities but in despair over the direction of history itself, and implicit in his opposition to war was the fear that atomic energy, rather than helping to liberate humanity, would merely be "at the service of the rulers; it will change their strength but not their aims." The opportunities for reducing that strength, however, were slipping fast. "Already," he wrote, "the great imperialisms are jockeying for position in World War III."[40]

World War II exposed too much brutality and turpitude to foster the illusion that it would end all other wars. But neither did it, as Macdonald feared, end all civilization; and few Americans who reflected upon the global conflict of 1939–1945 regarded their nation's political and military aims as unjust. The devastation that World War II produced can barely be measured. That is why the testimony of those who recorded its bestiality must be remembered.

7
The Root Is Man

In 1946 Macdonald's closest collaborator, Nicola Chiaromonte, went to a New York pier to meet a friend he had not seen in five years, Albert Camus. In the interim Camus had ceased to be a promising playwright and poet and had become an intellectual and moral symbol of the French Resistance. Soon after his arrival the author of *The Stranger* and *The Myth of Sisyphus* addressed an audience at Columbia University, where he warned that any man is "an actual or potential assassin" who "speaks of human existence in terms of power, efficiency and 'historical tasks.'" Claiming to speak for a generation of Europeans that had come to know both absurdity and terror, Camus announced: "We reject any ideology that claims control over all of human life." And that night, in two sentences, he encapsulated a mood and an ethic that would reverberate far beyond the lecture hall: "We have learned . . . that we cannot accept any optimistic conception of existence, any happy ending whatsoever. But if we believe that optimism is silly, we also know that pessimism about the action of man among his fellows is cowardly."[1]

Camus and Macdonald were soon to work together, primarily through Chiaromonte, in the formation of Europe-America Groups. The purpose was to provide material aid, moral support, and intellectual solidarity to European exiles from Bolshevik and Nazi totalitarianism. Hopes for Europe-America Groups were never quite realized, but Camus published several issues of a *Bulletin d'Information des Groupes de Liaison Internationale* in Paris. The lead article of the first issue was a reprint of Macdonald's *Politics* article on the Soviet Union and pacifism.[2]

Gloom saturated the intellectual atmosphere of the immediate postwar years. Professor Arnold Toynbee appeared on the cover of *Time* (the story itself was written by Whittaker Chambers), and the surprisingly large number of Americans who at least skimmed the single-volume summation of *A Study of History* wondered if the West could respond to the challenges which had doomed the twenty-five previous civilizations. Professor Friedrich von Hayek's best-seller, *The Road to Serfdom*, detected totalitarian tendencies in liberal planning; and the "severly intellectual" economist, noted Eric Goldman, "found himself lecturing up and down the country to rapt anti-New Deal audiences."[3] Nor were the young, presumably the avatars of hope, immune to the chastened reevaluation of the liberal faith. From Reinhold Niebuhr's sermons Arthur Schlesinger, Jr. sensed the unfolding of "a new dimension of experience—the dimension of anxiety, guilt and corruption." In the range of his influence and the nature of his message, Niebuhr himself was reminiscent of Jonathan Edwards's earlier ministry of fear. Norman Podhoretz remembered that "complexity became a key word in the discourse of the period. . . . Very much aware of how complicated and difficult all problems were, very much alive to the danger of ideologies and enthusiasms and passions. . . . [we were] poised, sober, judicious, prudent."[4] In such inhospitable soil other books of the period, like Paul and Percival Goodman's *Communitas* (1947), a consciously utopian creation of the standards of urban excellence, or Saul Alinsky's *Reveille for Radicals* (1946), a manual for community organizers, could scarcely fructify.

Macdonald, who deeply admired Camus's *Combat* editorials and who translated "Neither Victims nor Executioners" for the readers of *Politics*, would have been a poor journalist had he not caught the temper of his times. He too felt among the disinherited; he too had passed through the crucible of war scarred and repentant, haunted like Camus by the need to forge an intellectually coherent ethic which would recognize the sources of despair while defying its effects.

The ideological, moral, and political bankruptcy of Marxism had become obvious to Macdonald by the end of the war; and beginning in November 1945 *Politics* sponsored Second Avenue discussion evenings which set the tone for the magazine's intellectual reorientation. Among the discussants were Lewis Coser, who explained the "Failure of European Resistance"; Chiaromonte, who advocated utopian rather than scientific socialism; Goodman, who proposed decentralization as an alternative to the welfare state; Lionel Abel, who found omens of "The General Acceptance-in-Advance of World War III"; and the editor-publisher himself, who gave the audience a preview of what became a two-part essay published in the spring and summer of 1946, "The Root Is Man."[5]

Macdonald's most ambitious philosophical statement began with its author trekking across familiar territory. Mentioning Rizzi's *Bureaucratisation du Monde*, which he had not been able to read, he continued the dispute with Trotsky over bureaucratic collectivism. Macdonald repeated his contentions that the Soviet Union was the most dangerous threat to the working class, that the proletariat's failure to seize revolutionary opportunities called Marxism itself into question, and that the masses had become culturally corrupted. Bureaucratic collectivism had been undreamt of in the stacks of the British Museum, and what most troubled Macdonald was that socialism had failed.[6]

Mr. Dooley once took note of a meeting in which "Mrs. Vanderhankerbilk give a musical soree f'r th' ladies iv th' Female Billyonaires Arbeiter Verein. . . . Th' meetin' was addhressed be th' well-known Socialist leader, J. Clarence Lumley, heir to th' Lumley millyons."[7] But though the rich had lost interest in socialism by 1945, Macdonald was surprised to learn from the discussion evenings that the magazine's New York readers at least were still predominantly Marxist. The thrust of his essay was therefore a critique of the ideological system to which he himself had so recently adhered—"very much against my own temperament," he admitted.[8] "The Root Is Man" consequently gives the impression that Macdonald was assaulting a hitherto impregnable fortress. In fact he was charging through an open door: as early as 1938 *Partisan Review* had to abandon a symposium on the dialectic because the editors could find no one to defend it.[9]

What was unusual about Macdonald's critique, however, was its perspective. Unlike Eastman, Hook, or Wilson, for example, he was not primarily interested in exposing the mythic and unscientific aspects of Marxism. On the contrary, he insisted that, for all its errors, Marxism belonged within a scientific framework; and since Hiroshima, science itself required critical scrutiny. Macdonald distinguished between "Progressives" and "Radicals." The former embraced most of the left wing, from Stalinists and Trotskyists to social democrats and liberals; the latter included anarchists, conscientious objectors, and "renegade Marxists" like Macdonald himself. The former, Macdonald asserted, viewed history in terms of progress and science without reference to moral values; the latter "reject[ed] the concept of Progress . . . judge[d] things by their present meaning and effect . . . [and] redress[ed] the balance by emphasizing the ethical aspect of politics." In other words, "the Progressive makes History the center of his ideology. The Radical puts Man there . . . [stressing] the individual conscience and sensibility."[10]

Just as Trotsky had once accused Macdonald of attempting to convert him into a "Macdonaldist," the author of "The Root Is Man" almost performed the same plastic surgery operation on Karl Marx himself, who was not around to protest. Macdonald took the title of his essay from the pre-*Communist Manifesto* period, when Marx had purportedly criticized statism from the perspective of individual liberation: "As a moralist, Marx viewed the individual as the End and society as the Means." Macdonald regretted that Marx had spent so much time poring over statistics in the British Museum, "instead of making his theory of alienation the cornerstone of his intellectual effort."[11] Classifying Marx as a Radical who had inauthentically become a Progressive, "The Root Is Man" could be stamped with the only imprimatur which still mattered to many radical intellectuals; and Macdonald could expatiate more authoritatively on the virtues of anarchism.

In the 1930s the philosophy of Proudhon and Kropotkin had not interested him, and in fact he had never even met any of its living followers. But as an editor in need of articles "with unhackneyed ideas and some emotional force,"[12] Macdonald soon realized that anarchists like Chiaromonte and Goodman could submit pieces which were free of the pall of Marxist orthodoxy and could therefore validate his own transition from Progressive to Radical.

Chiaromonte's influence was the more decisive. Since their first meeting in 1944, he emerged as Macdonald's closest friend, "morally and intellectually, also personally. Chiaromonte was [the] one person, except my poor dear father, that gave me the feeling of being valued for myself, individually, not for my brains (though also for them too) or achievements, just for myself." Chiaromonte was a survivor of Mussolini's fascism, a veteran of the Spanish Civil War, and a refugee from the French defeat of 1940. He helped shape Macdonald's realization that the state was a greater threat than the bourgeoisie,[13] and Hiroshima taught Macdonald what even a supposedly democratic government could wreak with a modern arsenal. With the war-making machine "grinding away according to its own logic," the relentlessly efficient violence of contemporary warfare would be not the midwife of social change but the destroyer of worlds instead. Macdonald concluded that the trade unions had become an essential prop in the Permanent War Economy and that the class struggle was about as likely to bring forth social upheaval as dynastic succession within the House of Windsor.[14]

Going back to the root, he argued that Marxism shared with the belief in science and progress the paternity of eighteenth-century liberal optimism. Just as Marxist ideology obscured the fact that the working class was no longer imbued with revolutionary potential, nor was the Soviet Union its representative, so too the faith in progress and science had led to disaster. The ascending staircase of history had suddenly ended in thin air, contaminated with radioactive dust. But was the atomic bomb a perversion of the inherently humane ends of science, or was "the very triumph of the scientific organization of matter (and of men) . . . the root of our trouble"?[15]

As he had argued that the power of the entrenched capitalist class could not be destroyed by the countervailing power of the proletariat, Macdonald also maintained that scientifically induced disaster could not be vitiated by better science but only by values derived from outside its boundaries. His attempt to distinguish between the realm of fact and the realm of values forced him to embark on an enterprise inaugurated by the *Critique of Pure Reason* and *Critique of Practical Reason*. Macdonald questioned the position of the Goodmans' forthcoming *Communitas* that "a conflict between technological efficiency and human good is theoretically impossible," and he argued that moral conceptions were alien and sometimes hostile to the scientific method.[16] But the metaphysics then became muddled—Immanuel Kant he wasn't—when Macdonald claimed to be constricting merely the scope of science. The two realms were thus presented as allied rather than opposed. In fact he held out a slight hope of "scientifically grounding socialism . . . along the Utopian and anarchist (and today Reichian) lines,"[17] even though Reich's ethic was purportedly grounded in physiology and even though the distinctions drawn in Engels's *Socialism: Utopian and Scientific* would be inexplicably lost. The appeal for the imposition of human meaning upon technological means was unexceptionable; but, as Macdonald described it, the position of the Progressives was not significantly different. Calling John Dewey "the greatest living theorist of Progressivism, as defined in this article," Macdonald criticized pragmatism in terms which were less technical than political—and, incidentally, quite pragmatic. Judging ideas by their consequences, Macdonald noted that Dewey had supported two world wars; therefore something must be wrong with the philosophy that he professed.[18]

In rejecting Dewey's Science, Macdonald posited without elaboration a set of moral absolutes derived from prophets and poets. In rejecting Marx's History, he subscribed to the existentialist dictum that, with the future itself in doubt, the present must be infused with its own meaning. In rejecting Tolstoy's God as superfluous, he reiterated that "the root is man, here and not there, now and not then."[19] Arguing that the crisis of civilization was so profound that "only an alternative which is antithetical to the existing system can lead one to the abolition of that system," Macdonald called for the creation of a society "whose only aim, justification and principle would be the full development of each individual, and the removal of all social bars to his complete and immediate satisfaction in his work, his leisure, his sex life and all other aspects of his nature."[20]

The editor, who had elevated negativism into policy, who had considered the demolition of "the illusions and hypocrisies of the liberals and the labor movement" a worthy object of his magazine, felt compelled to suggest approaches to utopia.[21] Having denied the viability of mass action, he advocated "symbolic individual actions, based on one person's insistence on his own values, and through the creation of small fraternal groups which will support such actions, keep alive a sense of our ultimate goals, and both act as a leavening in the dough of mass society and attract more and more of the alienated and frustrated members of that society." Such groups should not be physically separated from the mass society; they should be organized according to principles of pacifism and noncoercion; and they should meet the state's coercion not only with draft refusal but with "sabotage, ridicule, evasion, argument."[22]

Not since the "Ten Propositions" five years earlier had Macdonald swum so far away from solid ground, and the undertow of his argument swept him beyond the point of meeting serious objections to his plea for small economic and political units. Could the town meeting repel the modern aggressor? "This is one more reason for giving up war (rather than the town meeting)." Would scientific research be made more difficult in such a society? "Let us by all means hamper it." How could a powerful and repressive government be challenged? "Encourage attitudes of disrespect, skepticism, ridicule towards the State and all authority, rather than . . . build up a competing authority." Violence should be met only with nonviolence, "which throws the enemy off balance . . . and confuses his human agents, all the more because it appeals to traitorous elements in their own hearts."[23] Although he recognized that man was both good and evil, Macdonald's pacifist absolutism ignored the practical difficulties of reaching those hearts hardened by the very historical forces he had so sensitively explored.

Instead of appealing to the enemy's human representatives, or to the proletariat, Macdonald pleaded the case for anarchist communities to the intelligentsia. For "what we are looking for represents so drastic a break with past traditions of thinking and behaving that at this early stage only a few crackpots and eccentrics (i.e., intellectuals) will understand what we're talking about, or care about it at all." In politics as in mechanics, cranks make revolutions; and Macdonald's individualism was directed toward a drastic change which was at least as much psychological as political: "We must emphasize the emotions, the imagination, the moral feelngs, the primacy of the individual human being once more."[24]

Not many intellectuals took Macdonald up on the suggestion to form anarchist communities founded upon pacifism. Richard Rovere was "deeply impressed" by Macdonald's struggle to justify the reorientation of radicalism, but doubted the viability of pacifism. He added that Macdonald had failed to meet "the libertarian criticisms of socialism," as represented in Hayek's warning in *The Road to Serfdom*, "that planning and liberty are incompatible. Historically, the evidence to date is all on their side." Even Chiaromonte, whose anarchism was more durable and more sophisticated, was disappointed: "Not only is the existence of superhistorical values, but also the validity of such positions as nonviolence and anarchism, are assumed rather than redemonstrated. No fresh argument is offered, no attention paid to the difficulties involved."[25]

The inevitable Marxist counterattack came at close quarters from Coser and Howe, who subjected "The Root Is Man" to friendly fire. Coser, who wrote for *Politics* under the nom de plume of Louis Clair, condemned Macdonald's pursuit of individual sensibility rather than collective action and his stress upon moral purity rather than political engagement. In "Digging at the Roots or Striking at the Branches," Coser feared that Macdonald's version of radicalism was doomed to historical irrelevance. Irving Howe, then a member of the editorial board of the Shachtmanite *Labor Action*, typed up a twenty-two-page reply to "The Root Is Man," identifying himself as "a *practicing* Marxist, that is, one who functions in a group." In "The Thirteenth Disciple," Howe objected to Macdonald's dismissal of the working class and obituary notice for a revolutionary movement, his snobbish preference for a "community of intellectuals and other saints." Howe also noticed, as did Chiaromonte, that Macdonald had left unexplained the philosophical warrant as well as the historical source of the moral values that were presumably required for human salvation.[26] It is worth noting that Howe later thought better of "The Root Is Man," considering it "in many ways the most poignant and authentic expression of the plight of those few intellectuals—Nicola Chiaromonte, Paul Goodman, Macdonald—who wished to dissociate themselves from the postwar turn to *Realpolitik* but could not find ways of transforming sentiments of rectitude and visions of utopia into a workable politics."[27]

Macdonald's attempt to infuse philosophy into his iconoclasm was taxing as well as poignant. The essay had taken him approximately two years to complete, but not only because of the frenetic demands of a one-man magazine. Before publication of "The Root Is Man," he admitted to the "intrinsic difficulties of an extremely broad subject (the problem being largely what *is* the subject)" and to his "own incompetence and dilatoriness (perhaps also I am not too happy about the conclusions being forced on me by reality as I see it)." And between the publication of the two parts, Macdonald further confessed to "feel[ing] a little fatigued by the rarified atmosphere of the magazine of late."[28]

Authorial anguish may help explain why "The Root Is Man" is more a period piece than an article which can reach beyond its immediate audience, and why it is also a sample of Macdonald's driest writing. It is as though he wrote the essay under the burden of obligation rather than with the breath of conviction. He believed that *someone* had to offer a prolegomenon to a new radicalism, not that he was equal to the task. What he once surmised in Simone Weil's "Factory Work" is applicable to "The Root Is Man": "By the time she wrote this article, Weil was pretty much disillusioned about Marxist socialism and the working-class movement. She probably felt some responsibility to give a 'positive' conclusion to her criticism and, reacting against Marxism, went in the other direction. The very tone of the writing suggests that her positive ideas did not come so spontaneously to her as her criticisms."[29]

8
The Pacifist Dilemma

When Macdonald had believed in the possibility of mass action, he had done little more than write and edit articles and sign manifestoes—even as a member of the Socialist Workers party and then the Workers party. When he felt the restricted scope of radical involvement, he plunged more eagerly into the practice of what he preached. The contemplative life and the politically active life are not so different as is commonly supposed, since both ineluctably depend upon the spoken, if not the written, word. Macdonald's "activism" therefore represented an extension more than an alteration of his previous engagements in politics.

During the war Macdonald had become impressed with "how much serious and original thinking is being done by CO's." He was pleased that the conscientious objectors and the historic peace churches were articulating a more fundamental opposition to government than a refusal to fight in its wars. Since the phoenix of revolt had not arisen from the ashes of Stalingrad and Hiroshima, Macdonald came to appreciate the validity of "individual protest. . . . Radicals must be more concerned about individual morality than they have been in the past."[1] What he expressed philosophically in "The Root Is Man" was expressed practically when he joined with younger pacifists emerging from the prisons and Civilian Public Service camps.

Macdonald's new associates had already practiced some of the principles espoused in his magazine. David Dellinger, also a Yale alumnus, was a socialist divinity student who had refused to register for the draft and had therefore spent the war years in prison, where he had engaged in hunger strikes to protest racial segregation and other penal conditions. George Houser, like Dellinger a former seminarian, had lived in voluntary poverty in Harlem and had been incarcerated for noncooperation with Selective Service. James Peck, a labor organizer in the 1930s, had helped make Danbury the first federal prison to desegregate its dining facilities when he went on a hunger strike in 1943; and he was to participate in the first direct action against nuclear testing after the war. Bayard Rustin was an alumnus of City College, a former organizer for the Young Communist League, a field secretary for the Congress of Racial Equality, and a conscientious objector who had served three years in jail.[2] The blazing convictions of the new generation of pacifists were often startling—"You mean they put you in here for *not* killing?" Louis Lepke asked one conscientious objector[3]—and the head of "Murder, Inc." was not the only one taken aback.

The Fellowship of Reconciliation, for example, did not approve the prison-hardened language of civil disobedience and draft resistance; and the traditional pacifists succeeded in keeping control of the 14,000-member organization. But the tinier War Resisters League was ripe for a takeover; and Abraham Kaufman, its executive director for nineteen years, decided to resign in 1947. Roy Kepler, an advocate of direct action, replaced him.[4] The League's executive committee included Dellinger, Houser, Peck, and Rustin, plus older proponents of militant nonviolence like Macdonald and A. J. Muste, who was then executive secretary of the Fellowship of Reconciliation and exerted no small influence upon younger pacifists. Muste once warned that "anyone is on very dangerous ground when he suggests there is something I haven't joined at one time or another."[5] While not openly advocating illegal acts, the executive committee of the War Resisters League resolved in 1947 to promote "political, economic, and social revolution by non-violent means."[6]

Macdonald also joined the Committee for Non-Violent Revolution, a predominantly socialist group which mixed pacifism and anarchism in its February 1946 organizing manifesto. Its members pledged themselves to nonviolence "as the instrument of mass revolution" and promised to "appeal to workers to leave war jobs and to soldiers to desert."[7] But how to persuade workers to refuse cooperation in peacetime with the Permanent War Economy was more challenging than phrasing a manifesto, as Macdonald and other members of the C.N.V.R. quickly discovered.

Peck, an organizer for the Workers Defense League, suggested that a picket line be formed in July 1946 at Oak Ridge, Tennessee. The aim was to protest both the atomic tests on Bikini and the development of atomic energy for warlike purposes. In the two planning sessions that were held in Macdonald's apartment, a half-dozen pacifists committed themselves to participation in the demonstration. The host himself declined on the grounds that he could not spare the time, especially in case of arrest.[8]

In any event Oak Ridge was not picketed because the C.I.O. feared interference with its organizing drive and urged Peck's contingent to stay away. Macdonald alone saw no reason to accede to the C.I.O. plea and in fact urged a confrontation. He noted that the union had meekly accepted its place at Oak Ridge, truckling to the government in order to exclude the rival A. F. of L.[9] Union leadership thus confirmed the point of Macdonald's earlier wisecrack that "it's a wise worker who knows his own fatherland,"[10] but he blamed the cancellation of the picket line on "a cultural lag." His Marxist colleagues assumed, quite incorrectly, that pacifism and support for the unions were compatible; and he wanted the increasing evidence of conflicting interests to be exposed rather than concealed. "It takes courage to risk probable arrest by the police and army in picketing an atomic bomb plant, but it also takes courage to clash with the unions, those sacred cows of Marxian doctrine; and the latter kind of courage, I suspect, will be increasingly needed by radicals in the future."[11]

A picket line was eventually set up in Washington, D.C., but Macdonald was not among the eleven arrested for parading without a permit.[12] David Dellinger thereupon accused Macdonald of parlor pacifism: "Serious revolutionaries require the courage to set aside intellectual duties, on occasion, in order to participate directly in the current struggles." And he pointedly asked Macdonald, "Did you not feel a little strange at being a) the only member of the committee who favored carrying out the demonstration, as originally planned; b) the only member of the committee who could not spare the time to participate?" Macdonald replied lamely that editing *Politics* was itself a "deed";[13] but his definition of a radical act sounded suspiciously like *Partisan Review's* earlier justification for printing Eliot's "Burnt Norton." Dellinger resented the writers' bloc, whose members defined themselves as intellectuals first and revolutionaries thereafter.

But even those who sought to create a center of radical activity rather than, as *Politics* claimed, "a center of consciousness on the Left" felt frustrated; and the Committee for Non-Violent Revolution was incorporated into Peacemakers in 1948. A chief purpose of the organization was to promote draft resistance by "taking politically radical steps in furtherance of pacifism."[14] Macdonald joined the Peacemakers' executive committee, which also included Dellinger, Houser, Kepler, *Politics* contributor Milton Mayer, Muste, and Rustin. In January 1947 Macdonald joined Dellinger, Houser, Mayer, Muste, Rustin, Donald Harrington, and Scott Nearing, among others, in signing an open letter which called for defiance of the Selective Service System. They branded the draft "an integral part of a consistent pattern . . . including the maintenance of huge military machines, the development of atomic and biological weapons, the scramble for colonies and raw materials." Advocating civil disobedience, the signatories in possession of draft cards promised to mail them to President Truman. The others pledged themselves to "write a letter to the President, expressing our solidarity and agreement with this action."[15]

Sixty-three men destroyed their draft cards on Lincoln's birthday in New York City, in the presence of policemen, F.B.I. agents, master of ceremonies Bayard Rustin, and speakers David Dellinger, A. J. Muste, and Dwight Macdonald. The editor of *Politics* told the audience of about 200 persons that "when the State—or rather, the individuals who speak in its name, for there is no such thing as the State—tells me that I must 'defend' it against foreign enemies . . . then I say that I cannot go along." Birth on American soil had been "quite involuntary" and no social contract bore his signature; he therefore claimed the right of civil disobedience against military induction.[16]

Macdonald was not prosecuted, and the Republican-controlled Congress permitted the bill establishing universal military training to die in the House Rules Committee later that year. In 1948, however, the issue was joined again, with Rustin's mentor, A. Philip Randolph, organizing the League for Non-Violent Civil Disobedience Against Military Segregation. An infuriated Senator Wayne Morse warned Randolph that civil disobedience in the event of a Russian attack could merit prosecution for treason; Randolph shot back that, before such an invasion, Congress still had time to abolish Jim Crow. Congress enacted a conscription law, and in July Truman ordered the desegregation of the armed forces.[17] For Macdonald it was a bitter victory; the abolition of a Jim Crow army which he had demanded four years earlier had come only in the aftermath of the first peacetime conscription law in American history.

Macdonald's plunge into pacifist activity deepened his hostility to the Soviet Union, whose course, he feared as early as March 1946, was leading to permanent militarization rather than the withering away of the state. He was disgusted by Stalin's most recent justification for socialism—that it wins wars—and noted characteristically: "On the evidence of Stalin's barbarous oratorical style alone, one could deduce the bureaucratic inhumanity and the primitiveness of modern Soviet society."[18] He added that "already, Stalin's Russia has taken the place of Hitler's Germany as a ruthless totalitarian power that is out to upset the Anglo-American status quo."[19] A year later he continued to refuse a choice between the Kremlin and the State Department. Nevertheless, in his analysis of the Truman Doctrine, the member of the executive committees of the War Resisters League and Peacemakers conceded that against Soviet imperialism "only a firm stand, backed by a show of force, will be effective. . . . Such a policy is more likely to postpone World War III than a 'soft' policy. But only to postpone it."[20]

With an honesty which bobbed to the surface with the inexorability of a cork, Macdonald's writing was revealing a certain ambivalence about American foreign policy which was not hitherto discernible. The accidental citizen still denounced his government as imperialist and still insisted that "power-plays by the U.S. State Department" could be rectified by "pacifist or social-revolutionary [tactics] or perhaps some new combination of both."[21] Yet he gradually found himself driven toward another *faute de mieux*. Two months after he expressed tentative support of the Truman Doctrine, *Foreign Affairs* published its most famous article, "The Sources of Soviet Conduct." There "X" marked the spot where George Kennan articulated "containment" as the ramification of the "firm stand" which Macdonald reluctantly advocated.

If the editor of *Politics* began to lose his assurance in delineating appropriate responses in the world arena, he nevertheless proved to be a devilishly competent tour guide in "Wallaceland," which was "the mental habitat of Henry Wallace plus a few hundred thousand regular readers of the *New Republic*, the *Nation*, and *PM*. It is a region of perpetual fogs, caused by the warm winds of the liberal Gulf Stream coming in contact with the Soviet glacier. Its natives speak 'Wallese,' a debased provincial dialect."[22] The Baedecker to "Wallaceland" was Macdonald's first book, *Henry Wallace: The Man and the Myth*, which was quarried primarily from his March-April and May-June 1947 articles in *Politics*. In the previous eight years, the subject of his book had risen from Secretary of Agriculture to vice president, then fallen to Secretary of Commerce and then to editor of the *New Republic*. By 1947 Communists and fellow-travelers were among the purveyors of a Wallace-for-president boomlet, and Macdonald warned: "A large power-mass like the Soviet Union exercises a tremendous gravitational pull on an erratic comet like Henry Wallace. In the past year . . . Wallace's Comet appears to have become a satellite of the larger body." Macdonald did not believe that Wallace would seek the presidency the following year;[23] but, even though the Americans for Democratic Action had been formed in part to inoculate liberals against the totalitarian bacillus, the author of what might be called an anticampaign biography was taking no chances. It was published the week its protagonist happened to announce his candidacy.

Macdonald toasted Wallace like a marshmallow. The former vice president, whom he had interviewed in 1946, "never analyzes a problem: he barges around inside it, throwing out vague exhortations." He was considered "a man not of principle but of principles—all of them all together all at once." Wallace was, for example, a believer in a people's capitalism defined as "a system of economic privilege in which *everyone* is a member of the elite. As for the class struggle, he wants everybody to win it."[24] Macdonald exhibited, as the purest sentence in "Wallese," "New frontiers beckon with meaningful adventure." He announced that "Wallese" was the secret of his rival editor's political success, for he offered "the liberals a commodity they crave: rhetoric which accomplishes in fantasy what cannot be accomplished in reality."[25]

Macdonald blamed Wallace's muddleheadedness not only for the peculiarities of his "style" but also for his willingness to become a dupe of the Stalinists. He was the sort of goodwill tourist who could visit Soviet Asia, accompanied by Owen Lattimore, and praise "men born in wide free spaces"—remarks which were delivered, Macdonald wrote, "to the assembled and stupefied prison-camp wardens of Irkutsk." The former vice president was therefore easy prey for Communist influence.[26] But when charges of Communist domination were first raised, one of the leading figures in Wallace's Progressive Citizens of America retorted: "Says who and so what? If . . . [our] program is like the Communist line, that is purely coincidental."[27] Macdonald had retained enough of his Marxism to minimize the importance of coincidence; and without considering valid domestic goals which he may have shared with Wallace, he damned the future candidate for behaving like a Soviet pawn.[28]

Although Macdonald was generally able to cite chapter and verse, a book so unrelieved in its exposure of Wallace's sins and follies ran the risk of caricature. Even *Time* deplored "the kind of recklessness that creates sympathy for the victim."[29] The book nevertheless had its admirers. Arthur Schlesinger, Jr. praised the initial account in *Politics* as "brilliant—the best thing written anywhere on him"; and Czeslaw Milosz, then an official in the Polish embassy in Washington, later a Nobel laureate in literature, used Macdonald's assessment of the Wallace movement in preparing his diplomatic reports. Sociologist David Riesman told Macdonald "how extraordinary a job of analysis" the *Politics* editor had performed. Riesman even compared Macdonald's dissection to "Freud in analyzing a dream, though without his dogmatism."[30]

The book sold only abour 3,500 copies, however, and seems to have exerted little if any impact upon the candidacy of the former vice president. *Henry Wallace: The Man and the Myth* is not even mentioned in the only historical account devoted to the Progressive party campaign, Karl M. Schmidt's *Henry A. Wallace: Quixotic Crusade, 1948*. In a broader historical treatment, Norman D. Markowitz's *The Rise and Fall of the People's Century*, Macdonald's book is mentioned only briefly, in an appendix, where it is referred to as a "tirade."[31]

Macdonald carried out his own campaign of Wallace *delenda est* when he spoke on several campuses. He "compared Wallace's demagogy to Hitler's . . . [and] spoke of Communism and Fascism as similar political formations, [but] a perceptible shudder ran through the audience." He then realized that the students had not attained "the level of sophistication I had reached in 1938"—when Macdonald had reached the age of thirty-two. "The experience of the thirties is not theirs; USSR to them is the wartime ally of the 'peace-loving democracies' against fascism."[32] Macdonald may well have exaggerated the extent of the postwar generation's naivete. In 1948 the Cold War was plainly in earnest, and domestic fears of Communism were rising. An American Legionnaire dean at the University of Illinois prohibited Macdonald himself from speaking on Wallace to the Socialist Study Club; and its president, an undergraduate named Albert Shanker, later president of the American Federation of Teachers, protested the violation of free speech—in a letter to *Politics*.[33]

Macdonald had wanted to denounce Wallace even more extensively, particularly under the auspices of the liberal Students for Democratic Action. He complained to the head of its parent organization, James Loeb of Americans for Democratic Action, that he should have been sponsored more energetically. Loeb's excuse—that Macdonald's analysis of Wallace was "completely negative"—drew this reply: "I have not yet learned to destroy a man's political reputation in a positive way."

Macdonald pointed out that "S.D.A. groups did sponsor me in Min-neapolis and at Antioch College . . . I found the attitude of Mayor [Hubert] Humphrey, of Minneapolis, who attended my first talk there . . . much more sensible than that of the A.D.A. central office. But of course in Minneapolis they have a real fight on with the Commies, and consequently want to get their knife into Wallace even at the risk of being 'completely negative.'" As though taking to heart the Marxist criticism of "The Root Is Man," Macdonald urged Loeb to commit the A.D.A. more energetically to "mass meetings and political action." And in the pages of *Fellowship* Magazine, Macdonald debated James Peck, who took the affirmative on the question, "Should Pacifists Vote for Henry Wallace?"[34]

In the general election Wallace lost badly; Macdonald was not sufficiently aroused to actually cast a vote in 1948. As an anarchist he found none of the candidates or parties appealing. Though Macdonald had voted for Al Smith in 1928, Roosevelt in 1932, and—here his memory blurred—Roosevelt or Norman Thomas in 1936, he successfully restrained his enthusiasm for the Democratic and Republican nominees in 1948. His opinion of Strom Thurmond of the Dixiecrats needed no elaboration. Macdonald considered the DeLeonites and the Trotskyists bush-league Bolsheviks, "midget totalitarians, in no significant way different from the American Communist Party except that they are smaller and look to native instead of Russian fuhrers and witch doctors." He also resisted the blandishments of the Greenback Party despite its intriguing proclamation of a program that was "neither right, left, nor center, but combining the best elements of all three."[35] That left Wallace—and Norman Thomas.

"My objection to Norman Thomas," Macdonald had written one election earlier, "can be put briefly: he is a liberal, not a socialist. . . . [His] role has always been that of the fighting crusader in small matters (like Hagueism and other civil liberties issues) and the timid conformist in big matters (like the . . . war)." He was offended by Thomas's "opportunism, his moral cowardice . . . his mealy-mouthed pulpit respectability . . . his comfortable liberalism, emotionally lukewarm and intellectually sterile." Yet Macdonald was still baffled by the task of classifying the Socialist tribune: "No one could ever accuse Norman Thomas of being an economic determinist, or of possessing, indeed, any theory of historical development. Nothing is excluded as impossible; one might call him a typical American pragmatist were it not that he refuses to learn from experience." Thus, in contrast to intellectuals like Bell, Hook, McCarthy, Mills, Phillips, Rahv, and Wilson, all of whom supported Thomas at least in part to undermine support for Wallace, Macdonald hoped that Thomas's vote would be small enough to erode his influence among Socialists.[36]

For all his sardonic skepticism, Macdonald sometimes picked out some curious silver linings. As a Trotskyist he had interpreted the inertia of the masses as proof of the failure of liberal reform and of "Win the War" as a galvanic rallying cry. In 1948 he detected in the refusal of forty-seven million Americans to march to the polls an anarchism of temperament if not of principle: "So healthy a degree of civic irresponsibility . . . is some cause for optimism in a dark age." Truman's victory over the opinion polls was hailed as "the Waterloo of the scientific method"— its Aboukir would be more accurate. Nor could Macdonald conceal his delight that Time, Inc. was perplexed by Dewey's defeat: "So shaken by November 2 were Luce's satraps . . . that an official phone call was put through to Sidney Hook humbly requesting light on the catastrophe."[37]

The following spring the ubiquitous philosophy professor strode into the Waldorf Hotel and asked permission to address the delegates of the Cultural and Scientific Conference for World Peace. Its sponsors knew that Hook had come to denounce the theory of the class nature of science, and therefore denied his request. They quickly learned, as did Macdonald, that Hook was "a man of considerable energy and bellicosity"; and at a meeting held in Macdonald's apartment, the Americans for Intellectual Freedom was born. Hook became the Clausewitz of the cultural Cold War by setting up an alternative conference at Freedom House and placing loudspeakers in Bryant Park. There thousands could hear the Waldorf Conference's claim to represent American culture punctured by educators like Hook and George Counts, biologists like George Biddle and Herman Muller, pacifists like Muste and historians like Schlesinger and Bertram Wolfe.[38]

Accompanied by Mary McCarthy, Elizabeth Hardwick, and Robert Lowell, Macdonald decided to pay three dollars to attend the Waldorf Conference, which must have struck him as the Second American Writers' Congress redivivus. He had no doubt who was behind the Conference: he simply spotted "all the old familiar Stalinoid names" like Howard Fast, F. O. Matthiessen, Clifford Odets, Frederick Schuman, I. F. Stone, and Paul Sweezy, added "some political illiterates," subtracted "every known opponent of the Communists," and concluded,

QED, that he was attending an operation of a party front, an instance of submission to Moscow. Along with some colleagues from the Americans for Intellectual Freedom, Macdonald decided to trouble the oily waters of the session on writing and publishing.[39]

The 1949 model of Granville Hicks was the critic Louis Untermeyer, whose categorization of Hook as "a dirty, four-letter word" provoked a protest from the floor; and Untermeyer thereupon complied with Lowell's demand for a retraction. Macdonald was impressed by the poet's incisiveness and clarity throughout the sessions. Macdonald himself listened patiently to the panelists' speeches, cherishing Professor Matthiessen's description of Captain Ahab as a "common man." When the meeting was thrown open to the floor, Macdonald was on his feet, despite "some commotion." He protested the presence on the panel of A. A. Fadayev, the secretary of the Union of Soviet Writers, whom Macdonald identified as "primarily not a writer but a State functionary." Macdonald then asked Fadayev of the whereabouts of authors like Boris Pasternak, Isaac Babel, and Anna Akhmatova; he inquired why Fadayev's own novel had been rewritten in the wake of political criticism; and he questioned Fadayev about his attacks upon American culture and civil liberty delivered in Wroclaw, Poland, the previous fall.[40]

"With angry gestures, his flushed face thrust forward aggressively," Fadayev offered his interlocutor an animated set of answers. He lied that Babel was still alive, asserted that "the Politburo's criticism has helped my work greatly," and boasted that his knowledge of American literature was superior to Macdonald's command of Russian literature. At least Fadayev was indisputably correct in his conclusion: "The point of view of my questioner is familiar: it is that of an enemy of the Soviet Union." Mary McCarthy, another veteran of the 1937 campaign, then asked Matthiessen if he considered Fadayev's response to Macdonald adequate. The Harvard literary historian assured her that "Mr. Fadayev met the questions directly, in fact head-on." Macdonald agreed, "in the sense that he collided violently with them," but Macdonald deplored Untermeyer's refusal to permit him to expose Fadayev's mendacity. Other dissidents took the floor, however; and Macdonald later gloated that "the organizers of the Conference had done a slipshod job. . . . They had evidently calculated on an idyllic rather than a dramatic work of art. Comrade Fast will certainly hear from headquarters about this."[41]

Then came the surprise ending to the story. Comrade Fast invited the dissidents to a reception, and Macdonald was amazed to find the

Stalinoids very *simpático*: "We had a common culture and even (oddly enough) political background: that is, we read the same books . . . shared the same convictions in favor of the (American) underdog . . . and against such institutions as the Catholic hierarchy and the U.S. State Department." Even educational backgrounds were similar: Corliss Lamont had graduated from Phillips Exeter Academy four years ahead of Macdonald, Paul Sweezy three years after him. In striking contrast to the bonhomie were the numerous pickets outside the Waldorf, whose patriotic purification rites led them to treat all those inside the hotel as damaged goods. In fact they booed Macdonald "as roundly as any other delegate (since their hatred was directed against all alien-appearing intellectuals)." According to Norman Mailer, who dramatically resigned from the Progressive party at the Conference, the delegates were confronted with the "all but open incitements to violence in the New York tabloids"; and Macdonald got a taste of a different variety of anti-Communism. The picketers "marched under the (to me repulsive) banners of religion and patriotism" instead of the third camp or the Peacemakers,[42] and they were to be the harbingers of the sterile and often indiscriminately woolly anti-Communism of the succeeding decade.

Poised between the random hysteria of the canaille outside and the cultivated geniality of the Stalinoids inside, Macdonald stood at the pathetic epicenter of independent radicalism. The Waldorf Conference exposed the stark alternatives and the narrowness of the choices. Macdonald had already given up reading *PM* before it folded, because its Soviet apologetics had opened too wide a "gap . . . between our respective methods of thinking and behaving."[43] He had once been able to give the *New Republic* and the *Nation* a reading that was razor-close, but now they simply annoyed him when they did not bore him. Yet he did not even bother to engage in controversy with the social democratic, indubitably anti-Communist *New Leader*, since "the whole level is so low, the terrain so marshy, that one would have to spend most of one's energy defining what the argument is about."[44] The Waldorf Conference epitomized the poignancy of Macdonald's plight and adumbrated the price that radical intellectuals would still have to pay for too many Kronstadts.

On 19 June 1948 the Soviet Union had clamped a blockade upon all surface traffic into West Berlin, and for a year only the airlifts of the United States Air Force kept its inhabitants alive. The same kinds of Americans who had dropped bombs on the city in 1945 were unloading food packages four years later. "There is indeed a logic to both actions," Macdonald observed, "but it is not a human, not a rational or ethical logic. It is rather the logic of a social mechanism which has grown so powerful that human beings have become simply its instruments."[45]

Nor did he find cause to praise the heroism of the West Berliner, who had "about the same chance of determining his own fate as a hog dangling by one foot from the conveyor belt of a Chicago packing plant." That others applauded the courage of those who had so recently been held accountable for Nazism merely corroborated the thesis of "The Responsibility of Peoples." Macdonald was pleased that West Berliners demonstrated "enough primitive sense of their own materialistic interests, enough distaste for the police state even when bedecked with red banners, to prefer Western 'decadence' and 'stagnation' to the dynamism of the terrible Utopia offered by the East." Their preference for the West was "a modest enough triumph,"[46] but it presented what Macdonald called "the pacifist dilemma."[47]

The Soviet Union was, after all, "the most militarist, imperialist, anti-democratic and reactionary nation in the world."[48] Sadly enough, only a "most reactionary organization whose purpose is mass slaughter," the American military, seemed capable of resisting Soviet advances. A. J. Muste's petitions could not adequately protect the West Berliners' trade unions, their freely elected government, their already limited liberties. While chafing at the unimaginative strategy of the State Department, Macdonald praised "the happy inspiration of the Marshall Plan"; and in renouncing pacifism, he urged a hard line against "comrades Stalin, Molotov, Vishinsky, et al. These gentlemen would interpret any showing of brotherly love by the West as simply weakness."[49]

Soviet imperialists would have been less vulnerable to nonviolent resistance than British imperialists, yet Macdonald also recognized that Gandhi's own "life work had been in vain." Like the Berlin blockade, the internecine outcome of Indian independence deepened Macdonald's sense of the futility of nonviolent tactics. And like Trotsky's assassination, the murder of the Mahatma early in 1948 came as an emotional shock. Both men had been executed not by their oppressors but by "the scum that had frothed up from their own heroic struggle to liberate mankind: young fanatics representing a new order. . . . The assassins killed not only two men, but also two cultures. Which makes it all the more painful." Gandhi's death not only emptied the vessel of Macdonald's pacifist faith but also touched his anarchist sensibility: "Gandhi was the last political leader in the world who was a person, not a mask or a radio voice or an institution. The last on a human scale. . . . He practiced tolerance and love to such an extent that he seems to have regarded the capitalist as well as the garbage-man as his social equal."[50]

In the same issue of *Politics* which contained his eulogy of Gandhi, its editor confessed to "feeling stale, tired, disheartened, and . . . demoralized." He blamed his exhaustion upon "the ever bleaker and bleaker political outlook," the tedium of research necessary to interpret a complicated world, and "the psychological demands of a one-man magazine which, at first stimulating, have latterly become simply—demands."[51]

He did have editorial help as well as exceptionally loyal readers, however. Help consisted largely of "Theodore Dryden," the nom de plume of Irving Howe, then still a Trotskyist. For fifteen dollars per week, Howe "did editorial chores, reworking pieces, and writing a 'Magazine Chronicle' praising or attacking articles in other magazines." Macdonald was "a brilliant journalist," Howe recalled, but "a hard boss, charmingly irascible, at once bright and silly." The former employee stressed Macdonald's "deadly eye for dead prose, especially the weighty sort of deadness I brought with me, but he was insensitive to styles not immediately transparent or journalistically 'clean,' like Harold Rosenberg's epigrammatic prose." But as *Politics* neared its demise, Howe too found the magazine "boring." He was replaced by Thomas B. Morgan, freshly graduated from Carleton College, who arrived in New York for an interview. "You've got a job," Macdonald told him, handing Morgan a broom. "Sweep out the room. We've just folded."[52] (Morgan would later marry a daughter of Nelson Rockefeller and buy the *Nation*.)

The inexorable death of *Politics*, in 1949, was due in part to financial causes. Contributors were paid only five dollars per printed page, yet printing costs doubled in the roughly four years of the magazine's existence—mostly because of the wage increases that the powerful New York printing unions had won. Macdonald recalled: "As a friend of the working class, I couldn't object. But as a publisher, I couldn't continue."[53]

Hopes that the magazine might be resuscitated were kindled at home and abroad. One devoted friend of the magazine was T. S. Eliot, who called *Politics* "the brightest spot in American journalism, so I very much hope that some way will be found to keep it going." Eliot's own politics were quite unlike those of the magazine he admired, but he was eager to meet its editor during a visit to the Unitd States late in 1948. A diverting incident occurred. Eliot climbed the three flights of steps to the Macdonalds' apartment, joining the poet John Berryman and his wife, who recalled that Macdonald's "manner remained unchanged no matter to whom he was speaking. Eliot seemed at ease." Because of the new Nobel laureate's shyness, only one other person was invited, Paul Goodman, who showed up with his hair unkempt, his clothing ripped and stained, and mud on his shoes. Berryman introduced the guest of honor to Goodman, who leaned forward and asked: "I didn't get it. What's the name?" "Eliot. Tom Eliot" was the amused reply. Later, after the guest of honor departed, Macdonald berated his chief American contributor: "Goodman, my God! *What manners* ! You knew damn well who he was." Goodman blamed his shortsightedness.[54]

Eliot's hope that *Politics* might be saved was shared by others. Mary McCarthy participated in plans to keep the magazine going, as did Arendt, whom Macdonald considered more on his own "wave-length than anybody else." (Interestingly enough, her teacher Karl Jaspers learned that Arendt had survived the Second World War only because, in its aftermath, Melvin Lasky had brought Jaspers a copy of *Politics* and mentioned her name.[55]) From Paris, as late as 1953, Milosz wrote Macdonald: "It is a pity that you do not continue to publish *Politics*. That publication had more influence than the editor could suppose." But by then it was too late. As Macdonald wrote Eliot, the magazine had seemed to be valuable to more readers, "in a personal, unique way," than he had realized. But he had to write for money, "as the family is broke."[56]

But finances were not the only cause of death. Its raison d'être of impassioned independence was disintegrating. And the final issue itself was a mirror test which showed that Macdonald's radicalism was no longer breathing. Muste had written a letter expressing his conviction that "two ethically symmetrical power-systems confront each other." Macdonald could no longer adhere to pacifism, however, because he now discriminated between the Soviet Union and the United States and feared one power-system as a threat to peace.[57] In an article entitled "The Uncommon People," he relished the unpredictability of human beings; but aphorisms like "Judges sometimes act as decently as pickpockets" defined the remains of Macdonald's anarchism.[58] He had been unable to extend the contours of his individualism from psychology to politics, and therefore a magazine named *Politics* could no longer be justified. Macdonald could not make anarchism more operative in his own country than he could consider pacifism an effective antidote to injustice in the world. Revolutionary socialism, nonviolent resistance, anarchism—by an ineluctable paradox, they had to be jettisoned only after they had been championed and then tested for their limitations.

9
L'Envoi

With faded hopes for the pollination of pacifist communities, Macdonald resigned from the executive committee of the War Resisters
League in the spring of 1949. In a letter to its executive secretary,
Macdonald deemed pacifism ethically defective because nonviolence
would have the effect of surrendering even more millions to Soviet
tyranny. The War Resisters League had failed "to suggest a reasonably
workable pacifist approach to the problem of Stalinist aggression."[1] Its
former chairman, Evan Thomas, resigned the following year after a
lifetime of pacifist struggle that now seemed of questionable value: "I am
less certain than I formerly was of the best ways to resist this worst of all
mankind's evils." His older brother, Norman, who had usually been at
least ambivalent about American foreign policy, supported the strategy
of containment after the 1948 Communist coup in Prague. Roy Kepler
discovered after a cross-country tour that year that Peacemakers was
rapidly becoming an extinct organization.[2]

The following year, even as Macdonald was resigning from the
W.R.L. executive committee, he quit the Peacemakers as well, for the
same reason. He felt "a growing doubt about pacifism as a political tactic
today, a doubt as to both its possible effectiveness and also its ethical
justification." Macdonald also told Muste of his lessening interest in the
work of organizations and committees.[3] Albert Einstein, a pacifist who
had uttered a simple, poignant "Oh, weh" upon hearing the first news of
Hiroshima, sighed fatalistically to Muste in 1950: "The men who possess
the real power in this country have no intention of ending the cold war."[4]
Others distanced themselves even further from the credo of nonviolence. Lord Bertrand Russell, who had been jailed for his pacifist

convictions in World War I, urged the United States to use its nuclear monopoly if necessary to force the Soviet Union into a world government.[5] These were among the indices of the travail of pacifism.

Without a magazine in which to express his remaining convictions, Macdonald turned in 1951 to the *New Leader*—which he had once scorned for having nothing to recommend it except anti-Communism—for the publication of a three-part series conceived in a spirit of piety rather than of critical scrutiny. He called Hannah Arendt "the most original and profound—therefore most valuable—political thinker of our times," and he concluded from her *Origins of Totalitarianism* that "a fundamentally new way of thinking (and, above all, of feeling) is necessary if we are to escape destruction."[6] Yet the book reviewer himself made no moves in that direction, perhaps because Arendt's emphasis upon the lunatic similarities between Nazis and Communists served to harden a Cold War posture of implacable opposition, perhaps also because her insistence upon the efficiency of totalitarian rule confirmed his sense of impotent resignation.

In the winter of 1952, plagued by the either/or which had doggedly pursued him since the middle of the "low, dishonest decade" of the thirties, Macdonald explicitly made a choice. To a Mount Holyoke College audience, he announced: "I Choose the West." He hastened to add: "I support it critically . . . but in general I *do* choose, I support Western policies." Temperamentally incapable of yes-saying, Macdonald staked out a position defined far more by anti-Communism than by reconciliation to America: "I choose the West because I see the present conflict not as another struggle between basically similar imperialisms as was World War I but as a fight to the death between radically different cultures. . . . Soviet Communism . . . is a throwback not to the relatively humane middle ages but to the great slave societies of Egypt and the Orient." Without affirming or repudiating the validity of his position in World War II, Macdonald finally adopted in 1952 the argument of virtually the entire left intelligentsia in 1942: "I prefer an imperfectly living, open society to a perfectly dead, closed society."[7]

Macdonald's speech was part of a debate, but he did not clarify who was asking him to make such a choice, or why the choice was indeed necessary, or what the practical consequences were. In fact his adversary in the debate, Norman Mailer, found himself unable to choose, thus extending the tradition of the early *Politics*. *The Naked and the Dead*, published four years earlier, had dramatized an American military society which strikingly resembled the tyrannical, irrational world of total-itarianism; yet in the novel some human beings prove resilient enough to place limits upon oppression, a toughness Macdonald did not dare to hope for in the Russian people.[8] But the clue to Mailer's position could be found in his contribution to a *Partisan Review* symposium that summer, in which he insisted that "the great artists—certainly the moderns—are almost always in opposition to their society." Mailer proclaimed the necessity of critical independence at a time when "no one of the intellectuals who find themselves now in the American grain ever discuss—at least in print—the needs of modern war. . . . Nor is it polite to suggest that the prosperity of America depends upon the production of means of destruction, and it is not only the Soviet Union which is driven toward war as an answer to insoluble problems."[9]

Mailer's warning against the atrophy of the critical intelligence was quickly substantiated, as Macdonald's choice of the West cut short his own attention span for politics. With Marxism, anarchism, and pacifism discarded onto the proverbial scrap-heap of history, Macdonald could find no new grand scheme for change. For some, like Daniel Bell, the exhaustion of ideology gave the West an opportunity to effect incremental improvements in the public realm. But for Macdonald, who had once attempted to thrash out the difference between a degenerated workers' state and a bureaucratically collectivist state, a politics without heroic possibilities and grandiose ideas and memorable speech was simply banal. Since technocracy was itself a large part of the terror of modern life, he "lost . . . interest in politics and in economics, for the simple reason that I don't see very much that can be done in these fields now."[10] Here his attitude was the opposite of proponents of the "end of ideology," for whom the reform of the polity became a genuine possibility with the abandonment of "metapolitics." Though he still considered himself something of a pacifist fellow-traveler, he feared appeasement of the Soviet Union. Having written valiantly on politics since 1937, he could not bear to watch "the whole ghastly newsreel flickering through once more in a second showing."[11]

In 1951 Macdonald joined the staff of the *New Yorker*, the very magazine at which he had sneered in his first contribution as editor of *Partisan Review*.[12] Once more he could write *pour épater les bourgeois*; and in going "against the American grain," he could crush many "midcult" pretensions. Macdonald's choice of the *New Yorker* was also a strange vindication of a scorched-earth policy. He had begun his journalistic career with *Fortune*; then called Time, Inc. "proto-fascist" in the pages of the *Nation*; then scoffed at the *Nation*'s editor, Max Lerner, in the pages of *New International*; then mocked the *New International*'s "revolutionary kibitzers" from his bastion at *Partisan Review*; then blue-penciled the editorial style and policy of Rahv and Phillips in the columns of *Politics*, only to be given the freedom of the *New Yorker*'s slick pages to deflate the cultural ambitions of many of his readers.

Macdonald's retreat from radicalism was symptomatic of the new temper. In England Arthur Koestler, who wrote his last political essays in 1950, pleaded: "Now the errors are atoned for, the bitter passion has burnt itself out; Cassandra has grown hoarse, and is due for a vocational change." In 1952–53 William Phillips, who told Koestler in 1946 that liberals still risked being tempted by totalitarianism, became a regular contributor to the stiffly conservative *American Mercury*.[13] Alfred Kazin, who had spoken Yiddish in his Brownsville home and picked up socialism as if by osmosis, and whose first book had fathomed the depths of alienation among American writers, made so proprietary a reference to Francis Parkman's *Oregon Trail* in *Partisan Review* that he was kidded: "*Our* forests, Alfred?"[14]

Our forests—as well as "Our Country and Our Culture," which was the title of a *Partisan Review* symposium in 1952. Nearly all the participants seemed to agree with Philip Rahv that "we have gained a sense of immediate relatedness to the national environment" and that the rejection of utopias made sense.[15] Two survivors of a heroic bohemian past, Max Eastman and John Dos Passos, publicly supported Senator Robert Taft for the Republican presidential nomination in 1952. In 1953 Macdonald's old antagonist, Granville Hicks, appeared as a friendly witness before the House Un-American Activities Committee. He was accompanied by a former member of his Harvard cell-group, Daniel Boorstin, who had celebrated *The Genius of American Politics* the year before Hicks wrote that he "liked America in 1938, but I like it even better in 1954."[16]

Also pleased with America was the new conservative journal, the *Freeman*, whose managing editor, Suzanne LaFollette, had been secretary of the Dewey Commission to hear Trotsky's side of the story. One of its editorials illuminated the resurgent anti-Communism of the right that had so appalled Macdonald at the Waldorf Conference: "Why do so many sincere anti-Communists hate Joe McCarthy? Personally we think it is a matter of pique or wounded amour-propre. Here the boys, from Sidney Hook to Arthur Schlesinger, had been carrying an anti-Stalinist

torch, honorably but without any important results. " The editors, dem-
onstrating a sure instinct for le mot juste, then described "a pop-off guy
with a gift for dramatizing the issue, [who] muscled in on what had been
an intellectuals' preserve. Action followed. . . . It was enough to burn any
good intellectual to see Joe carrying off something that had never been
carried off before."[17] It did not seem to matter to the McCarthyites that
their hero could not have found a Communist in Red Square. The
coarseness of this brand of anti-Communism, by publicists unfit to
fertilize George Orwell's aspidistra, was to dominate much of the rhetoric
of public life in the 1950s.

The pop-off guy from Wisconsin did not madden all intellectuals,
however. James Burnham resigned from the advisory board of Partisan
Review in 1953 because of its hostility to McCarthy; but the editors'
parting salvo at Burnham, in which they expressed their dislike for "the
new anti-anti-McCarthy attitude," was scarcely calculated to echo
through the ages. And Commentary managing editor Irving Kristol, also
a former radical, produced a curiously ambivalent article about
McCarthyism in 1952 in which he denied that "it is necessary to protect
Communism in order to defend liberalism."[18] Macdonald's own position
during the 1950s was sensible, balanced, and admirable. The anti-
Stalinism that kept the most regular beat of his politics did not so
dominate his concerns that he ignored the fragility of civil liberties. A
test case was his stance toward his former comrades. He had long
regarded the Shachtmanites as "no more than a variant of Stalinism,"
which may be why the Department of Justice put the Workers party on its
list of subversive organizations in 1947. Party members were harassed,
fired from their jobs, and given dishonorable discharges—all without
hearings or formal charges. In 1956 Macdonald joined Daniel Bell and
Norman Thomas on the stand as expert witnesses in the defense of what
now called itself the Independent Socialist League. Macdonald fully
supported the group's political rights but hoped that the government's
lawyers would not inquire why Macdonald had resigned. Omitting mention of the "undemocratic nature" of the Shachtmanite sect, Macdonald
told the court that the party was "not an action group but a propaganda
and educational society. . . . The question of 'overthrowing the government' by non-Constitutional means—or indeed any means—never
came up when I was there," he recalled telling defense attorney Joseph
Rauh, "since there were only five hundred or so of us, and we weren't
lunatics." The sect was dropped from the Department of Justice rolls of

subversive organizations, possibly to avoid an invalidation of the entire attorney general's list by the Supreme Court.[19] Macdonald's intense opposition to totalitarianism did not weaken his powers of discrimination and proportion.

Nor did he abandon politics entirely. The opposition to the Waldorf Conference in 1949, organized in Macdonald's apartment, was transformed two years later into the American Committee for Cultural Freedom, itself an independent affiliate of the Congress for Cultural Freedom. The A.C.C.F. proposed to "counteract the influence of mendacious Communist propaganda," as Macdonald and others had done at the Waldorf Conference; to protect academic freedom; and to oppose "thought-control." The membership of the A.C.C.F. never exceeded six hundred, and ran the gamut of the anti-Stalinist intelligentsia. Its right flank included both Burnham and Whittaker Chambers (despite his reservations about belonging to the same group as J. Robert Oppenheimer). Its first chairman was the indefatigable Hook; its first secretary, Irving Kristol. The A.C.C.F. was funded by public contributions and by the Congress for Cultural Freedom, whose first director, Michael Josselson, was a C.I.A. agent. It is still not known how much money from the C.I.A. was funneled into the A.C.C.F.; but by 1957 the organization largely ceased its activities against "thought-control," due in no small measure to financial anemia.[20]

Macdonald played a minor role in the A.C.C.F., and felt the dilemma of a leftist anti-Stalinist obliged to unite with those less devoted to other values that Macdonald cherished. It was not enough to detest Soviet depredations of human freedom, he believed; by the early 1950s, the intellectual defenses of these depredations had crumbled anyway. The A.C.C.F. was supposed to combat the threats to political and cultural liberty in the United States as well. Less than a year after the organization was established, but over two years after Senator McCarthy had inaugurated his reckless attacks upon the loyalty of other Americans, Macdonald urged the A.C.C.F. to condemn both the man and the ism. His allies included Rahv, Schlesinger, and Diana Trilling; their opponents included Phillips and Karl Wittfogel, a former Communist who had survived a Nazi concentration camp. A split in the organization was threatened. A milder resolution was introduced by Bell and Kristol that circumspectly did not name any demagogues; it criticized both Communism and "certain types of anti-communism." The resolution was postponed. Bell's separate resolution, denouncing by name the junior senator from Wisconsin, later passed unanimously. Some hemorrhaging of membership could not be avoided. Burnham resigned in 1954 because he perceived the A.C.C.F. as anti-McCarthy, and Schlesinger withdrew a year later because the A.C.C.F. was, in his view, obsessed with the receding domestic danger of Communism.[21] Macdonald, who quit in 1954, later remarked in a private letter to a radical sociologist that Kristol and Bell "have long fascinated me by the acuteness of their specific criticisms of our institutions and the blandly unimaginative way they accept the status quo in general."[22]

As an editor of *Encounter*, Kristol was apparently decisive in rejecting an article that Macdonald submitted to the magazine that was rather derisively and one-sidedly anti-American. Having spent a year in London as an advisory editor to *Encounter*, Macdonald returned to the United States in 1957 to discover "an unhappy people . . . a people without style, without a sense of what is humanly satisfying." Americans seemed incredibly prosperous, possessing more "than Fourier, Proudhon, or Marx could have imagined possible." Yet the "terrible shapelessness" and joylessness of the national life was due to a deprived sense of tradition and of community, resulting in public manners that were "either bad or non-existent," shocking levels of violence, the ugliness of the human environment, eerie isolation, and the inability to form decent contacts with other peoples. Macdonald wrote: "Americans appear to other nations to be at once gross and sentimental, immature and tough, uncultivated and hypocritical, shrewd about small things and stupid about big things. In these antinomies fatally appears our lack of style."[23] The article was emblazoned with the same title as an early short story by Delmore Schwartz, "America! America!"

Encounter initially accepted the article by its former advisory editor, then rejected it, then reaccepted it, then finally re-rejected it. Kristol complained of the "bad impression" made by "an American, writing for an English publication, [who] seems determined to say the worst about his own country. It leaves a bad taste in people's mouths. . . . Your article," he wrote Macdonald in 1958, "is . . . in the nature of rock-throwing." Macdonald characterized his article instead as "a note of major questioning of the U.S. way of life. . . . I'm most distressed about the kind of life we've developed over here, and I think it both my privilege and duty to say so. If it leaves a bad taste, well really, I have never cared about that." As though inadvertently proving his own point about the lack of community feeling in America, Macdonald added: "I don't seem to feel a kind of group loyalty that many others do feel." From Paris, Michael Josselson explained to Macdonald that "the sympathy and confidence of the foundations has [sic] been won through hard labor, . . . without [which] . . . *Encounter* and much else would cease to exist. A certain amount of diplomacy and tact" was therefore required, and Josselson feared that the publication of articles like "America! America!" would jeopardize the future of the magazine.[24]

Macdonald was obliged to follow such advice, and his article was published elsewhere. It appeared first in the American *Dissent*, where it was prefaced by the author's own account of the *Encounter* rejection, then in the British *Twentieth Century*, and finally—paradoxically enough—in another magazine sponsored by the Congress of Cultural Freedom, the Italian *Tempo Presente*, cofounded by Ignazio Silone and Chiaromonte. Less than a decade later, the significance of the *Encounter* episode was cast in a more sinister light with the revelations of the C.I.A. subsidies. Macdonald was "convinced that [editors Stephen] Spender and Kristol didn't know about the C.I.A. financing." But the Paris office did, of course. In an angry letter to Josselson, Macdonald noted that the secret financing of a magazine by an espionage agency had occurred "just as all my more radical friends insisted . . . I, like a damned fool, denied [it] on the grounds they didn't have any hard evidence (as of course they didn't—and couldn't). . . . I've been played for a sucker." He insisted that he would never have worked or written for *Encounter* had he known what *Ramparts* magazine disclosed in 1967 about the C.I.A. funding.[25]

Kristol himself was more studied and casual in his response to the revelations; and in seeking to minimize the imputation of outside interference in the editorial life of *Encounter*, he later told one interviewer that Macdonald was scheduled to have been his own successor in coediting the magazine. "Could the C.I.A. really have 'endorsed' *him*?" Kristol parried. "Dwight has spent a fruitful life and distinguished career purposefully being a security risk to just about everyone and everything within reach of his typewriter." Such drollery fudged the question of the propriety of an espionage agency subsidy, since not even Macdonald charged that there was much, if any, pressure upon the actual editorial decisions at *Encounter*. As Peter Steinfels also pointed out, "the incident does not support Kristol's point but indicates that *someone*, whether or not the C.I.A., was standing watch." Macdonald did not replace Kristol, Steinfels reports, because of the opposition of Hook and "other ideological elders." Instead Kristol's successor was another former

Trotskyist, Melvin Lasky, who admitted his own knowledge of C.I.A. funding dating to 1963, and who remained as an *Encounter* editor even after Spender and another British editor resigned in the wake of the scandal.[26]

It was fitting that "America! America!" was first printed in *Dissent*, since the socialist magazine founded by Howe and Coser in 1954 was hardly unaware of the shadow of its celebrated predecessor in independent radicalism. Writing to Macdonald in 1953, Coser acknowledged that *Dissent* "will be by no means as good as *Politics* used to be [,] but it will at least be an effort to provide a forum for dissenters of various stripes and hues." Four years later Coser was still bewitched by the "almost mystical aura that *Politics* has acquired among the younger generation." The Brandeis University sociologist had reread back issues of Macdonald's magazine: "It still stands up beautifully, wish we could fully emulate it." But *Dissent* didn't, Macdonald agreed. Or so he implied in 1959, reviewing an anthology of articles from what he called "the best left-wing political magazine we have, which makes it all the more depressing." Macdonald praised the seriousness and critical stance of the *Dissent* circle, whose editorial board included other *Politics* alumni like Travers Clement, Frank Marquart, Meyer Schapiro, and George Woodcock. He welcomed so undoctrinaire an approach to socialism. But "the very idea of socialism is no longer interesting," Macdonald concluded; "it is at once banal and ambiguous." There was a certain "mandarin quality" to the magazine, a dullness from which only some dissenters of the 1950s— for example, Goodman, Mills, and Mailer—contrived to escape.[27] *Dissent* upheld the socialism which had once been bound so closely to the anti-Communism of the New York intellecturals. But as Macdonald realized when he explicitly chose the West, the cause of the democratic left was for the immediate future honorable but lost.

After the death of *Politics*, Macdonald transformed himself from an intensely political intellectual to a formidable cultural critic. The transformation coincided with changes in his personal life as well, as he divorced his wife, Nancy, the mother of their two sons, and in 1954 married Gloria Lanier. Macdonald's mother died in 1957. He was still, in the phrase that Spiro Agnew would later make famous, a nattering nabob of negativism, an incessant—and incessantly vibrant—foe of the American public culture.

His studies in the expression of mass culture and his literary and cinematic essays are beyond the scope of this book, but one curious aspect of his criticism should be mentioned. In a general sense Macdonald realized that social and political arrangements shaped the possibility, to quote Confucius, that "ceremonies and music will flourish." But the passions of his politics did not dictate his aesthetic judgments; his responses to novels and films usually did not stem from his radicalism. The fact that Macdonald championed a society that would reduce depersonalization and would enhance the autonomy of the masses did not require him to share their tastes. He wished to promote the self-respect of common citizens without sentimentalizing—or sharing—their cultural habits. Macdonald believed in defending the melancholy complexity of modern art that had been forged in his youth, and therefore he was often accused of elitism and snobbery.

Such charges do not do justice to his work as a practicing critic, for he rarely wrote about the rarified. He specialized in the documents of "midcult" and its uneasy relationship with high art and folk traditions. He took far more seriously than most of his critical peers the overly ambitious, the theoretically inflated, the ponderous monuments of mass culture—from pretentious best-sellers to Biblical revisions to indulgent dictionaries to the *Syntopicon*. Macdonald wrote sympathetically of such artist-entertainers as Mark Twain, and was one of the first American intellectuals to plumb the greatest of the mass arts: film. He cared enough about popular taste to dream that it could be improved. His negativism and elitism—or, rather, his skepticism—therefore had prophylactic value. And like his political writings, Macdonald's cultural criticism was bereft of theory, which he suspected added misleadingly to the weight, like a butcher's thumb upon the scales. The acuity of his opinions and the liveliness of his wit, decanted mostly in the *New Yorker*, *Esquire*, and *The New York Review of Books*, blessed him with a much wider following than ever read *The New International*, *Partisan Review*, or *Politics*. Such a shift in focus also made Macdonald a symptomatic figure, especially in the 1950s, the decade that Daniel Bell had characterized as "the exhaustion of political ideas."

Whatever persisted of radicalism in the late 1950s, according to another *Politics* contributor, Nathan Glazer, included little more than opposition to New Dealish bureaucracy, hopes invested in anti-colonialism, support for urban renewal and for initiatives toward a thaw in the Cold War. Among the "mild radicals" still around, Glazer mentioned Goodman, Howe, Mills, Michael Harrington—and Dwight Macdonald. They were not without programs or ideas. But for all the impact such figures had on the policies of the United States, they might as well have adopted the Essene Manual of Discipline. It therefore fell to Howe to suggest the epitaph for his generation's radicalism: "From a doctrine it became a style, and from a style a memory."[28]

10
The New Left's Ancestral Voice

Less than a decade after Howe's eulogy, radicalism was once again to become a style; and about a decade after that, it was to become a doctrine as well. While it was still a style, however, the legacy of *Politics* was to be felt in ways that perhaps none of its contributors or readers in the 1940s could have suspected. When Macdonald had been shopping around for a name for his new magazine, he almost selected *New Left*, until C. Wright Mills suggested *Politics* instead. Nearly two decades later Mills applied the phrase used to describe Britain's angry young radicals to their American cousins, and the "New Left" was born.[1]

This chapter is an attempt to discover meaning in a coincidence of names, to elucidate a connection between a magazine and a movement separated across the gulf of a generation, and to expose intellectual roots of the radicalism of the 1960s. Some writers have been skeptical of such an enterprise. Howard Zinn, a former advisor to the Student Non-violent Coordinating Committee, argued in 1965 that "SNCC's new radicalism comes from nowhere in the world but cotton fields, prison cells, and the minds of young people reflecting on what they see and feel. . . . Its radicalism is not an ideology but a mood." Jack Newfield, a founder of the Students for a Democratic Society and author of a fine general account of the early movement, insisted that "the New Radicalism is authentically new in its vague weaving together of anarchist, existential, transcendental, Populist, socialist, and bohemian strands of thought. *It is not the logical outgrowth of the older radical traditions in the West.*" Newfield added: "It is not built upon the same discontents as the Old Left—the depression and the threat of fascism—but upon newer discontents like powerlessness, moral disaffection, and purposelessness of middle-class life—all of which are the special products of an abundant, technocratic urban culture."[2]

While it is true that the New Left valued the deed above the word, its activists were usually well educated. S.N.C.C. volunteers read books in prisons, if permitted; and of necessity they communicated ideas in churches and fields. Replying to the accusation that, unlike Depression radicals, New Leftists did not read books, a leader of Students for a Democratic Society claimed: "We read different books."[3] Whatever differences separate the radicalism of the 1930s from that of the 1960s, authentic and serious social criticism did not grind to a halt with the revelation of the Nazi-Soviet Pact or the attack on Pearl Harbor. The "newer discontents" were first exposed in *Politics* magazine from 1944 to 1949, in the reconstruction of a radical critique emptied of the weight of the betrayals of Kronstadt and Warsaw and immune to the seductions of the Roosevelt coalition. Like Thoreau and Debs, DuBois and Goldman, Macdonald can be considered the New Left's ancestral voice, prophesying war aginst the technocrats and the liberals as well as against the racists and the militarists. *Politics* did not die intestate: its legacy was to be sustained, distorted, and extended by heirs born at the time of the little magazine's half-life and committed to making operational ideas which Macdonald had already articulated.[4]

The core of this interpretation consists of two layers of argument. The first draws a parallel between *Politics* and the New Left in terms of common ideas, approaches, aims, and definitions of evil; the second partially explains the parallel by examining intellectuals who either wrote for or read Macdonald's magazine and who subsequently influenced the new radicalism of the 1960s. But since neither Macdonald nor the New Left was noteworthy for succumbing to what Emerson called "the hobgoblin of little minds," definitions must be imposed upon the purportedly random impulses and sensibilities which have characterized the journalist and the activists.

Politics was nurtured in a Marxist hothouse, and its editor-publisher soon realized that his attitudes had been artificially heated. He did not explicitly repudiate Marxism until "The Root Is Man" (1946), which appeared after two years of struggling out of the ideological debris. In the wake of Hiroshima, Macdonald became a pacifist; in the face of the Berlin blockade, he abandoned his faith in a nonviolent alternative in the international arena while maintaining certain anarchist sentiments. Within the brief span of three years, Macdonald and other contributors thus enunciated what the historian Marvin Meyers termed a persuasion—"not a consistent doctrine, not a finely articulated program but . . . a broad judgment of public affairs informed by common sentiments and beliefs about the good life in America."[5] The *Politics* persuasion might be summarized as follows: recognition of the insidious threat of depersonalization; repudiation of the belief in progress or salvation by science; abhorrence of a political economy girded with weaponry; moral outrage against the claims of Communism, disparagement of liberalism; advocacy of decentralization and nonviolent direct action viewed as alternatives to both the class struggle and the two-party system; and an emphasis upon the individual conscience rather than mass organizations as the catalyst of radical action.

Delineating the *Politics* persuasion is easy compared to generalizing about the New Left, which, like shaking hands with the Tar Baby, becomes stickier the more one grapples with it. Staughton Lynd mentioned a peculiar difficulty in describing the contours of the New Left, in that its continuous absorption of young recruits made it "appear to an observer that over a period of time [that] the organization is forever relearning the same lessons."[6] This view actually implies a deeper ideological continuity than may be apparent from the outside and would strengthen a case for the persistence of the New Left's earliest intellectual undercurrents. These impulses and strategies can be most readily labeled anarcho-pacifist and, to avoid the confusion with the later history of the movement, might be considered the predominant persuasion of the "classical" New Left. While anarcho-pacifism was the chief intellectual inspiration of the movement in the early- to mid-1960s, chronology alone is not a useful instrument of analysis.

For the "classical" New Left was a tendency which occurred after there were colored people, but before there were blacks. After Che Guevara had become a successful revolutionary and an unorthodox economist, but before he had become an icon and a poster. After Joseph Heller's *Catch-22* helped shape a vision of war, but before Timothy Leary's League for Spiritual Discovery marketed a vision of peace. When a phrase like "the beloved community" came more easily to the lips than "up against the wall, motherfucker." When Berkeley's free speech campaign resulted in the dirty speech controversy, but before trashing and destruction of property were devised as a tactic to undermine American imperialism. After policemen were denounced for brutality, but before they were vilified as pigs. Before Frantz Fanon's definition of manhood as violence against oppressors was accepted, but also before Paul Goodman was condemned for "male chauvinism." When Jerry Rubin went to Berkeley and Abbie Hoffman to Mississippi, but before they forged the cap-pistol politics of the Youth International Party. When Bayard Rustin was still the only Negro leader to wear an Afro haircut, but before Congressman Mendel Rivers (D—S.C.) clipped his John Calhoun-length locks so that a tonsorial sign of subversiveness could be maintained. After William Kunstler decided to become the attorney for Freedom Riders in Jackson, Mississippi, but before he refused to defend Weathermen in Chicago. When it was considered more challenging to create a "free university" than to shut down an old one. When the object of civil disobedience was deliberately to crowd the jails rather than to elude the F.B.I. Before blacks sought to be *plus royaliste que* Le Roi Jones and Charles 37X Kenyatta, and while "black and white together" still meant the gruesome discovery of the bodies of the martyred Chaney, Goodman, and Schwerner.

The locus classicus of the New Left's anarcho-pacifism is the S.D.S. Port Huron Statement, written by Tom Hayden in 1962 as a declaration of independence from the League for Industrial Democracy. The statement marked a divergence from the staples of earlier radical manifestoes, which usually condemned class exploitation and material injustice, and updated a form of analysis already incorporated in the *Politics* persuasion. In 1946 Macdonald had lamented that "the trouble is everything is too big. . . . A style of behavior which refuses to recognize the human existence of the others has grown up of necessity, [and it] breaks down human solidarity, alienates people from one another." In 1962 Hayden defined "the contemporary malaise" as "the felt powerlessness of ordinary people, the resignation before the enormity of events. But subjective apathy is encouraged by the *objective* American situation—the actual structural separation of people from power, from relevant knowledge, from pinnacles of decision-making." As Macdonald made depersonalization the theme of his magazine, as he unapologetically applied moral standards to political behavior, as he spurned the Stalinist timetable of transformation to communism, so too S.D.S would "oppose the depersonalization that reduces human beings to the status of things—if anything, the brutalities of the twentieth century teach that means and ends are intimately related, that vague appeals to 'posterity' cannot justify the mutilations of the present. . . . Men have unrealized potential for self-cultivation, self-direction, self-understanding, and creativity. It is this potential . . . to which we appeal, not to the human potentiality for violence, unreason, and submission to authority."[7]

What had stunted man was the abuse of science, the dependency upon a technology which denied a sense of place in the world, the banality and impersonality of bureaucratic control. As a Trotskyist Macdonald had condemned the bureaucratic corruption of the Soviet Union; and while his criticisms of the bureaucratic style were usually leveled at the East, his personalist ethic obviously had wider applicability. Hayden claimed that "power in America is abdicated by individuals to top-down organizational units, and it is in the recovery of this power that the movement becomes distinct from the rest of the country and a new kind of man emerges."[8]

But while Macdonald was deeply dissatisfied with the actualization of some of Kafka's forebodings, no contributor to *Politics* reached the pitch of intensity invoked in the speeches of Berkeley's Mario Savio, whose followers were purportedly willing to "die rather than be standardized, replaceable, and irrelevant." Macdonald pleaded for the humane utilization of science and for a nuclear-free world, but he never stated the case for sabotage as forcefully as Savio did from the steps of the University of California administration building: "There is a time when the operations of the machine become so odious, make you so sick at heart, that you can't take part, you can't even tacitly take part. And you've got to put your bodies upon the gears and upon the wheels, upon the levers, upon all the apparatus, and you've got to make it stop. And you've got to indicate to the people who run it, to the people who own it, that unless you're free the machine will be prevented from working at all."[9]

But the bureaucrats were not the only enemy Macdonald and the New Left shared. In November 1965 the president of S.D.S. urged the approximately 20,000 peace marchers assembled in Washington to "name the system that creates and sustains the war in Vietnam—name it, describe it, analyze it, understand it, and change it." Carl Oglesby asked the audience to "think of the men who now engineer that war—those who study the maps, give the commands, push the buttons, and tally the dead: Bundy, McNamara, Rusk, Lodge, Goldberg, the President himself.

"They are not moral monsters.

"They are all honorable men.

"They are all liberals."[10]

The New Deal and the Great Society—"He was like a daddy to

me," Lyndon Johnson once said of Franklin Roosevelt—provoked more visceral hatreds than the policies of conservatives or reactionaries. The inanity of the *American Mecury* could never arouse in Macdonald the same superbly modulated vituperation as the liberal weeklies; his admiration for Roosevelt consisted of a grudging respect for the president's success in posing as a humanitarian statesman; his first book attempted to get at the mind of Henry Wallace—by aiming right between the eyes. Oglesby confessed to feeling sickened at a government which "can send two hundred thousand young men to Vietnam to kill and die in the most dubious of wars, but . . . cannot get a hundred voter registrars to go into Mississippi."[11] It was Secretary McNamara, not General Westmoreland, whose car was rocked by antiwar students; it was Hubert Humphrey, not Richard Nixon, who was heckled in the 1968 presidential campaign.

Oglesby acknowledged that his conversion to radicalism was a response to "those who mouthed my liberal values and broke my American heart." Hayden seconded him: "My own disenchantment with the U.S. didn't really come because of its failures in Negro rights and foreign policy, but with the realization . . . that responsibility for these things lies with the most respectable people in society . . . people in the North with connections with the foundations, corporations and banks and the Democratic Party, who parade in their own suburban communties as liberals."[12] No wonder then that New Left politics often displayed the wrenching emotions of parricidal impulses: Nixon's endorsement of "black power" in 1968 generated far less resentment than Johnson's "we shall overcome" speech in 1965. Even as the Black Panther party newspaper was approving Sirhan Sirhan's murder of Robert Kennedy, Hayden was seen weeping in the rear of St. Patrick's Cathedral, where the senator's body lay in state.[13] Animating the antiliberalism of the New Left was not only Oedipal ambivalence but—as the speeches of Oglesby and Hayden reveal—the pain of betrayal as well.

The shock of broken faith may also account for a difference between Macdonald and the New Left, however. The *Fortune* writer who was radicalized during the Depression, who might have joined the Communists had it not been for that "bloody Sunday" at William Phillips's house, and who drew inspiration from the career of the brilliant but doomed Trotsky, could not forget how Stalinism had soiled the socialist ideal; and his radical anti-Communism was a natural reaction to the purges, the labor camps, the Warsaw uprising, and the Berlin blockade. But the "classical" New Left had no such shocks to absorb: the Bay of Pigs was nearer than Budapest; the Marines' invasion of the Dominican Republic more recent than Kim Il Sung's invasion of South Korea; sheriffs Laurie Pritchett and Jim Clark more menacing than the jailers of Ivan Denisovich. American Communists were not executioners but could present themselves as victims. They were not cynical manipulators of the American Writers' Congress or of some C.I.O. unions or of the Progressive party, but the beleaguered opponents of H.U.A.C. and J. Edgar Hoover and local vigilantes. S.D.S. became a wholly disowned subsidiary of the League for Industrial Democracy, for example, in part because the importance of anti-Communism was perceived so differently. H. Stuart Hughes, the Ur-practitioner of the "new politics" of left-liberalism, recalled an incident from his 1962 Senate campaign in Massachusetts: "To my young supporters—this was the difficulty between us—the Communist danger was never quite as real as it necessarily was for my own generation. I remember shouting at them one night: 'If you kids don't shut up, you'll force me to give an anti-Communist speech'—a most effective way of getting silence."[14]

The incapacity to conceive of anti-Communism as anything other than either paranoic or potentially lethal became evident in a song by the New Left's most resonant troubadour, Bob Dylan. "With God on Our Side" finds no purpose in any previous American wars—even before the growing military involvement in Vietnam. Dylan mocks the propaganda that has promoted hostility to the Soviet Union as well as the comfortable assumption that the Americans fight under divine dispensation. As medieval Catholicism cannot be understood apart from Aquinas, so allusion to Dylan is obligatory to any study of Sixties radicalism. In "Subterranean Homesick Blues," which is the Growing Up Absurd of folk rock, he warns, "Don't follow leaders," and adds "You don't need a weatherman to know which way the wind blows"—the line which an S.D.S. faction used in 1969 to discredit the allegedly clumsy ideology of the rival Progressive Labor party. But Dylan encapsulated the new radicalism in the final stanza of "A Hard Rain's A-Gonna Fall," written during the 1962 missile crisis. He responds to the threat of nuclear destruction with a desire to engage in the nonviolent struggle in the South, where hunger and misery are rampant and where black identity remains to be forged. Yet Dylan also vows that, before humanity is submerged in the hard rain of nuclear catastrophe, he will at least have discovered himself, will have found his own voice before coming to the end of his song.[15] Here was an example of what S.D.S.'s Richard Flacks called "the overpersonalization of the movement, a situation in which one's personal needs and hang-ups are increasingly acted out in the larger arena."[16] Here was also a hint of the preoccupation with the self which would later hurl Dylan and substantial segments of the new radicalism into drugs and privatism.

When Dylan sang about going "to the depths of the deepest dark forest," two philosophy students had already been there; and in 1965 Robert Penn Warren published his interviews with the "Two for SNCC," Robert Moses and Stokely Carmichael. Moses was the more authentic representative of the classical New Left, so that when the movement changed, he disappeared. In the back of an empty Jackson, Mississippi, auditorium, the denim-clad mystic who left Harvard graduate school to become S.N.C.C.'s first voter registration worker described what he had read in prison: "Camus talks a lot about the Russian terrorists—around 1905. What he finds in them is that they accepted that if they took a life they offered their own in exchange. He moves from there into the whole question of violence and non-violence and comes out with something which I think is relevant in this struggle." Moses explained: "It's not a question that you just subjugate yourself to the conditions that are and don't try to change them. The problem is to go on from there, into something which is active, and yet the dichotomy is whether you can cease to be a victim any more and also not be what he calls an executioner. The ideal lies between these two extremes—victim and executioner."[17] Camus's essay "Neither Victims nor Executioners" appeared in America first in *Politics*, and was reprinted in *Liberation*, in Macdonald's translation.

Unlike Moses, Carmichael told Warren that he "had always been oriented to the left, from an economic point of view—not an economic determinist but certainly a great proclivity for that sort of thing." He found himself impressed by the conduct of the Freedom Riders and the students who had first engaged in sit-ins. Warren asked, "You mean a human approach, a moral approach?"; and the Howard University senior replied, "It seemed to me this was euphemistic—I think men always cover up their actions with moral issues. So I began to think seriously whether this was an economic problem or whether the students were right, whether non-violence and love was [sic] the thing."[18] Within a year of the interview, of course, Carmichael led S.N.C.C. out of its "classical" period, out of the civil rights movement and into the black liberation movement. And in advocating "black power," Carmichael frequently cited Lewis Carroll:

> " . . . When I use a word," Humpty Dumpty said, in a rather scornful tone, "it means just what I choose it to mean—neither more nor less."
> "The question is," said Alice, "whether you *can* make your words mean so many different things."
> "The question is," said Humpty Dumpty, "which is to be master—that's all."

It is a coincidence that, a year before Carmichael's family moved to the United States from Trinidad, Macdonald also quoted this passage and called the author of *Alice in Wonderland* "peculiarly relevant to modern politics," to the rectification of names. It was in that phase of the "movement" that Carmichael deliberately missed the point of Camus's essay. A journalist overheard him tell an associate: "We are the victims and we've got to move to equality with our executioners. Camus never answers that question, does he? We are the victims, they are the executioners. Every real relationship is that—victim and executioner. Every relationship . . . "[19]

Also relevant to the politics of the New Left were the findings of psychologist Kenneth Keniston, whose *Young Radicals* implicitly helps substantiate a connection with the *Politics* persusasion. In 1967 he conducted intensive interviews with seventeen activists—an admittedly small sample—prominent in Vietnam Summer, and he showed how many radicals were seeking political fulfillment of the ethical norms inculcated at home. Many of their parents were liberal and "principled" (not synonymous); and out of the recognition that society and its authoritative figures were not fulfilling those principles, young activists were created. "These radicals stand on their own feelings of inner rightness," Keniston wrote; and this "inner rightness" generated their fear of government by "power elite," their rejection of liberal politics, their advocacy of decentralization, their revulsion at bureaucratic manipulation, their ambivalence toward technology.[20]

"The technology of death has hung like a sword over the lives of this post-modern generation," the Yale psychologist argued, explaining the radicals' adoption of a nonviolent ethic in a manner that echoed Macdonald's essays on "The Bomb" and "The Responsibility of Peoples":

"These young men and women were born near the end of the most savage, wanton, and destructive war in the history of the world. . . . The lessons of that war for this generation are summarized in the names of three cities: Auschwitz, Hiroshima, Nuremberg. . . . and their lessons— the bureaucratization of genocide, the clean ease of the unthinkable, and the ethic above nationality—have marked post-modern youth."[21]

If the cluster of ideas and impulses associated with the "classical" New Left bears strong resemblance to the *Politics* persuasion, the explanation may be that in history— unlike plane geometry—parallel lines can meet. Two men in particular, C. Wright Mills and Paul Goodman, entwined the magazine to the movement.

"Mills first became known in the intellectual world at about the time Dwight Macdonald was publishing his lively radical magazine *Politics*," Irving Howe recalled. "Only Macdonald's personal zest as editor . . . created the possibility—perhaps the illusion—of preserving some sort of the left-wing community. Into this depressing scene there suddenly barged the bear-like figure of Mills." His politics have been described by Ralph Miliband in terms which fit Mills snugly into the *Politics* persuasion: "There was in Mills a not very dormant anarchist. His whole personal system of feeling was anti-elitist, anti-bureaucratic, anti-state." Like Macdonald, the sociologist "found the Communists morally, intellectually, and politically impossible; the various Trotskyite sects were too disputatiously futile for a serious man to bother with; and the social democrats were, so to speak, too social democratic for his robust political tastes." According to Miliband, Mills was committed to the rectification of names: "Mills was a moralist as well as a moral man. . . . With a right to denounce crime goes the duty to locate the criminals, and to expose them." And, as with Macdonald, his "critique of American liberalism is one of the dominant themes of his work throughout."[22]

Thanks to Daniel Bell, who had introduced Macdonald to Arendt as well, Macdonald and Mills became acquainted in 1943 and took an immediate liking to one another. Both were, the ex-editor recollected, "congenital rebels" who "liked to argue long and loud. . . . He was passionate, generous, crotchety, imaginative; even our chief difference—he the hot generalizer, me the cold rationalist (*raisonneur*), added interest to our meetings." As the editor of *Politics*, Macdonald welcomed and appreciated Mills's stimulating counsel; but by 1949 they were beginning to diverge politically. Mills had agreed to serve on a board of contributing editors, were the magazine to be resuscitated. Even if it had been, however, Macdonald expressed to Mills "the depth of the differences between us—on such questions as the labor movement, the possibility of socialist action today, the application of scientific thinking to politics, etc."[23]

What shattered their friendship was the review of Mills's study of the "new" middle class, *White Collar*, that Macdonald published in *Partisan Review* in 1952. Macdonald found it "boring to the point of unreadability," "horribly abstract," far from the incisiveness of which Macdonald knew Mills was capable: "I wish he hadn't done it." The sociologist was infuriated, taking personally the reviewer's response to *White Collar*. He even complained to Columbia University colleagues about Macdonald's attack, from which Mills professed to have learned little; and when Richard Hofstadter, for example, was insufficiently supportive, Mills's friendship with the historian was smashed up too. When Norman Thomas asked Mills to participate in a panel discussion with Macdonald, he refused, insisting that they did not inhabit the same political and mental universe. "I hold quite firmly to certain now old-fashioned beliefs, including socialist and humanist and certainly secular ideals; I do not think Dwight is capable of fixing his beliefs in any warrantable way. I believe in reflection and in empirical research," Mills added. "Dwight has made a fetish of confusion and drift, which is now his charming style and serves for such trademark as he has." Macdonald's reaction typified his own capacity to be both "mentally aggressive" and personally generous; he did not understand why they could not be friends just because he did not like Mills's book. But the overtures failed.[24]

Though Mills defined himself in 1952 in terms of fixity of belief, he too was to transform himself in the course of the decade into the maverick academic that the New Left found congenial. Macdonald and Goodman, Theodore Roszak once fleetingly remarked, had done in the pages of *Politics* "an even shrewder job of analyzing technocratic America than Mills was ever to do—and without relinquishing their humanitarian tone. But it was Mills who caught on [with the New Left]. His tone was more blatant; his rhetoric, catchier. He was the successful academician who suddenly began to cry for action in a lethargic society. . . . And by the time he finished playing Emile Zola [,] he had marked out just about everybody in sight for accusation."[25]

Mills's 1960 defense of the Cuban revolution as a non-Communist assault upon social injustice, his luridly mistitled but striking *Causes of*

World War Three, above all his description of an American society ruled by an alliance of leading capitalists, military men, and politicians, rather than organized as a pluralist democracy, were seized upon for the sense of commitment and rage that these works imparted. His 1960 essay, "On the New Left," which S.D.S. later reprinted as a pamphlet, recycled themes that Macdonald had developed in *Politics*—the same insistence upon the dysfunctional role of the labor movement, the same scorn for the current practice of parliamentary democracy, the same contempt for American expansionism, the same yearning for the efficacy of non-violent direct action, the same desire to transform intellectuals—faute de mieux—into the vanguard of social change.[26]

The counterforce to the "power elite" that Mills had proposed in 1956—an invigorated and disciplined civil service—was soon down-played, and contradicted the *Politics* persuasion. Mills died in 1962 at the age of forty-six. He had helped inspire a movement in the wilderness, but he was not destined to see a promised land of participatory democracy— at least not north of Havana. Whether his influence would have pre-vailed had he lived longer is problematic; he himself was hardly an activist, and young radicals tended to judge the separation of words from deeds rather harshly.

The fate of having lived through and beyond the epoch of the "classical" New Left cursed Paul Goodman. The only major contributor to *Politics* besides Macdonald who was native-born, he was a highly eccentric figure in radical circles. For Goodman was a pacifist who refused to participate in the war against fascism, a social theorist more interested in the creation of meaningful work than in the triumphs of the labor movement, an anarchist and therapist who considered the desire for power a symptom of psychological aberration, a self-proclaimed utopian who has engendered more practical ideas than "practical" men, and a sexual ideologue who, he recalled, was condemned by the radicals, such as C. Wright Mills, as a 'bedroom revisionist.'"[27]

Macdonald acknowledged in 1946 that his "own thinking has been influenced by [Goodman's] ideas, where it has not, independently, come to conclusions similar to his. . . . We all know that we live in a corrupt and alienating society, and that we don't *really* get much pleasure or satisfaction from the things which our social institutions, from the business world to the colleges and government bureaux, trap us into doing; and it makes us angry to have someone quite simply insist on this commonplace and unmentionable fact. . . . The sort of revolution Good-

man proposes involves not only political institutions but also our every-
day, personal way of living and thinking." Macdonald much admired
Goodman's thoughtfulness and published as much of his writing "as I
could get . . . when nobody else would," he recalled. But they "were
never pals. Nothing personal between us . . . always felt constrained."
Macdonald was eventually troubled by the shrillness and severity of
Mills's pamphleteering against America; but he never lost his admiration
for Goodman's "shrewd, original, deeply imaginative mind—it was
always *working*."[28]

Goodman ushered in the decade of the 1960s with *Growing Up
Absurd*, which advanced a far more sophisticated case for his "crazy
young allies" than they themselves could make and argued that their
alienation was understandable and praiseworthy in a society which
denied them a natural maturation. After the publication of the book,
Goodman was able to dip into his legendary trunk of previously rejected
manuscripts on so many topics that he was called—in a strange phrase
that perhaps only Macdonald could have fully appreciated—"the thinking man's Max Lerner."[29] He was the only writer to be cited consistently
by representatives of Berkeley's Free Speech Movement; he lectured on
countless campuses and even, once, in the citadel of the military-
industrial complex; he was a familiar figure on peace marches and at draft
resistance meetings. Yet by the end of the decade, Goodman had soured
on the revolt he had stimulated: "Except for a few . . . I am not impressed
by their moral courage or even honesty. For all their eccentricity they are
singularly lacking in personality. They do not have enough world to have
much character." Nor was Goodman's own role always acknowledged: "I
am often hectored to my face with formulations that I myself put in their
mouths, that have become part of the oral tradition, two years old,
author prehistoric."[30] Yet, through the vicissitudes of the past decades,
Goodman's thought remained anchored in the *Politics* persuasion—"to
dispel the mesmerism of abstract power. . . . to live communally and
without authority, to work usefully and feel friendly, and so positively to
replace an area of power with peaceful functioning."[31]

A very different Nestor of the New Left was Herbert Marcuse. A
Hegelian seeking to blend Freud and Marx, a refugee who served in the
Office of Strategic Services in the Second World War, he was never
connected with *Politics* magazine. Only with unseemly dexterity could
Marcuse be fitted into the framework of the "classical" New Left. He was
hardly without influence; but, according to Carl Oglesby, "Marcuse's

importance to the New Left has probably by this time [1969] been badly overstated." The former S.D.S. president revealed an unsuspected gift for understatement in explaining that Marcuse "is not the kind of writer whose books explode one out of the study," and the philosopher himself conceded that "very few students . . . have really read me, I think."[32]

I. F. Stone was also an influence upon the New Left independent of *Politics*. His *Weekly* upheld many of the same sparkling, trenchant, and thoughtful standards as Macdonald's own experiment in personal journalism. Stone was endowed with the same nose for nonsense and the same eye for fine print and had a much better memory. During the Vietnam War, Stone noted the effects of the diminution of man, as in his romantic tribute to the National Liberation Front: "When General [Curtis] Le May said we could win the war by bombing them back into the Stone Age, he was speaking up from the depths of our deepest horror. What fate could be worse than to put people back to the Stone Age— without refrigerators, supermarkets, even toilets. . . . Down there in the jungle, unregenerate, ingenious, tricky, as tiny as a louse or a termite, and as hard to get at, emerged a strange creature whose potency we had almost forgotten—Man." The journalist added: "To sit down now and deal with him is to admit that the Machine is lost to Man, that our beautifully computerized war, with the most overwhelming firepower ever mustered, has failed."[33]

Stone's journal, Paul Jacobs and Saul Landau reported, was "trusted by almost the entire left. He is one of The Movement's few heroes."[34] In the 1940s however the contributor to the *Nation* and *PM* was the very prototype of the liblab that made Macdonald see red. Stone did, after all, sign the August 1939 denial that totalitarianism was common to Germany and the Soviet Union. He did exclaim in 1944, to Macdonald's dismay, that "we may count our country fortunate in having in a single generation two leaders of the stature and vision of Franklin D. Roosevelt and Henry A. Wallace." He did admit, with irony, that he had been "a poor dupe" for Wallace in 1948.[35] He did lend his name to the Cultural and Scientific Conference for World Peace at the Waldorf-Astoria Hotel in 1949. What distinguished Stone from the *Politics* persuasion was not only a less astringent anti-Communism but an absence of anarchist proclivities. Neither Macdonald nor Goodman could have written, as Stone did in 1961, that he was "becoming optimistic" about President Kennedy's prospects for drawing America back from the brink of nuclear annihilation.[36] For all of Stone's radicalism, he lacked an instinctive distaste for the power of the nation-state.

Stone and perhaps Marcuse serve as reminders that the New Left was seeded by a variety of intellectual influences, and the effect of Mills and Goodman—both thinkers of idiosyncratic integrity—was not necessarily related to their association with *Politics* magazine. Apart from a few young pacifists, the militants of the sixties do not appear to have thumbed through back issues of *Politics*, nor even to have been aware of the magazine's existence.[37] But the bonds between the *Politics* persuasion and the "classical" New Left could be drawn tighter had there been radical intellectuals old enough to have absorbed *Politics* but too young to have contributed to it. Such persons exist.

Noam Chomsky was a high school student during the Second World War and was skeptical of the validity of American involvement, despite his emphatically Jewish family background. He found himself "on the fringes of the left wing of the Zionist youth movement, never joining because of certain political disagreements, but enormously attracted . . . by what I saw as a dramatic effort to create . . . some sort of libertarian socialism in the Middle East." At least until 1947, Chomsky opposed the creation of a Jewish state because of his interest in the maintenance of the "potentially free, collective form of social organization as embodied in the kibbutz and other socialist institutions." He also became "anti-Bolshevik after a brief flirtation with Trotskyites of various shadings."[38]

As a postwar undergraduate at the University of Pennsylvania, Chomsky read *Politics*, which "in some respects answered to and developed further these interests and rather vague points of view," especially toward anarchism. Macdonald's essays, "The Root Is Man" and "The Responsibility of Peoples," were especially important to Chomsky, as an adolescent and later. He later called "the revival of anarchist thinking in the 'New Left' and the attempts to put it into effect . . . the most promising development of the past years"; and he first met Macdonald while helping to organize draft resistance after the escalation of the Vietnam War. The linguistics professor "admire[d] him greatly as an independent, thoughtful person. I don't agree with everything he has said . . . naturally, but he is one of the few people who I think must be taken seriously, over a long stretch."[39]

Chomsky immersed himself in anti-war activities in 1965 and

collected his political essays into *American Power and the New Mandarins* four years later. While comparisons between the ends and means of the Second World War and the Vietnam War constitute a separate question too complicated to be explored here, it is worth noting the resemblances between Macdonald's and Chomsky's criticism. Macdonald is mentioned at the beginning and end of Chomsky's most famous essay, "The Responsibility of Intellectuals," which asserts that Macdonald's insights into the problem of collective guilt for atrocities "have lost none of their power or persuasiveness. . . . The issues that Macdonald raised are as pertinent today [1967] as they were twenty years ago." Curiously though, Chomsky seemed unaware that he had contradicted the central proposition of "The Responsibility of Peoples." Macdonald had exempted the German people from war guilt, while Chomsky wished to hold considerable (though unspecified) numbers of Americans responsible for the military intervention in Indochina. He proposed "to ask ourselves whether what is needed in the United States is dissent—or denazification. . . . To me it seems that what is needed is a kind of denazification."[40]

Chomsky would apparently have begun his "kind of denazification" with those labeled the "new mandarins"—the intellectuals who create and accept the rationale for American intervention in Vietnam, the realpolitiker who serve as policymakers, administrators, and advisors for the war machine. They bore some resemblance to the group Macdonald ridiculed as liblabs, and in the intervening decades the liblabs had become decision-makers instead of kibitzers. While Macdonald's targets were usually his fellow journalists and Chomsky's have often been his fellow academicians, both the liblabs and the new mandarins have been committed to a pragmatic liberalism alien to the moral standards by which Macdonald and Chomsky have judged political behavior.

Rhetoricians with an unwholesome gravitation toward force majeure seem to have been especially annoying: what Max Lerner was to Dwight Macdonald, Arthur Schlesinger has been to Noam Chomsky. In a 1945 piece on Lerner's visit to Germany, for example, Macdonald mocked his admiration for "Soviet generals, people's generals, democratic generals, very inspiring generals altogether, generals on the Right Side, the People's Side, the Yalta Side. Yes, they were clearly Max Lerner's kind of people—the progressive, democratic and victorious people, not like those wretched German farmers with their shabby clothes and shell-wrecked homes and hungry faces and their callous and cowardly refusal to lick the boots of an accredited *PM* war correspondent."[41] Chomsky assailed Schlesinger's *The Bitter Heritage* (1966), an *anti*war tract, for insufficient disagreement with the assumptions underlying American intervention. Schlesinger's "pray[er] that Mr. [Joseph] Alsop may be right" in his hawkish optimism and his pragmatic criticism of the Johnson administration's escalation are little more than "a willingness to tolerate any barbarism, so long as it can succeed, and to raise our twitters of protest only when total victory seems beyond our grasp." Chomsky recites examples of the devastation and suffering inflicted upon South Vietnam, and then notes that "all of this arouses in . . . [Schlesinger] feelings of great compassion—for President Johnson. ('No thoughtful American can withhold sympathy as President Johnson ponders the gloomy choices which lie ahead.')"[42]

Just as Macdonald lampooned the liberal weeklies' attempts to keep Roosevelt and Churchill at the forefront of progressive humanitarianism, so Chomsky scored Schlesinger's desire to account for the Vietnam War as "the politics of inadvertence." Macdonald was enraged at "the official apologists, from Max Lerner to President Conant of Harvard, [who] envisage at most only a little face-lifting" on American social institutions, who were unaware "that modern technology has its own antihuman dynamics." Chomsky anathematized Senator Mike Mansfield, a very mild opponent of escalation, as "the kind of man who is the terror of our age. . . . What I find most terrifying is not Curtis Le May . . . but rather the calm disquisitions of the political scientists on just how much force will be necessary to achieve our ends."[43]

Chomsky sought to uphold the *Politics* tradition "that the policies of governments should be judged by their effects and not by the reasons advanced to justify them. And to apply the rule to 'us' as well as to 'them.'"[44] In both cases the rules were more heatedly invoked against "us," if only because the American apologetics of war seemed more obtrusive and exalted and therefore more insidious. Macdonald of course opposed the means of fighting the Second World War but not the objective of eliminating fascism; and while fiercely exposing American racial hatred and imperialist designs against Japan, he made no attempt to justify the Greater East Asia Co-Prosperity Sphere. By contrast Chomsky not only condemned both the means and ends of American involvement in Vietnam, he also dismissed a Communist threat, as Macdonald could not do in *Politics* in his assessment of the Axis powers. And in judging "us" as well as "them," Chomsky twisted his youthful skepticism into a mildly perverse historical interpretation of the Second

World War: "In noting the all-too-obvious parallels between Japanese fascism and contemporary American imperialism in Southeast Asia, we should also not overlook the fundamental differences; in particular the fact that Japan really was fighting for its survival as a great power, in the face of great-power 'encirclement' that was no paranoid delusion."[45]

Chomsky was widely admired by the New Left, which bestowed a distinctive honor upon a slightly younger intellectual—a button expressing a preference for "Lynd not Lyndon." And while Staughton Lynd himself denied his own preeminence—"We spread the charisma around," he told the New York Times—no one else so unerringly personified the "classical" New Left.[46]

Like Chomsky's, Lynd's parents were educators; and he "grew up in a certain well-known subculture of the 1930s, where there was a good deal of admiration for the Soviet Union, a good deal of sympathy for the organization of the C.I.O., and so forth. And the framework of ideas was much more Marxist or quasi-Marxist than religious." Lynd's "years of coming-to-maturity after World War II involved a continuing dialogue between the hard-boiled centralizer and the sensitive anarchist, the Commissar and the Yogi, the Marxist and the pacifist, a dialogue which . . . expressed itself in a most erratic sequence of personal actions."[47] The sequence included serving as national youth organizer for the Wallace campaign and briefly joining the Shachtmanites and the Cannonites; the other side of the ledger included organizing an anarchist club at Harvard and reading Politics.[48] Lynd was particularly impressed by Simone Weil's famous interpretation of the Iliad, by a report on the Macedonia Cooperative Community in Georgia, and by the concept of the "permanent war economy" which Walter Oakes (a pen name for Edward L. Sard) published in the first issue of Politics and which Lynd long considered a central insight into postwar America.[49] Just as Chomsky had lived on kibbutzim, so the future historian and labor attorney spent three years at Macedonia: "I was not sweating out the Eisenhower years in the belly of the whale. When I rejoined society I found that many of my colleagues were emotionally fatigued."[50]

Strengthened for the 1960s, Lynd combined peace campaigns with civil rights, authorship with activism. In 1962 he joined Howard Zinn and S.N.C.C. staffers in setting up a picket line in Atlanta to protest the Caribbean embargo during the missile crisis; he also led the first group of southern blacks in an antiwar protest to the White House; he directed the Freedom Schools in Mississippi in the summer of 1964; and he organized the first massive peace march on Washington in the following year.

A baffled Jack Newfield once called Lynd's politics akin to "a tortured mixture of Thoreau and John Brown" (an overload, since Thoreau approved the Harpers Ferry raid and compared the guerrilla leader to Christ). Lynd's alternative vision of politics combined personalism and *beaux gestes*. Nor did it exclude the dream of a sit-in at the seat of government, as in his description of the 1965 peace march: "It seemed that the great mass of people would simply flow on through and over the marble buildings, that . . . nothing could have stopped that crowd from taking possession of its government. Perhaps next time we should keep going. . . . until those who make policy for us, and who like ourselves are trapped by fear and pride, consent to enter into dialogue with us and with mankind."[51] In whose name, with what democratic legitimacy, the marchers would have kept going, Lynd did not specify.

Like Chomsky and Macdonald, Lynd could not believe in the inadvertence of America's wars: "Many people in a sense still treat the war as a kind of automobile accident. You know, you were just on your way to something that you very much wanted to do . . . and then suddenly came this annoying and really unexpected eventuality." On the contrary "American policy in Vietnam is consistent with other aspects of its foreign policy since 1945, and in some respects before that." Like Macdonald he has denied the "responsibility of peoples": "The people did not, in any very meaningful sense, decide upon our present Vietnam policy." Like Macdonald, Lynd nurtured a deep suspicion of coalition politics, and his attack on the social democrat Bayard Rustin for seeking a Negro civil rights-liblab coalition echoed Macdonald's criticism of Norman Thomas: "The coalition . . . [Rustin] advocates turns out to mean implicit acceptance of Administration foreign policy, to be coalition with the marines."[52]

But an important discontinuity weakens the parallel between Macdonald and Lynd. After 1937 Macdonald was a consistent critic of Soviet Communism. As a Trotskyist he was appalled by its bureaucratic degeneration, as an anarcho-pacifist he concluded that means had so corrupted ends that he eventually was to "choose the West." But Lynd, like Mailer in the Mount Holyoke debate, could not make the choice; and he judged the Vietnam War in a way in which Macdonald obviously could not regard the Second World War: "I don't believe that violence never accomplishes anything good," he told an interviewer in 1967. "I would prefer not an N.L.F. victory but a coalition between them and neutralist elements in the area presently controlled by Saigon. . . . Although I may be a *personal* pacifist, I am by no means of the opinion that both sides are equally guilty or that it is a matter of indifference how the struggle ends."[53] When he visited North Vietnam in 1965, he traveled not only with Tom Hayden but also with the Communist historian and propagandist Herbert Aptheker—company that Macdonald would not conceivably have kept. But Lynd's appeal for medical aid for all combatants was of a piece with Macdonald's repeated insistence upon the humanity of the enemy and with the *Politics* relief and rescue program. Nor should it be forgotten that, in his 1945 list of actions to be considered in reducing the danger of nuclear warfare, Macdonald included "sabotage."[54]

Perhaps then the *Politics* persuasion and the "classical" New Left are historically connected. If a common approach and sensibility have been demonstrated, then the meaning of the recent past may become clearer. For if the thread of continuity between the radicalism of the 1940s and the 1960s did not snap, Macdonald's renunciation of the leftism of the 1930s may well have signaled not only the persistence of earlier forms of injustice. His switch to an anarcho-pacifism bereft of immediate antecedents also reflected the vicissitudes of American politics, especially the permanent war economy. The parallel with the generation of radicals born with the atomic age would therefore suggest broader continuitites, allowing the 1930s to recede into an earlier epoch.

For the radicalism of the Great Depression focused upon the working class and how it could be organized into parties and unions. But by the end of the Second World War, as Macdonald informed other radicals, even the Congress of Industrial Organizations had accepted the place that it was offered within the prevailing political economy. Macdonald realized more quickly than his Marxist friends that major social change could no longer be expected from the proletariat, as demonstrated by the unions' refusal in 1946 to permit a pacifist picket line at Oak Ridge. The C.I.O. defined its interest in terms of job security; the C.O.'s insisted upon the primacy of preventing a nuclear catastrophe. Similar lines were drawn in the 1960s. The unions had become essential to the extension of liberal reform, from economic security to civil rights; but their rather consistent support of American foreign policy saddened and outraged young radicals. A dissidence centered upon the dispossessed was superseded by a radicalism which sometimes concerned only the privileged;

the appeals to individual conscience and to "the beloved community" were rarely anchored in the nexus of class interest or economic necessity. In civil rights as in the labor movement, the 1940s marked a caesura. In the 1930s Negro progress was measured by symbolic gestures, like Jesse Owens in Berlin, Robert Weaver in the "black cabinet," Marian Anderson at the Lincoln Memorial; and the New Deal helped poor Negroes because they were poor, not because they were the special victims of a cruelly racist society. Only in the 1940s did the ticking of the civil rights time-bomb become audible. The Freedom Rides began in 1947, not 1961. A. Philip Randolph in 1948, not Stokely Carmichael in 1966, first called for black resistance to the draft. Rustin helped organize his first march on Washington in 1941, not 1963; and he, not Malcolm X, made the first pilgrimages to Africa to internationalize the blacks' struggle. And Conrad Lynn, who helped organize antidraft and antiwar activities in the 1960s, had received support for his campaign against a Jim Crow army from Macdonald in the very first issue of *Politics*.

Both disenchantment with the unions and the battle for civil rights intersected in the 1940s on the issue that Macdonald considered the most important for radicals: human survival through the avoidance of war. In his sensitivity to the implications of the atomic bomb, Macdonald not only exemplified a dominant tendency in postwar radicalism but refracted a structural change in American life as well.

In 1945 a young army captain published in the *Atlantic Monthly* an article which vigorously supported an obvious departure from American military tradition: a program of peacetime conscription. The captain insisted that military policy and foreign policy were inseparable, that "peace is too important to be left to the civilians"; and he advocated the draft not because it would maintain civilian control but because it would discipline American youth: "A boy will learn to know Americans he would not otherwise meet; we think he will face and learn from a kind of American discipline he would not otherwise find. I believe that to know what military service means greatly helps a man in search of rounded education."[55] That Captain McGeorge Bundy later became special assistant for national security to two liberal presidents adds a fine touch to the picture of what the first issue of *Politics* feared would become a "permanent war economy."

If Bundy, the beau ideal of the new mandarins, personified a continuity of postwar foreign and military policy, Dwight D. Eisenhower repersented a slight discontinuity. In 1946 the chief of staff wrote a memorandum urging the army "to promote the development of new resources, if our national security indicates the need. It is our duty to support broad research programs in educational institutions, in industry, and in whatever field might be of importance to the Army." Eisenhower insisted "that all those civilian resources which by conversion or redirection constitute our main support in time of emergency be associated closely with the activities of the Army in time of peace."[56] Fifteen years later the retiring president recognized, albeit briefly, how ominous such military and civilian cooperation had become, and his warning against the aggrandizement of the "military-industrial complex" was to be repeated frequently in the years to come.

Eisenhower was probably as unaware of the publication of *The Power Elite* as Macdonald was certainly ignorant of the general's memorandum ten years earlier. But the editor of *Politics* nevertheless sniffed danger very early in the formation of the "military-industrial complex." Not only did he foresee the postwar arms race by the late spring of 1944, but he also brought to the attention of his readers a speech by Charles E. Wilson, who had gone from General Electric to the War Production Board. In 1944 Wilson asserted, according to Macdonald, that "he no longer considers 'war' and 'peace' as distinct and divisible conditions, and that war-making is as normal and legitimate a form of business enterprise as soap- or steel-making."[57] Several months later, when Roosevelt suggested a labor draft and peacetime conscription, Macdonald sensed "a great step forward in the militarization and state regimentation of our society; the recognition of war as not a 'mistake' or 'accident' which better management may hope to avoid 'next time' but as a permanent feature of The American System."[58]

Despite Macdonald's warnings, the Department of Defense was soon directing the biggest planned economy in the world outside the Soviet Union; and almost two-thirds of all American engineers, technicians, and scientists were participating in defense projects.[59] It is not necessary to share Macdonald's anarcho-pacifism, which he himself of course repudiated, to lament the tragic misuse of American human and physical resources committed to meeting the threat of Soviet power. It is not necessary to believe in the realization of utopian visions to wonder why the major powers and often the minor powers elected to pursue peace by means of an arms race. Nor is it a disparagement of other issues to underscore the centrality of the question of modern war, which continues to bedevil humanity and has, if anything, grown far more acute than at the time *Politics* was published. It is not to Macdonald's discredit that his insightfulness and ethical sensitivity did not resonate deeply enough, though it is noteworthy that he himself could not envision an alternative to deterrence and the balance of terror. The quest for substitutes, either in terms of policy or in terms of civic action, was begun as early as 1945 in the pages of *Politics*. And the fact that members of another generation, unwittingly, enacted the ideals Macdonald proposed in "Why Destroy Draft Cards?" (1947), testifies to the recalcitrance of a political problem still too intimidatingly difficult to be resolved, too dangerous to be neglected.

11

A Critical American

An ancient Chinese curse—"May you live in interesting times"—
was inflicted on Macdonald himself in the 1960s. He left the staff of the
New Yorker in 1965, having written on a wide variety of topics, from
nineteenth- and twentieth-century literature to philanthropy (which
resulted in a 1955 volume, *The Ford Foundation*). He produced a brilliant
and distinctive anthology of *Parodies* (1960), and he wrote monthly film
reviews for *Esquire* from 1960 to 1966. For the next two years he wrote a
monthly column for *Esquire* on politics, his own having become once
again "theoretically . . . radical." Macdonald told an interviewer in 1970
that, without believing in any sort of revolution, he did not "feel
particularly conservative" either. Indeed he continued to find Paul
Goodman's brand of anarchism especially attractive, including Goodman's opposition to student extremism.[1]

Macdonald had, in other words, survived to offer his own critical
evaluation of the "classical" New Left. With the *New Yorker*'s Richard
Rovere, he engaged in a 1967 colloquy with Tom Hayden of S.D.S. and
Ivanhoe Donaldson of S.N.C.C., neither of whom sought to press an
intellectual paternity suit. Macdonald announced the verification of his
prophecy in "The Root Is Man," that "small groups without any idea of
appealing to the masses in the way that all Marxist parties do" had
actually accelerated social change. He also acknowledged the New Left's
programmatic superiority to the Old Left and praised the southern civil
rights movement as well as Hayden's attempt to organize the poor in
Newark. But Macdonald argued that the New Left's overwhelmingly
youthful leadership and membership undermined its claim to "be taken
seriously," and he urged its spokesmen to show more concern with the

relationship of means to ends. Nor could Macdonald share the New Left's extremism—later symbolized by a *Ramparts* cover portrait of a freckle-faced Little Leaguer holding a Viet Cong flag, with the caption defining alienation as "when your country is at war and you want the other side to win." Macdonald warned Hayden and Donaldson that the presumption of American malevolence made no more sense than the reflex-belief in its benevolence—advice which Macdonald himself did not take until late in the history of *Politics*.[2]

But his most fundamental disappointment transcended rational argument: the new radicals simply lacked the "intellectual and moral style . . . my own generation had." Criticizing the New Left's "principled refusal to learn from the past, from history,"[3] Macdonald sensed that the young activists regarded learning as an encumbrance. He himself remained not only a critical American but a radical *intellectual*, invoking a tradition in which revolutionaries were at least partially the products of the enemy's libraries. Marx had arrived at the British Museum every morning at nine and left every night at its closing; Lenin had journeyed from Geneva to the British Museum with the sole intention of rendering more invulnerable his argument in *Materialism and Empirio-Criticism*; Mao Zedong had labored assiduously in the library of Peking University. Lenin had wept over Turgenev; Trotsky had held up to Bernard Shaw the corrosive example of Jonathan Swift. Yet when Louis Kampf, an M.I.T. professor who served informally as a faculty advisor to the New Left, refused "to take the rectionary and mercenary objectives of Balzac as merely an adjunct to his artistry," this radical president of the Modern Language Association may not have realized that he was sneering at Marx's favorite novelist.[4] For the Old Left at its best, as for Dwight Macdonald, "bourgeois culture was a mark to surpass and not something to be rejected"; and he vigorously urged the veterans of multiversities and jails to "go to a library . . . and look up all those big dull books. . . . Sort of smarten up a bit."[5] Or as the ex-Trotskyist Leslie Fiedler told a student audience: "We went in for Talmudic exegesis. You go in for holy rolling."[6]

The next year the Low Library of Columbia University was among the buildings struck by the Students for a Democratic Society; and after climbing into some of the revolutionary bastions on campus, Macdonald publicly supported both the strike and the sit-ins. He conceded that much of the activity was illegal, and honestly reported the 6 June 1968 poll of Columbia students by the Bureau of Applied Social Research (cofounded by C. Wright Mills): 68 percent against the S.D.S. tactics, only 19 percent for them. Yet Macdonald, a believer in close scrutiny of means and ends, justified the Columbia "disturbances" as "beneficial," because S.D.S. was so manifestly opposed to American intervention in Vietnam and to the alleged complicity of the university itself in the perpetuation of racism and poverty. "The follies and the injustices of the Establishment, in these two cases, are so extreme and so indurated," he asserted in a letter to the New York Review of Books, "as to make necessary the use of extralegal pressures." He sponsored an S.D.S. fundraiser in his apartment, in which its leader, Mark Rudd, was chief speaker. Macdonald told his wife, Gloria, that Rudd was "a no-good charmer"; but doubts about the personnel, the tactics, the sheer "nihilism" of the activists were suppressed as the revolutionist emeritus made a public appeal for funds.[7] Along with Harold Taylor, the president of Sarah Lawrence, and psychoanalyst Erich Fromm, Macdonald spoke at a "counter-Commencement" intended to draw attention to necessary reforms within the academy itself. Despite some hissing by students and outsiders, including Tom Hayden (seated next to the speaker's wife), Macdonald condemned the effort to use the university "to pry open our society for the benefit of social revolution," and he counselled strongly against "indefinite" application of sit-in tactics. Macdonald later described the "para-Commencement" as "spirited and friendly and dignified," even though little seems to have come of the work of Columbia's "Students for a Restructured University."[8]

Though he was later surprised that Rudd chose to "go in for narodniki-anarchist-19th century explosions," Macdonald continued to express sympathy for the dissident spirit of the young radicals. In a letter to an old friend who had become dean of Phillips Exeter Academy, Macdonald also praised the undergraduates of the late 1960s as "the best generation I've known in this country, the cleverest and the most serious and decent (though I wish they'd read a little—also I hate the obscenity bit)."[9] He became a more familiar figure on campuses in the 1970s, teaching courses in film, literature, and anarchism at such institutions as Northwestern, Hofstra, the University of Texas, the University of Wisconsin, the University of Massachusetts, and the State University of New York. He had maintained his distance as a rationalist rather than a romantic, without abandoning his vaguely radical yearnings for a drastic revision of the status quo.

Macdonald's eminence was greater in the 1960s than it had ever been before, extending beyond the boroughs of New York City. His cultural rather than political criticism was probably responsible for his high reputation among the intelligentsia; but, no longer confined to "little" magazines, he exerted some political influence as well.

Perhaps the most important and effective political article he ever wrote appeared in the *New Yorker* on 19 January 1963. "Our Invisible Poor" was drawn primarily from *The Other America*, a report on the perpetuation of mass poverty that the democratic socialist Michael Harrington had published—"to friendly, if modest, reviews," he recalled—in 1962. Harrington's book was at the point of disappearing when the *New Yorker* review—about as long as the magazine had ever published—"had the effect of a second publication date and made poverty a topic of conversation in the intellectual-political world of the Northeast corridor." President Kennedy's advisor, Theodore Sorensen, read Macdonald's review and passed it on to the President, who then read Harrington's *cri de coeur* itself.[10] Another advisor, Arthur Schlesinger, Jr., unaccountably credited John Kenneth Galbraith's *The Affluent Society* (1958), which minimizes the importance of the problem, as well as *The Other America* in leading to the formal declaration of war on poverty. Daniel Patrick Moynihan of the Department of Labor told Macdonald that his review had also contributed to the *casus belli*.[11] The defeats were appalling however. As recently as 1982, Moynihan estimated that "one-third of all children born in America during 1980 will likely spend some portion of time on welfare before reaching the age of eighteen."[12] It is a war that neither liberalism nor conservatism has been able to win.

A terribly lethal war galvanized most of Macdonald's political energies, however. During Kennedy's presidency and at least the first year of Johnson's term in office, Macdonald seems barely to have noticed the mounting escalation of the American military intervention in Vietnam. But by 1967 he wrote in *Esquire*: "I can't get away from it, and I can't get used to it." So haunted had he become by the destructiveness and folly of the intervention that he implicitly repudiated his earlier sense that peoples are not "responsible" for the policies of their governments. Sadly, he assumed some civic responsibility by admitting: "In the last two years, for the first time in my life, I'm ashamed to be an American."[13] Like the young whom he came to admire, Macdonald found himself increasingly opposed to the dominant forces of American society; he put on some of his radical armor again. Susan Sontag wrote in 1968: "Only within the last two years (and that very much because of the impact of the Vietnam war) have I been able to pronounce the words 'capitalism' and 'imperialism' again."[14] But Macdonald himself shied away from such terms, and never developed a systematic explanation for the American involvement. Nor did he say a kind word (Sontag herself said many) for the Viet Cong, the National Liberation Front, or the North Vietnamese government. He could however almost pronounce the word "pacifism" again. Because his moral and practical objections to the conflict ("they always go together somehow") were so intense, he could once again join with pacifists despite his general disagreement with their views. Macdonald described the war as "an accident that has turned into a disaster," but wrote no essays with the sweep or flashing penetration of his *Politics* articles. "As an old commie fighter," he rated "Johnson about as, I imagine, old Indian-fighters rated General Custer: rash, hot-headed, vain and alarmingly ignorant of the nature of the enemy."[15]

In print Johnson was called "the most dangerous President in American history."[16] In private, in a letter to Chiaromonte, Johnson's "vigorous and terrifying will" was compared to Stalin and Hitler, "the worst President we've had, the one who's done dirt more than any other on the best of our political traditions." In a letter to Mary McCarthy, the alarm was sounded that Johnson "seems to be out of control rationally and morally." Seeing no purpose to the casualties, no political benefit to justify such carnage, and no prospect of American victory in any case, Macdonald realized that "for once, only time in my memory, there is *nothing* to be said on the other side," the side that supported the conflict. It also reminded him of the Peloponnesian War. Vietnam was proving, "as with Athens, that despite all the good things about our internal political-social-cultural life, we have become an imperialist power, and one that, partly because of these domestic virtues, is a most inept one." It was a shrewd point, and it summarized Macdonald's hostility to the military intervention.[17]

Macdonald's condemnations of the Vietnam conflict exhibited much the same devastating skill in marshaling significant facts and rhetorical force that he had earlier demonstrated in *Politics*. His indignation was tempered by a biting wit; he got down to personalities, wondering about the blindness and ineptitude of American leaders; he made clear the bases of his own opposition, even though devoid of a systematic philosophy. During the Second World War, *Politics* was too isolated to make any impact on the conduct of the conflict. Macdonald's objections to the Vietnam war were also both practical and moral, but in the 1960s his influence was impossible to measure because of the opposite reason: by the time he began his monthly columns on the subject in *Esquire*, opposition to the war had already crystallized among most intellectuals and liberals. However distinct and cogent, Macdonald's voice was one of many in the pages of *Partisan Review*, *Commentary*, the *New York Review of Books*, and other house organs of the intelligentsia.[18]

Perhaps an even more striking difference was how Macdonald expressed his antiwar sentiments. After Pearl Harbor there were genuine dangers that dissent might be interpreted as treason, and the Smith Act was applied viciously to stifle the publication of right-wing and profascist magazines or (in the case of the Minneapolis Trotskyists) to resolve an internal Teamsters dispute. During total war the fears of domestic repression were more warranted than during the Johnson and Nixon presidencies, when several respected government officials seemed to harbor doubts about the wisdom of American involvement in Indochina.

One of them—or so it was perceived—was Adlai Stevenson, who was serving as ambassador to the United Nations in 1965, when a declaration against the war was addressed to him by Artists and Writers Dissent. Stevenson agreed to talk to eight of the signatories on 21 June. The delegation included Macdonald, Goodman, Muste, Muste's biographer Nat Hentoff, and David McReynolds of the War Resisters League. The meeting lasted almost one and one-half hours, with Macdonald, Goodman, and McReynolds arguing the most vigorously against American interventionism in the Dominican Republic and in Vietnam. They also urged the ambassador to resign his position in protest against the deepening willingness of the Johnson administration to employ force abroad. Stevenson refused, insisting that he was a team player who would not violate the "rules of the game." Macdonald got the impression that Stevenson was about to break down and cry, but the ambassador's composure was maintained; his manner was courteous, gracious, attentive, decent—and troubled. After the meeting was over, Stevenson told the delegation: "You honor me by coming. I do not have the chance often these days to have this kind of dialogue." When he suggested that the delegation should see him again, Macdonald, who had broken his own anarchist principles by voting for Stevenson in 1952, asked: "What about the same time, same place tomorrow?" A slight sign of distress momentarily crossed the ambassador's face, and then a laugh. Shortly thereafter Goodman wrote Stevenson even more bluntly, urging him to denounce the lies of the Johnson administration and then to get himself fired.

Stevenson was still working on a draft of a reply when he died less than three weeks later, in London; the declaration of the Artists and Writers Dissent was in his briefcase.[19]

Macdonald also ventured to Washington for two events which mixed the political anxieties and passions of the decade with a bracing pinch of the human comedy. He was invited to the first and only White House Festival of the Arts in June 1965. Horrified by his host's foreign policy, the distinguished critic participated as a "critical observer" rather than as an honored guest: "I sacrificed, not for the first time, consistency, and possibly even good taste, in the interest of a larger objective"— which a startled Ralph Ellison described as "boring from within at the White House." He was certainly not bashful. Professor Eric F. Goldman, the presidential advisor who organized the festival, soon discovererd that this "heavy, quick-moving man with a bearded, interesting face and a clever tongue" was urging other intellectuals and artists to sign his petition denouncing American military interventionism. Macdonald for his part noticed that "Goldman . . . looked most unfestive throughout his festival—the only really happy-looking people, in fact, were Duke Ellington and his bandsmen." Macdonald must have sought signatures with the industriousness of a Stakhanovite; for "his furious activity," Goldman recalled, "left his sports coat wilted, his shirt damp, his face dripping perspiration, his shirt and undershirt pulled out with round pink belly showing, and he made no attempt to repair himself in the break provided before dinner."[20]

Then, in the Rose Garden, Macdonald got into eyeball-to-eyeball, toe-to-toe confrontation with Charlton Heston, whom he branded a Hollywood lackey for refusing to sign his petition. The actor inquired where Macdonald had been during civil rights demonstrations and whether his behavior in his host's home was not lacking in taste. Heston further called Macdonald's activity "arrogant" for presuming to know more about foreign policy than the president. Macdonald then began shouting at the star of *Ben-Hur*, who walked away; and the critic joined the other guests at dinner. There, the hapless Goldman noticed, "he sneered at the exhibits and attacked the President personally in a voice that carried across tables and made other guests squirm." After all, the eristic intellectual later wrote in *The New York Review of Books*, "arguments are part of the New York ambience I'm used to."[21]

Over two years later Macdonald returned to Washington; and this time he was joined by Robert Lowell, who dedicated to Macdonald his poem for the occasion—the first mass march on the Pentagon. Mailer, who "was unquenchably fond of Macdonald," was also present and, like Goldman, yielded to a ventral fixation, describing his own activities in the third person: "Not a minute would go by before he would be poking Macdonald's massive belly with a finger." The novelist proclaimed that among his generation of writers, he "was the one who had probably been influenced most by Macdonald, not so much from the contents of Macdonald's ideas which were always going in and out of phase with Mailer's, but rather by the style of Macdonald's attack." Like the Spock-marked young radicals whom Keniston observed standing "on their own feelings of inner rightness," Mailer had learned from his Mount Holyoke debating opponent to "look to the feel of the phenomenon. If it feels bad, it is bad."[22] The admiration was mutual. Macdonald hailed Mailer's review of Lyndon Johnson's book, My Hope for America (1964), as "a masterpiece of political criticism. . . . It's the kind of thing I used to do myself twenty years ago, even down to the semantic analysis." The reviewer replied: "When it comes to writing this sort of thing, you're my mentor. Those pieces you used to do on politics taught a whole gang of us how to write."[23]

Three years later the two journalists addressed a fund-raising rally. It was the night before the march across the Arlington Memorial Bridge. Mailer, who later paid sly tribute to Macdonald as "one of the oldest anti-Communists in America" and a critic "full of the very beans of that old-time Wasp integrity," delivered a crapulous speech. Macdonald, Time magazine clucked, "was aghast at the barroom bathos, but failed to argue Mailer off the platform. Macdonald eventually squeezed in the valorous observation that Ho Chi Minh was really no better than Dean Rusk." Mailer, for his part, was furious that Macdonald had even tried to interrupt the flow of drunken obscenities. Nor did he have much respect for Macdonald as a rabble-rouser, and described how his "mentor" generally "gesticulated awkwardly, squinted at his text, laughed at his own jokes, looked like a giant stork, whinnied, shrilled, and was often inaudible." That night, the war correspondent for The Armies of the Night recalled, Macdonald was "somewhat less impressive than ever."[24]

The account that Mailer managed to produce however became a classic of the sixties, no doubt because no antiwar activist was more idiosyncratically bellicose than the novelist-as-historian. None of the marchers was less suited to the vaguely pacifist and nonviolent mentality that animated so many of those who challenged the Pentagon; and unlike

Macdonald, Mailer acknowledged that, in logical terms, the case for intervention was about as strong as the case against it. Such empathy may have given *The Armies of the Night* its permanence. In any event Macdonald began his very favorable *Esquire* review of the book with a tour de force that elicited a letter from Mailer: "I thought your parody of my style was superb. The best parody—with one exception—I've ever seen. . . . Yours had me laughing all the way, and like all marvellous parody gave me a rare hint of my vices."[25]

Thirty-five thousand marchers nevertheless had swarmed into range of the nerve-center of the military -industrial complex, with apparently no greater immediate effect upon American policy than Macdonald's petition campaign within the walls of the White House itself. Isolated in the 1940s, engagé in the 1960s, he sagged with the exhaustion of "too many Pentagon marches, Sheep Meadow demonstrations, draft-board picketings; too many years, decades, centuries of exposing 'the moral absurdities' of American society (it is wearying when your five-year campaign to dump Johnson succeeds and you get—Nixon); too many committees joined, petitions signed, speeches made, checks contributed. But what can you do?" he wondered in 1970. "It's necessary."[26]

If the zeitgeist would have fixed upon a motto, William Blake's line would have been suitable: "The tigers of wrath are wiser than the horses of instruction." Macdonald remained among the horses of instruction and never mastered the antinomian style and idiom of sixties radicalism. But he expressed more sharply and directly his antiwar rage and shame than three decades earlier, when his Trotskyism, his anarchism, and his pacifism had driven him outide the contours of the conventional wisdom.

Along with Chomsky, Dr. Benjamin M. Spock, Reverend William Sloane Coffin, and others, he "founded Resist in 1965 to give aid and comfort to draft resisters and it wasn't my fault I wasn't indicted . . . I tried."[27] He believed that civil disobedience was warranted, because (1) the Johnson Administration was "violating the spirit . . . of our Constitution" in waging so destructive and senseless a war, (2) by 1967 protests short of illegality no longer appeared to be tactically effective, and (3) the war and its apparatus, such as Selective Service, had become so personally "obnoxious" that something more drastic, but nonviolent, had to be effectuated. Following Chomsky's lead, Macdonald refused to pay a quarter of his federal income tax. In December 1967, he and Dr. Spock held a press conference in which they proposed to "shut down" a Manhattan induction center by attempting to prevent anyone from entering the building.

William F. Buckley, Jr. was furious at such a provocative and blatant attempt to interfere with the Vietnam War; and he phoned the U.S. Attorney, Robert Morgenthau, to ask whether Spock and Macdonald were going to be prosecuted. Morgenthau was noncommittal, telling Buckley that the U.S. Attorney's office did not disseminate advisory judgments. Buckley then challenged Macdonald to risk arrest more directly, inviting him to the offices of the National Review. Upon Macdonald's acceptance of the invitation, Buckley promised the presence of young men whom Macdonald would presumably counsel not to register nor serve in the military, plus a television camera, plus "a representative of the Justice Department." Macdonald refused, wondering how Buckley got into the act: "Who appointed him sheriff? Assuming the government needs more evidence of my law-breaking than I've given in writing and verbally (twice with TV cameras in action), why should I provide it in the office of the National Review," a magazine whose first eleven issues Macdonald had panned devastatingly in Commentary in 1956? Macdonald rejected such a "publicity stunt." But he continued to avow his interest in "a demonstration trial, which the press would not ignore, in which the immorality, and the illegality, of the Vietnam war could be thoroughly, dramatically explored by the defense."[28]

Three weeks later the Johnson administration moved to indict Spock, Coffin, and three others—but not Macdonald—for conspiracy to violate the Selective Service Act. But Macdonald still tried to get arrested. Along with Goodman, McReynolds, and four others, Macdonald accepted at the Overseas Press Club the draft cards of two young men, plus their written refusal to serve in the American military. The seven no longer eligible for induction submitted a cover letter to the Attorney General, indicating their support and encouragement of the illegal act. Again the critical American was not prosecuted, although the government brief in the Spock-Coffin case made clear that Macdonald was part of the same conspiracy associated with Resist.[29]

In 1973, with the Vietnam conflict still raging, Macdonald headed an organizing committee to celebrate the fiftieth anniversary of the War Resisters League. (Other members of the committee were Chomsky, Dellinger, Hentoff, Spock, Kay Boyle, Allen Ginsberg, and Dorothy Day—about whom Macdonald had written movingly in a New Yorker profile in 1952). The affair was a success, though Macdonald received a couple of refusals that indicated the flexibility of his own principles as well as the vigor of his own condemnation of the Indochina war. Herbert Marcuse declined Macdonald's offer to join in the celebration, "because I am not against 'any war.' (I would certainly support war against fascism.)" But given the likelihood that the "next war will . . . be waged against . . . antifascist and liberation movements," Marcuse added, a check for twenty-five dollars was enclosed. Arendt also refused, along somewhat similar lines: she was not a pacifist. Much as Macdonald himself had written in 1949, Arendt affirmed that "the nuclear deterrent is indeed more effective than pacifism could ever be. For the time being, war has become the luxury of small nations. . . . Pacifism, at any rate, is not likely to save us."[30]

Whatever their differences, Marcuse and Arendt both emanated from a tradition that was deductive and systematic, and were able to handle abstruse metaphysical concepts without even working up a sweat. They were willing to follow through the logic of their own first principles, and therefore could not include members of the War Resisters League in their choice of comrades opposed to the American involvement in Vietnam. Macdonald was no more of a pacifist than they. He had supported the Berlin airlift and the U.N.-sanctioned defense of South Korea, and more recently had been heartened by the Israeli victory in the Six-Day War of 1967. But Macdonald's openness of spirit—the very quality of mind and temper that had made him so receptive to the vicissitudes of politics—encouraged him to express solidarity with those who claimed to oppose "any war."[31] Untrained in German philosophy, Macdonald was fond of quoting the aphorism of Lord Melbourne: "Nobody ever did anything very foolish except from some strong principle."

The end of the war in Vietnam coincided largely with a decline in Macdonald's own commitment to establish his thoughts in print. He occasionally tackled cultural ephemera for which his own undiminished polemical skills seemed overmatched, like Norman Cousins's magazines and the now-forgotten film about campus revolt, Getting Straight. He produced anthologies of the writings of two special favorites, Poe and Herzen. His own film criticism, some of it dating back to 1933, was published as Dwight Macdonald on Movies in 1969; and the following year his writing from the 1940s and early 1950s, Memoirs of a Revolutionist, was reprinted as Politics Past. Immortality of a sort arrived in 1968 with the reprinting of the entire back file of *Politics*, with a respectful introduction by Arendt. It was, in his own estimate, his greatest achievement.[32]

He succumbed to heart failure in New York on 19 December 1982, at the age of seventy-six. A Unitarian funeral service was held.[33] Agee, Arendt, Chiaromonte, Goodman, and Mills were among those who had already faced what Henry James had called "the distinguished thing," which sanctioned the consoling hope that their legacies might be fully appraised and appreciated. What will survive of Macdonald's work, what his patrimony consists of, remains to be sorted out. As Arendt had pointed out in introducing the reprinted volumes of *Politics*, Macdonald's knack for significance did not prevent him from being wrong about many events; and in a crude sense the thoroughness of his opposition to such big events as the New Deal and the Second World War was mistaken. But out of such mistakes Macdonald still managed to fashion a response to his age that still vibrates with genuine feeling and penetration.

Despite the accusations of having embraced an ideology *du jour*, Macdonald was fairly consistent between 1938 and his death: a democrat and a libertarian (but not a liberal) in politics, an elitist and a classicist (but not a formalist) in the arts, an empiricist and a fox (rather than a hedgehog) by temperament. Compared to the dour ideologues of the Old Left and the earnest academicians who (perhaps more than journalists) are his true peers, Macdonald was more a swinger than a scold—open, colloquial, quick to admit his mistakes, a moviegoer. He was a controversialist who seemed to have made few bitter enemies.

Because he wrote so engagingly, he was in some quarters dismissed too easily. Of course no claim can be advanced for Macdonald as a theorist; he repudiated Marxism, remained indifferent to Freudianism, religion, structuralism, and other systems of thought. Macdonald dismissed as naive the cult of unadorned facts, without ever building a system of his own (here he was comfortably nestled in the American grain). Few of his future readers are likely to read him for instruction on particular topics. But his best essays have already provided another kind of intellectual pleasure, the exhibition of a mind that was well-stocked and finely honed, independent, incisive, versatile, supple, and therefore uncommonly interesting. Its expression was so distinctive, so fresh and clear, that he exemplified the Confucian wisdom that politics could work well only if language corresponded to truth. He did much to foster the rectification of names. To be sure, he seemed to believe that anything longer or more grandiose than magazine articles fell outside his range. No matter. For in the interstices of ephemeral journalism and elaborate philosophy, Dwight Macdonald offered the compensation of an unsurpassed polemical intelligence. For the sake of good taste and good sense, he proved himself to be not only sensitive and honorable but extraordinarily resourceful in illuminating his time—and therefore foreshadowing our own.

Notes

1. Introduction

1. Leon Trotsky, *In Defense of Marxism: Against the Petty-Bourgeois Opposition* (New York: Merit, 1965), 182.

2. Irving Howe, *Decline of the New* (New York: Horizon Press, 1970), 211–14, 219–20, 222, 226–28, 235; Daniel Bell, *The Winding Passage: Essays and Sociological Journeys, 1960–1980* (Cambridge, Mass.: Abt, 1980), 127; Charles Kadushin, *The American Intellectual Elite* (Boston: Little, Brown, 1974), 30.

3. Barbara McKenzie, *Mary McCarthy* (New York: Twayne, 1966), 106; Woody Allen, *Without Feathers* (New York: Warner Books, 1976), 39.

4. Dwight Macdonald, "A New Theory of Totalitarianism," *New Leader* 34 (14 May 1951), 19n; Macdonald, *On Movies* (New York: Berkley Medallion, 1971), ix, xviii; Paul Goodman, "Our Best Journalist," *Dissent* 5 (Winter 1958), 83.

5. Howe, *Decline of the New*, 235; Freda Utley, *Odyssey of a Liberal: Memoir* (Washington, D.C.: Washington National Press, 1970), 290.

6. Macdonald, "A New Theory of Totalitarianism," 19n.

7. William Phillips, "Fashions of Revolt," *Commentary* 40 (October 1965), 88; Dwight Macdonald, "Politics Past," in *Memoirs of a Revolutionist: Essays in Political Criticism* (Cleveland: Meridian, 1958), 9

8. F. Anthony Macklin, "Please, high culture: An interview with critic Dwight Macdonald," *Film Heritage* 8 (Spring 1972), 34.

9. Morris Dickstein, *Gates of Eden: American Culture in the Sixties* (New York: Basic Books, 1977), 34.

10. Macklin, "Please, high culture," 18.

11. Malcolm Muggeridge, *The Most of Malcolm Muggeridge* (New York: Simon and Schuster, 1966), 66.

12. Dwight Macdonald, "A Good American," in *Discriminations: Essays and Afterthoughts, 1938–1974* (New York: Grossman, 1974), 387.

13. Harry Roskolenko, *When I Was Last on Cherry Street* (New York: Stein and Day, 1965), 158.

2. From Fortune to Partisan Review

1. Dwight Macdonald to author, 20 December 1970, in possession of author; Macdonald, "Politics Past," 7; James B. Gilbert, *Writers and Partisans: A History of Literary Radicalism in America* (New York: John Wiley & Sons, 1968), 169.

2. Dwight Macdonald quoted in Brendan Gill, "Happy Times," *Yale Alumni Magazine* (October 1973), 38; F. W. Dupee in Stanley J. Kunitz, ed., *Twentieth Century Authors*, first supplement (New York: H. H. Wilson, 1955), 291; Macdonald to parents, n.d. [1924?], in box 1, folder 7, Dwight Macdonald Papers, Yale University Library.

3. James Agee to Macdonald, 16 June [1927 ?] and 21 July 1927, in box 5, folder 64, Macdonald Papers; Macdonald, *Against the American Grain* (New York: Random House, 1962), 144, 159–61, 166.

4. Macdonald, "Politics Past," 7–8; Alfred Kazin, *New York Jew* (New York: Knopf, 1978), 43; Robert T. Elson, *Time Inc.: The Intimate History of a Publishing Enterprise, 1923–1941* (New York: Atheneum, 1968), 139.

5. Kazin, *New York Jew*, 53–54; Dwight Macdonald, "'Fortune' Magazine," *Nation* 144 (8 May 1937), 528.

6. Macdonald, "'Fortune' Magazine," 528; "A New Theory of Totalitarianism," 17; and "Politics Past," 14.

7. *New York Times* 10 February 1933, 15; "Editorial Comment," *New Masses* 16 (26 February 1935), 5.

8. Quoted in Edgar Kemler, *The Irreverent Mr. Mencken* (Boston: Little, Brown, 1950), 271–72.

9. Macdonald, "'Fortune' Magazine," 529–30; "Politics Past," 9; and *Discriminations*, 273; Elson, *Time, Inc.*, 253–55.

10. Macdonald, *Discriminations*, 171, 273; Macdonald to Henry R. Luce III, 23 October 1972, in box 29, folder 756, Macdonald Papers.

11. Macdonald, "'Fortune' Magazine," 528.

12. Ibid., 529, 530; Dwight Macdonald, "'Time' and Henry Luce," 144 (1 May 1937), 501; Macdonald, "Time, Fortune, Life," *Nation* 144 (22 May 1937), 585–86; Elson, *Time Inc.*, 254.

13. Daniel Aaron, *Writers on the Left* (New York: Avon, 1965), 348.

14. Malcolm Cowley, "The Record of a Trial," *New Republic* 90 (7 April 1937), 267–70.

15. Dwight Macdonald, letter to the editor, *New Republic* 90 (19 May 1937), 49–50; Macdonald, "Politics Past," 11.

16. American Committee to Defend Leon Trotsky, *News Bulletin* no. 6 (3 May 1937), 1, in unclassified section, Brandeis University Library.

17. Gilbert, *Writers and Partisans*, 110–13.

18. William Phillips in "Symposium: Thirty Years Later: Memories of the First American Writers' Congress," *American Scholar* 35 (Summer 1966), 510.

19. Ibid., 510–11; Leslie Fiedler, "*Partisan Review*: Phoenix or Dodo?," *Perspectives USA* 16 (Spring 1956), 93n.; Alfred Kazin, *Starting Out in the Thirties* (Boston: Atlantic-Little, Brown, 1965), 155; McKenzie, *Mary McCarthy* 22–23; Doris Grumbach, *The Company She Kept* (London: Bodley Head, 1967), 62–63; 74–78.

20. Mary McCarthy, *On the Contrary* (New York: Farrar, Straus & Giroux, 1961), 85; Phillips in "Symposium: Thirty Years Later," 509.

21. Interview with Philip Rahv, 4 May, 1970; Malcolm Cowley and Granville Hicks in "Symposium: Thirty Years Later," 511; Hicks, *Part of the Truth* (New York: Harcourt, Brace and World, 1965), 147.

22. Henry Hart, ed., *The Writer in a Changing World* (New York: Equinox Cooperative Press, 1937), 225; Phillips and Hicks in "Symposium: Thirty Years Later," 509–10; Malcolm Cowley, *The Dream of the Golden Mountains* (New York: Viking, 1980), 311–16.

23. Dwight Macdonald, letter to the editor, *Nation* 144 (19 June, 1937), .714; Henry Hart, letter to the editor, *Nation* 144 (26 June 1937), 741.

24. Gilbert, *Writers and Partisans*, 183.

25. Hicks, *Part of the Truth*, 148; Hicks, *Where We Came Out* (New York: Viking, 1954), 48; Hicks, "A 'Nation' Divided," *New Masses* 35 (7 December 1937), 11.

26. Hicks, "A 'Nation' Divided," 11; and Hicks, "The Writers' Congress," *New Masses* 23 (15 June 1937), 8–9.

27. William Barrett, *The Truants: Adventures Among the Intellectuals* (Garden City, N.Y.: Doubleday, 1982), 6, 70–74, 204–5; Alan Lelchuk, "Philip Rahv: The Last Years," in Arthur Edelstein, ed., *Images and Ideas in American Culture: The Functions of Criticism* (Hanover, N.H.: University Press of New England, 1979), 208–9, 218–19; Kazin, *Starting Out*, 160.

28. Mark Epernay, *The McLandress Dimension* (Boston: Houghton Mifflin, 1963), 2–3.

29. Quoted in Kazin, *Starting Out*, 157; Fiedler, "*Partisan Review*: Phoenix or Dodo?," 84, 86, 93; Howe, *Decline of the New*, 220; Bell, *Winding Passage*, 127–35.

30. Gilbert, *Writers and Partisans*, 4–6, 185, 191.

31. Dwight Macdonald to Leon Trotsky, 23 August 1937; Trotsky to Macdonald, 11 September 1937; and Trotsky to Macdonald, 20 January 1938, in box 53, folder 1283, Macdonald Papers.

32. Dwight Macdonald, "Laugh and Lie Down," *Partisan Review* 4

(December 1937), 49; Macdonald, "Cross Country," *Partisan Review* 4 (February 1938), 42–43.

33. Malcolm Cowley, "Partisan Review," *New Republic* 90 (19 October 1938), 311–12; Edmund Wilson to Cowley, 20 October 1938, quoted in Aaron, *Writers on the Left*, 349n.

34. "Staement of the L.C.F.S.," *Partisan Review* 6 (Summer 1939), 125–27.

35. Letter to the editor, *Nation* 149 (26 August 1939), 228; Gilbert, *Writers and Partisans*, 201–2; Aaron, *Writers on the Left*, 464.

36. Dwight Macdonald, "Socialist Stomatology," *New International* 5 (November 1939), 333.

37. Gilbert, *Writers and Partisans*, 194; Victor Serge, *Memoirs of a Revolutionary, 1901–1941* (New York: Oxford University Press, 1963), 360.

3. The Only Really Moral People

1. Isaac Deutscher, *The Prophet Outcast: Trotsky 1929–1940* (New York: Vintage, 1965), 419–20, 424.

2. Allen Ginsberg, "America," in *Howl and Other Poems* (San Francisco: City Lights, 1959), 31; Constance Ashton Myers, *The Prophet's Army: Trotskyists in America, 1928–1941* (Westport, Conn.: Greenwood, 1977), 137–42.

3. Irving Howe, *A Margin of Hope: An Intellectual Autobiography* (New York: Harcourt Brace Jovanovich, 1982), 40; John P. Diggins, *Up from Communism: Conservative Odysseys in American Intellectual History* (New York: Harper & Row, 1975), 161, 163–64.

4. Daniel Bell, *Marxian Socialism in the United States* (Princeton: Princeton University Press, 1967), 173–74; Max Shachtman, "Radicalism in the Thirties: The Trotskyist View," in Rita James Simon, ed., *As We Saw the Thirties* (Urbana: University of Illinois Press, 1967), 29–31.

5. Macdonald, "Politics Past," 14; Gilbert, *Writers and Partisans*, 236.

6. Macdonald, "Politics Past," 15, 17; Roskolenko, *Cherry Street*, 158; Gilbert, *Writers and Partisans*, 172n.

7. Macdonald, *Against the American Grain*, 124–25.

8. Roskolenko, *Cherry Street*, 158.

9. Deutscher, *Prophet Outcast*, 436–37; *Bulletin Oppozitsii*, no. 70 (1938), quoted in ibid., 438.

10. Macdonald and editors in "Discussion: Once More Kronstadt," *New International* 4 (July 1938), 212–13; Trotsky, *In Defense of Marxism*, 153.

11. Macdonald, "Kronstadt Revisited," *Discriminations*, 359–60; Macdonald to author, 20 December 1970; Diggins, *Up from Communism*, 181–84.

12. Whittaker Chambers, *Witness* (Chicago: Henry Regnery, 1952), 459–60.

13. Robert Wistrich, *Trotsky: Fate of a Revolutionary* (London: Robson, 1979), 172–75; Roskolenko, *Cherry Street*, 175.

14. Ibid., 175–78.

15. Ibid., 178–79.

16. Macdonald, "Politics Past," 17–18, 20; Diggins, *Up from Communism*, 13–14.

17. Editorial, *Fourth International* 1 (May 1940), 2.

18. Macdonald, "Politics Past," 18, 22; interview with I. Milton Sacks, 8 May 1970; Howe, *Margin of Hope*, 42.

19 Macdonald, "Reading from Left to Right," *New International* 4 (July 1938), 209, 211; and "Reading from Left to Right," *New International* 5 (July 1939), 221.

20. Macdonald, "The United States at War," *New International* 6 (April 1940), 73; "Why I Am No Longer a Socialist," *Liberation* 3 (May 1958), 4; and "Politics Past," 18.

21. Macdonald, "Notes on a War," *New International* 5 (November 1939), 332–33; and "Fascism: A New Social Order," *New International* 7 (May 1941), 85.

22. Macdonald, "Reading from Left to Right," *New International* 6 (June 1940), 104.

23. Vladimir Lenin, *State and Revolution* (New York: International Publishers, 1932), 15–20, 69–71; Leon Trotsky, *My Life* (New York: Charles Scribner's Sons, 1930), 341; E. H. Carr, *The Bolshevik Revolution*, vol. 1 (London: Macmillan, 1966), 240–53.

24. Max Nomad, *Aspects of Revolt* (New York: Bookman Associates, 1959), 99–101, 116–17; Trotsky, *My Life*, 129.

25. Bruno Rizzi, *La Bureaucratisation du Monde* (Paris, 1939), quoted in Deutscher, *Prophet Outcast*, 463–64; Daniel Bell, "The Strange Tale of Bruno R.," *New Leader* 42 (28 September 1959), 19–20.

26. Leon Trotsky, "The U.S.S.R. in War," *New International* 5 (November 1939), 327–32.

27. Diggins, *Up from Communism*, 186–98; James Gilbert, *Designing the Industrial State: The Intellectual Pursuit of Collectivism in America, 1880–1940* (Chicago: Quadrangle, 1972), 274–79; Michael Harrington, *Fragments of the Century: A Social Autobiography* (New York: Saturday Review Press, 1973), 70–75.

28. Dwight Macdonald, "The Burnhamian Revolution," *Partisan Review* 9 (January-February 1942), 76–77, 80, 84.

29. Myers, *Prophet's Army*, 169; Irving Howe, *Leon Trotsky* (New York: Penguin, 1979), 187; Macdonald to Howe, 6 July 1965, in box 23, folder 586, Macdonald Papers.

30. Macdonald, "Politics Past," 20–21.

31. Howe, *Margin of Hope*, 114; Macdonald, letter of resignation (Spring 1941) in box 148, folder 22, Macdonald Papers; Macdonald to Max Eastman, 9 March 1945, in box 14, folder 358, Macdonald Papers.

33. Shachtman to Macdonald, 17 May 1941, in box 47, folder 1143, Macdonald Papers; Daniel Bell, *The End of Ideology: On the Exhaustion of Political Ideas in the Fifties* (New York: Free Press, 1962), 306.

34. Albert Gates, "In Reply," *New International*, 8 (April 1942), 93.

35. Macdonald, "Trotskyism II: Revolution, Ltd.," *Memoirs*, 280–81; Irving Howe, *Steady Work: Essays in the Politics of Democratic Radicalism* (New York: Harcourt, Brace and World, 1966), 363.

36. Macdonald, "Trotskyism II: Revolution, Ltd.," 283.

37. Jack Barnes, introduction to James P. Cannon, *Letters from Prison* (New York: Merit, 1968), xi; Macdonald, "Trotskyism I: 'The Only Really Moral People,'" *Memoirs*, 274–75; Myers, *Prophet's Army*, 177–87.

38. Macdonald, "Trotskyism I: 'The Only Really Moral People,'" 272-73.

39. Ibid., 274.

40. James P. Cannon to Rose Karsner, 7 June 1944, in Cannon, *Letters from Prison*, 90.

41. Cannon to Karsner, 12 June 1944, in ibid., 93; Cannon to Karsner, 14 June 1944, in ibid., 95.

42. Macdonald, "Trotskyism II: Revolution, Ltd.," 278n.

4. Farewell to Partisan Review

1. Irving Howe, "The Dilemma of Partisan Review," *New International* 8 (February 1942), 21–22.

2. Dwight Macdonald in "Partisan Review Controversy," *New International* 8 (April 1942), 91; "A Statement by the Editors," *Partisan Review* 9 (January-February 1942), 2; Gilbert, *Writers and Partisans*, 248.

3. Archibald MacLeish in "Symposium: What Will I Do When America Goes to War?," *Modern Monthly* 9 (June 1935), 199, 201; MacLeish, "Post-war Writers and Pre-war Readers," *New Republic* 102 (10 June 1940), 789–90.

4. Edmund Wilson, *Classics and Commercials: A Literary Chronicle of the 1940's* (New York: Farrar, Straus and Giroux, 1950), 3–9.

5. Dwight Macdonald, "Kulturbolshewismus [sic] and Mr. Van Wyck Brooks," *Memoirs*, 207–8, 212, 214; and *Against the American Grain*, 208–9.

6. William Carlos Williams and Lionel Trilling in "On the 'Brooks-MacLeish' Thesis," *Partisan Review* 9 (January-February 1942), 39, 47.

7. Dwight Macdonald to Edmund Wilson, November 1941, *Partisan MSS*, quoted in Gilbert, *Writers and Partisans*, 228–29; Sherman Paul, *Edmund Wilson: A Study of Literary Vocation in Our Time* (Urbana: University of Illinois, 1965), 161n.

8. James T. Farrell, *The League of Frightened Philistines* (New York: Vanguard, 1945), 11; H. L. Mencken to James T. Farrell, 11 December 1940, in Guy J. Forgue, ed., *Letters of H. L. Mencken* (Boston: Northeastern University

Press, 1981), 451; V. J. Jerome, *Intellectuals and the War* (New York: Workers Library, 1940), 63.

9. Howe, *Decline of the New*, 220.

10. Fiedler, *"Partisan Review*: Phoenix or Dodo?," 89.

11. Quoted in Norman Podhoretz, *Making It* (New York: Random House, 1967), 100.

12. Interview with Rahv, 4 May 1970; Gilbert, *Writers and Partisans*, 232; Fiedler, *"Partisan Review*: Phoenix or Dodo?," 85, 89, 93.

13. Dwight Macdonald, "Notes on a Strange War," *Partisan Review* 7 (May-June 1940), 173-75.

14. Stephen Spender, "Defense of Britain," *Partisan Review* 7 (September-October 1940), 406.

15. Dwight Macdonald in ibid., 407-8.

16. Dwight Macdonald, "National Defense: The Case for Socialism," *Partisan Review* 7 (July-August 1940), 261, 264-66.

17. Gilbert, *Writers and Partisans*, 245.

18. Max Eastman in "As to Facts and Values: An Exchange," *Partisan Review* 9 (May-June 1942), 205.

19. Clement Greenberg and Dwight Macdonald, "Ten Propositions on the War," *Partisan Review* 8 (July-August 1941), 275-76, 278.

20. Interview with Rahv, 4 May 1970; Arthur Koestler, *The Yogi and the Commissar* (New York: Macmillan, 1945), 100.

21. Philip Rahv, "Ten Propositions and Eight Errors," *Partisan Review* 8 (November-December 1941), 499, 501-3.

22. "Reply by Greenberg and Macdonald," in ibid., 506-8.

23. Dwight Macdonald, "The (American) People's Century," *Partisan Review* 9 (July-August 1942), 294.

24. Karl Shapiro, letter to the editor, *Partisan Review* 8 (September-October 1941), 439.

25. Dwight Macdonald, "Roosevelt's Conservative War," *Partisan Review* 9 (November-December 1942), 476.

26. Elson, *Time Inc.*, 460-64; Norman D. Markowitz, *The Rise and Fall of the People's Century: Henry A. Wallace and American Liberalism, 1941-1948* (New York: Free Press, 1973), 40, 45-56; Macdonald, "The (American) People's Century," 297-98, 304-5, 308.

27. Quoted in Elson, *Time Inc.*, 464.

28. Interview with Rahv, 4 May 1970; Gilbert, *Writers and Partisans*, 234; Kazin, *Starting Out*, 72; Barrett, *Truants*, 83-84; Hook quoted in "Professor Out of Step," *Time* 101 (1 January 1973), 39.

29. Sidney Hook, "Failure of the Left," *Partisan Review* 10 (March-April 1943), 166, 169; Bell, *Marxian Socialism*, 180, 189-90.

30. Hook, "Failure of the Left," 168-69.

31. Ibid, 172, 175-76.

32. Dwight Macdonald, "The Future of Democratic Values," *Partisan Review* 10 (July-August 1943), 335; Macdonald to author, 20 December 1970.

33. Macdonald, "Future of Democratic Values," 328–30, 331–32, 337.

34. Interview with Rahv, 4 May 1970; Gilbert, *Writers and Partisans*, 251; Barrett, *Truants*, 80.

35. James Atlas, *Delmore Schwartz: The Life of an American Poet* (New York: Farrar, Straus and Giroux, 1977), 202–3, 255–56; Macdonald to Delmore Schwartz, 22 December 1942, in box 45, folder 1116, Macdonald Papers.

36. Letters from Dwight Macdonald and editors, *Partisan Review* 10 (July-August 1943), 382–83; Philip Rahv to Macdonald, 28 July 1943, in box 42, folder 1030, Macdonald Papers.

37. Letters from editors, *Partisan Review* 10 (July-August 1943), 383; James Burnham to Philip Rahv, 5 October 1943, *Partisan MSS*, cited in Gilbert, *Writers and Partisans*, 252n.; George Orwell to Rahv, 9 December 1943, in Sonia Orwell and Ian Angus, eds., *The Collected Essays, Journalism and Letters of George Orwell*, vol. 3 (New York: Harcourt Brace Jovanovich, 1968), 53.

38. Barrett, *Truants*, 80.

39. Quoted in Eric F. Goldman, *Rendezvous with Destiny* (New York: Vintage, 1956), 136.

5. Politics: *An Evaluation*

1. Dwight Macdonald, preface to *Politics* 1 (New York: Greenwood Reprint Corporation, 1968), n.p.; Macdonald to Philip Young, 27 May 1947, in box 61, folder 1433, Macdonald Papers; Macdonald to author, 20 December 1970; C. Wright Mills to Macdonald, 10 October 1943, in box 34, folder 855, Macdonald Papers.

2. Macdonald, preface to *Politics*, n.p.; Macdonald, "Politics Past," 26; interview with Sacks, 8 May 1970.

3. Dwight Macdonald, "War and the Intellectuals: Act II," *Partisan Review* 6 (Spring 1939), 4, 6–7, 15, 18–19; Randolph Bourne, *War and the Intellectuals: Collected Essays, 1915–1919*, ed. Carl Resek (New York: Harper & Row, 1964), 5–8, 12–14, 59–62, 71–82, 91–92, 117, 122–23, 130.

4. Quoted in Resek, introduction to Bourne, *War and the Intellectuals*, xiii.

5. Milton Konvitz to Macdonald, 26 October 1943, in box 26, folder 682, Macdonald Papers.

6. Macdonald, preface to *Politics*, n.p.

7. Ibid.; Macdonald, "Politics Past," 26; Lewis Coser, letter to *New York Review of Books*, 26 November 1968, in box 12, folder 288, Macdonald Papers.

8. Macdonald, preface to *Politics*, n.p.; Goodman quoted in Richard Kostelanetz, *Master Minds: Portraits of Contemporary American Artists and Intellectuals* (New York: Macmillan, 1969), 283.

9. Wilson, *Classics and Commercials*, 117; William L. O'Neill, *A Better World: The Great Schism: Stalinism and the American Intellectuals* (New York: Simon and Schuster, 1982), 79–81.

10. George Orwell to Philip Rahv, 1 May 1944, in Orwell and Angus, *Collected Essays*, 142; Orwell, "As I Please," 16 June 1944, in ibid., 172.

11. Malcolm Cowley, —*And I Worked at the Writer's Trade: Chapters of Literary History, 1918–1978* (New York: Viking, 1978), 151.

12. Utley, *Odyssey of a Liberal*, 290–91; Macdonald, "Why I Am No Longer a Socialist," 4.

13. Macdonald, "A Confession," *Discriminations*, 386.

14. Macdonald, "Trotsky is Dead," *Partisan Review* 7 (September-October 1940), 346–47.

15. Bell, *End of Ideology*, 306; Macdonald, preface to *Politics*, n.p.

16. Bell, *End of Ideology*, 307.

17. C. Wright Mills to Macdonald, 12 February 1944, in box 34, folder 855; and Seymour Martin Lipset to Macdonald, 4 October 1945, in box 28, folder 745, Macdonald Papers; Howe, *Margin of Hope*, 114–15; Howe, *Decline of the New*, 235.

18. Goodman, "Our Best Journalist," 83; Mary McCarthy to John Hay Whitney, 4 March 1961, in box 31, folder 780, Macdonald Papers.

19. Richard Rovere to Macdonald, 22 October 1945, 16 July 1946, and 31 January 1974, in box 44, folder 1081; and Waldemar Gurian to Macdonald, 28 October 1946, in box 20, folder 512, Macdonald Papers.

20. Daniel Bell to Macdonald, 19 July 1944, in box 7, folder 138, Macdonald Papers; Hannah Arendt, "He's All Dwight," *New York Review of Books* 11 (1 August 1968), 31.

21. Malcolm Cowley, "Ten Little Magazines," *New Republic* 116 (31 March 1947), 32; Granville Hicks to Macdonald, 13 February 1945, in box 22, folder 566, Macdonald Papers.

22. Gilbert, *Writers and Partisans*, 255–56; Dwight Macdonald, "'Partisan Review' and 'Politics,'" *Politics* 3 (December 1946), 403.

23. Philip Rahv to Arthur Schlesinger, Jr., 4 September 1947, *Partisan* MSS, quoted in Gilbert, *Writers and Partisans*, 189.

24. William Barrett, "The Resistance," *Partisan Review* 13 (September-October 1946), 487; James Burnham, "Politics for the Nursery Set," *Partisan Review* 12 (Spring 1945), 188–90.

25. William Phillips and Philip Rahv, "The Fugitives from Politics: Dwight Macdonald," *Partisan Review* 13 (November-December 1946), 612–13; Linda Kaye Kirby, "Communism, the Discovery of Totalitarianism, and the Cold War: *Partisan Review*, 1934 to 1948" (Ph.D. diss., University of Colorado, 1970), 172–80, 188.

26. William Phillips, "The Lions and the Foxes," *Partisan Review* 12 (Spring 1945), 190–91, 194.

27. Interview with Rahv, 4 May 1970.

28. Philip Rahv, "Disillusionment and Partial Answers," *Partisan Review* 15 (May 1948), 521, 524–26, 529.

29. Barrett, *Truants*, 6, 89; Eileen Simpson, *Poets in Their Youth: A Memoir* (New York: Random House, 1982), 162.

6. The Responsibility of Peoples

1. Dwight Macdonald, "Why Politics?'" *Politics* 1 (February 1944), 6–7.

2. Ibid., 6–7; Dwight Macdonald, "A Theory of 'Popular Culture,'" in ibid., 23; Macdonald, "By Way of Rejoinder," *Politics* 1 (July 1944), 179.

3. Dwight Macdonald, "Internationale into Nationale," *Memoirs*, 117.

4. Dwight Macdonald, "Mr. Churchill's Spades," in ibid., 127–29.

5. Dwight Macdonald, "'Twas a Famous Victory," in ibid., 151.

6. Cited in David M. Potter, *People of Plenty: Economic Abundance and the American Character* (Chicago: University of Chicago Press, 1958), 80.

7. Macdonald, "'Twas a Famous Victory," 152.

8. Dwight Macdonald, "'People's Capitalism,'" *Memoirs*, 288–89.

9. Macdonald, "Why Politics?," 8.

10. Dwight Macdonald, "The Prospects for Revolution," *Memoirs*, 129, 131–33, 137.

11. William Safire, *Safire's Political Dictionary* (New York: Random House, 1978), 127–28; Dwight Macdonald, "Three Worlds," *Memoirs*, 123–24.

12. Dwight Macdonald, "Warsaw," *Memoirs*, 146.

13. O'Neill, *Better World*, 75–78.

14. Dwight Macdonald, "'Here Lies Our Road!' said Writer to Reader," *Politics* 1 (September 1944), 251.

15. Dwight Macdonald, "'Why?'—Underside View," *Politics* 2 (April 1945), 102.

16. Dwight Macdonald, "Notes on the Psychology of Killing," *Memoirs* 79, 89.

17. Ibid., 90.

18. Dwight Macdonald, "My Favorite General," ibid., 93, 96, 99.

19. Quoted in ibid., 99.

20. Dwight Macdonald, "On the Conduct of the Lynn Case," *Politics* 1 (April 1944), 85–88; Arthur Garfield Hays, letter to the editor, *Politics* 1 (April 1944), 88.

21. Dwight Macdonald, "The Supreme Court's Moot Suit," *Politics* 1 (June 1944), 133.

22. Dwight Macdonald, "How 'Practical' is a Radically Segregated Army?," *Politics* 1 (July 1944), 184, 186.

23. Hannah Arendt, *The Jew as Pariah: Jewish Identity and Politics in the Modern Age*, ed. Ron H. Feldman (New York: Grove Press, 1978), 230.

24. Gordon Allport to Macdonald, 26 May 1944, in box 5, folder 69; Macdonald to Bruno Bettelheim, 29 February 1944, in box 8, folder 151; Bettelheim to Macdonald, 12 March 1944, in box 8, folder 151, Macdonald Papers.

25. Howe, *Margin of Hope*, 253; Stephen J. Whitfield, "The Holocaust and the American Jewish Intellectual," *Judaism* 28 (Fall 1979), 391–92, 394–96, 399, 401.

26. Dwight Macdonald, "The Responsibility of Peoples," *Memoirs*, 36, 42–43n.

27. Ibid., 45, 47–50.

28. Ibid., 64–65.

29. Ibid., 59–60, 62–63, 71.

30. Ibid., 61; Macdonald, "Why I Am No Longer a Socialist," 7.

31. Macdonald, "The Responsibility of Peoples," 60.

32. Hannah Arendt, *Eichmann in Jerusalem: A Report on the Banality of Evil* (New York: Viking, 1963), 149–53, 154–58, 167–75.

33. Hannah Arendt, *The Origins of Totalitarianism* (Cleveland: World, 1958), 405–406n.

34. Jean Malaquais, letter to the editor, *Politics* 2 (September 1945), 283; Dwight Macdonald, reply, *Politics* 2 (September 1945), 284.

35. Quoted in Isaac Deutscher, *Stalin: A Political Biography* (New York: Oxford University Press, 1949), 324.

36. Dwight Macdonald, "Two Footnotes to History," *Memoirs*, 104.

37. H. Stuart Hughes, *An Approach to Peace* (New York: Atheneum, 1966), 73–74; Michael Walzer, *Just and Unjust Wars* (New York: Basic Books, 1977), 255–62; Albert Speer, *Inside the Third Reich: Memoirs* (New York: Macmillan, 1970), 280–81, 284–86, 347n.

38. Macdonald, "The Responsibility of Peoples," 35; Robert MacIver and Reinhold Niebuhr, letters to the editor, *Politics* 2 (May 1945), 160; Lewis Coser to Macdonald, 1945, in box 12, folder 288; Willmoore Kendall to Macdonald, 1951, in box 25, folder 643, Macdonald Papers.

39. Quoted in Lawrence S. Wittner, *Rebels Against War: The American Peace Movement 1941–1960* (New York: Columbia University Press, 1969), 125; Walzer, *Just and Unjust Wars*, 263–69; Dwight Macdonald, "The Bomb," *Memoirs*, 169–70.

40. Ibid., 169–70, 172, 178; Macdonald, "Why I Am No Longer a Socialist," 4.

7. The Root Is Man

1 Nicola Chiaromonte, *The Worm of Consciousness and Other Essays* (New York: Harcourt Brace Jovanovich, 1976), 52–53, 56; Macdonald, preface to *Politics*, n.p.

2. Herbert R. Lottman, *Albert Camus: A Biography* (Garden City, N.Y.: Doubleday, 1979), 458–59, 461.

3. Chambers, *Witness*, 712; Eric F. Goldman, *The Crucial Decade—and After: America 1945–1960* (New York: Vintage, 1960) 7–8, 60–61.

4. Arthur Schlesinger, Jr., *The Vital Center* (Boston: Houghton Mifflin, 1962), xxiii; Norman Podhoretz, *Doings and Undoings: The Fifties and After in American Writing* (New York: Farrar, Straus, 1964), 107, 110.

5. Advertisement, *Politics* 2 (November 1945), 352.

6. Dwight Macdonald, "The Root Is Man," part one, *Politics* 3 (April 1946), 97–99.

7. Finley Peter Dunne, *Mr. Dooley: Now and Forever* (Stanford: Stanford University Press, 1954), 252.

8. Macdonald, "Why I Am No Longer a Socialist," 7; Macdonald, "Politicking," *Politics* 3 (January 1946), 31.

9. Gilbert, *Writers and Partisans*, 242.

10. Macdonald, "The Root Is Man," part one, 100.

11. Ibid., 105; Macdonald, "The Root Is Man," part two, *Politics* 3 (July 1946), 208n.

12. Macdonald, "Why I Am No Longer a Socialist," 7; reply by the editor, *Politics* 3 (May 1946), 141.

13. Macdonald to Miriam Chiaromonte, 19 January 1972, in box 10, folder 240, Macdonald Papers; Barrett, *Truants*, 90–91; Mary McCarthy, preface to Chiaromonte, *Worm of Consciousness*, xiv–xv.

14. Macdonald, "The Root Is Man," part one, 98, 101–2, 104, 112–15.

15. Ibid., 100, 102, 106.

16. Macdonald, "The Root Is Man," part two, 195–96, 205.

17. Ibid., 198–99.

18. Ibid., 211.

19. Ibid., 198, 205, 214.

20. Ibid., 208, 210.

21. Macdonald, "'Here Lies Our Road!' said Writer to Reader," 249.

22. Macdonald, "The Root Is Man," part two, 209, 213.

23. Ibid., 209, 212–13.

24. Ibid., 210, 214.

25. Richard Rovere to Macdonald, 16 July 1946, in box 44, folder 1081; and Nicola Chiaromonte to Macdonald, 1946, in box 10, folder 241, Macdonald Papers.

26. Richard King, *The Party of Eros: Radical Social Thought and the Realm of Freedom* (Chapel Hill: University of North Carolina Press, 1972), 39–43; Irving Howe to Macdonald, 1 August 1946, in box 23, folder 586, Macdonald Papers.

27. Howe, *Decline of the New*, 235; and *Margin of Hope*, 116–17.

28. Macdonald, "Politicking," *Politics* 3 (February 1946), 64; reply by the editor, *Politics* 3 (May 1946), 141.

29. Dwight Macdonald, comment on Simone Weil, "Factory Work," *Politics* 3 (December 1946), 377.

8. The Pacifist Dilemma

1. Dwight Macdonald, "Conscription and Conscientious Objection," *Politics* 2 (June 1945), 165; and "By Way of Rejoinder," *Politics* 1 (July 1944), 180.

2. Wittner, *Rebels Against War*, 56–57, 85–88, 91–92; Staughton Lynd, ed., *Nonviolence in America: A Documentary History* (Indianapolis: Bobbs-Merrill, 1966), xxxvii, xxxix–xi, 296, 520; James Finn, *Protest: Pacifism and Politics* (New York: Vintage, 1968), 328; Penina M. Glazer, "From the Old Left to the New: Radical Criticism in the 1940s," *American Quarterly* 24 (December 1972), 593–601.

3. Lowell Naeve, *A Field of Broken Stones* (Glen Gardner, New Jersey: Libertarian Press, 1950), 29, quoted in Wittner, *Rebels Against War*, 91n.

4. Wittner, *Rebels Against War*, 152–53.

5. Quoted in Nat Hentoff, *Peace Agitator: The Story of A. J. Muste* (New York: Macmillan, 1963), 108–11, 114, 115, 177.

6. War Resisters League Executive Committee Minutes, 11 June 1947, W. R. L. MSS, quoted in Wittner, *Rebels Against War*, 153.

7. "Report of the February Conference on Non-Violent Revolutionary Socialism, Chicago, February 6–9, 1946," quoted in Wittner, *Rebels Against War*, 154–55.

8. James Peck and Dwight Macdonald in "Atomic Bombs, Union Made," *Politics* 3 (August 1946), 245, 247.

9. Macdonald in ibid., 247.

10. Dwight Macdonald, "Comment: Russomania in England," *Politics* 1 (November 1944), 296.

11. Macdonald in "Atomic Bombs, Union Made," 247.

12. Ibid., 247.

13. David Dellinger, letter to the editor, and Dwight Macdonald, editor's reply, *Politics* 3 (November 1946), 365–66.

14. Wittner, *Rebels Against War*, 156–57; "Peacemeakers," *Politics* 5 (Spring 1948), 136.

15. Letter from David Dellinger, Donald Harrington, et al., *Politics* 4 (January 1947), 31.

16. Dwight Macdonald, "Why Destroy Draft Cards?," *Politics* 4 (March-April 1947), 54; memorandum of break with conscription committee, 12 February 1947, in box 161, folder 28, Macdonald Papers.

17. *New York Times*, 1 April 1948, 1, 10; Max Lerner, *Actions and Passions: Notes on the Multiple Revolution of Our Time* (New York: Simon and Schuster, 1949), 102; Bayard Rustin, *Down the Line* (Chicago: Quadrangle, 1971), 50–52.

18. Dwight Macdonald, "Stalin's February Ninth Speech," *Memoirs*, 183, 185.

19. Dwight Macdonald, "The Late War: A Trial Balance," ibid., 182.

20. Dwight Macdonald, "Truman's Doctrine, Abroad and at Home," ibid., 187.

21. Macdonald, "'Partisan Review' and 'Politics,'" 401; Macdonald, "The Late War: A Trial Balance," 183.

22. Macdonald, *Henry Wallace: The Man and the Myth* (New York: Vanguard, 1948), 24.

23. Ibid., 93, 166.

24. Ibid., 20–21, 27.

25. Ibid., 23, 25, 162.

26. Henry Wallace, *Soviet Asia Mission* (New York: Reynal and Hitchcock, 1946), quoted in ibid., 104; O'Neill, *Better World*, 150–51.

27. Hannah Dorner quoted in "Glamour Pusses," *Time* 44 (9 September 1946), 25.

28. Macdonald, *Henry Wallace*, 171–75.

29. "What is Henry Wallace?," *Time* 51 (15 March 1948), 118.

30. Arthur M. Schlesinger, Jr., to Macdonald, 15 April 1947, in box 45, folder 1109; Czeslaw Milosz to Macdonald, 21 December 1958, in box 34, folder 856; David Riesman to Macdonald, 13 August 1947, in box 43, folder 1059, in Macdonald Papers.

31. Macdonald to Roger N. Baldwin, 16 March 1951, in box 7, folder 116, Macdonald Papers; Markowitz, *Rise and Fall of the People's Century*, 340.

32. Dwight Macdonald, "USA v. USSR," *Memoirs*, 309.

33. Albert Shanker, letter to the editor, *Politics* 5 (Summer 1948), 202.

34. Macdonald to James Loeb, 22 April 1948, in box 6, folder 86, Macdonald Papers; O'Neill, *Better World*, 152; James Peck, *Underdogs and Upperdogs* (Canterbury, N.H.: Greenleaf, 1969), 59.

35. Dwight Macdonald, "The 1960 Campaign: An Anarchist View," *Discriminations*, 62; and "On the Elections," in *Politics* 5 (Summer 1948), 203.

36. Macdonald, "On the Elections," 204; and "Thomas for President?", *Politics* 1 (October 1944), 278, 280; W. A. Swanberg, *Norman Thomas: The Last Idealist* (New York: Charles Scribner's Sons, 1976), 287–91.

37. Macdonald, "On the Elections," 204.

38. Dwight Macdonald, "The Waldorf Conference," special insert, *Politics* 6 (Winter 1949), 32-A-B.

39. Ibid., 32-A.

40. Ibid., 32-B; Simpson, *Poets in Their Youth*, 190.

41. Macdonald, "Waldorf Conference," 32-B-C; O'Neill, *Better World*, 163–67.

42. Macdonald, "Waldorf Conference," 32-D; Norman Mailer, *Advertisements for Myself* (New York: G. P. Putnam's Sons, 1959), 409–10.

43. Dwight Macdonald, "Curiouser and Curiouser," *Memoirs*, 291.

44. Macdonald, "'Partisan Review' and 'Politics,'" 403.

45. Dwight Macdonald, "The Germans—Three Years Later," *Memoirs*, 75–76.

46. Ibid., 75, 78–79.

47. Dwight Macdonald, "The Pacifist Dilemma," ibid., 193, 197.

48. Macdonald, "USSR v. USA," 313.

49. Macdonald, "The Pacifist Dilemma," 194–95, and in *Politics* 5 (Summer 1948), 148; Macdonald, "Why I Am No Longer a Socialist," 4.

50. Dwight Macdonald, "Gandhi," *Memoirs*, 345–47, 349.

51. Dwight Macdonald, "A Personal Letter to 2500 People," *Politics* 5 (Winter 1948), 58.

52. Howe, *Margin of Hope*, 114–15; Macdonald to Richard Gillam, 23 November 1970, in box 18, folder 458, Macdonald Papers; "Old Left, New Broom," *Time* 108 (6 December 1976), 82.

53. Macdonald, preface to *Politics*, n.p.

54. T. S. Eliot to Macdonald, 15 August 1949; and Macdonald to Mrs. T. S. Eliot, 19 January 1965, in box 15, folder 366, Macdonald Papers; Simpson, *Poets in Their Youth*, 171–73; Barrett, *Truants*, 106.

55. Elisabeth Young-Bruehl, *Hannah Arendt: For Love of the World* (New Haven, Conn.: Yale University Press, 1982), 197, 212; Macdonald to Hannah Arendt, 30 August 1967, in box 6, folder 98, Macdonald Papers.

56. Macdonald to T. S. Eliot, 14 November 1949, in box 15, folder 366; and Czeslaw Milosz to Macdonald, 12 December 1953, in box 34, file 856, Macdonald Papers.

57. Macdonald, editor's reply, *Politics* 6 (Winter 1949), 57; O'Neill, *Better World*, 169–70.

58. Macdonald, "The Uncommon People," *Politics* 6 (Winter 1949), 60.

9. L'Envoi

1. Macdonald to Abraham Kaufman, 20 May 1949, in box 55, folder 1337, Macdonald Papers.

2. War Resisters League Executive Committee Minutes, 12 September 1949, W.R.L. MSS; and Evan Thomas to Sidney Aberman, 12 December 1950, W.R.L. MSS, cited in Wittner, *Rebels Against War*, 188n; Roy Kepler, "Report on a Country-Wide Trip," W.R.L. MSS, in Wittner, *Rebels Against War*, 211.

3. Macdonald to A. J. Muste, 19 April 1949, in box 35, folder 892, Macdonald Papers; Marty Jezer, *The Dark Ages: Life in the United States, 1945–1960* (Boston: South End Press, 1982), 293–95.

4. Quoted in Otto Nathan and Heinz Norden, eds., *Einstein on Peace* (New York: Schocken, 1960), 308, 519–20.

5. Sidney Hook, *Political Power and Personal Freedom* (New York: Criterion, 1959), 433; Barrett, *Truants*, 106.

6. Macdonald, "A New Theory of Totalitarianism," 17.

7. Dwight Macdonald, "I Choose the West," *Memoirs*, 197–98, 200; Christopher Lasch, *The New Radicalism in America, 1889–1963: The Intellectual as a Social Type* (New York: Knopf, 1965), 323–34.

8. Podhoretz, *Doings and Undoings*, 182–85; Walter B. Rideout, *The Radical Novel in the United States, 1900–1954* (Cambridge: Harvard University Press, 1956), 271–72.

9. Norman Mailer in "Our Country and Our Culture: A Symposium," *Partisan Review* 19 (May-June 1952), 300–1.

10. Macdonald, "Why I Am No Longer a Socialist," 4; Barrett, *Truants*, 91–92.

11. Macdonald, postscript to "I Choose the West," 201.

12. Dwight Macdonald, "Parajournalism II: *The New Yorker* and Tom Wolfe," *New York Review of Books* 6 (3 February 1966), 21.

13. Arthur Koestler, *The Trail of the Dinosaur and Other Essays* (New York: Macmillan, 1956), viii; Gilbert, *Writers and Partisans*, 257–58.

14. Podhoretz, *Making It*, 123.

15. Philip Rahv in "Our Country and Our Culture," 304–5.

16. Hicks, *Where We Came Out*, 3–4, 9, 183.

17. Quoted in ibid., 184–85, 188.

18. Editors' reply, *Partisan Review* 20 (November-December 1953), 717; Diggins, *Up from Communism*, 329–30; Irving Kristol, "'Civil Liberties,' 1952—A Study in Confusion," *Commentary* 13 (March 1952), 229.

19. Harrington, *Fragments of the Century*, 82–83; Macdonald, *Memoirs*, 283; Macdonald to Rowland———[?], 9 June 1956, in box 61, folder 1425, Macdonald Papers.

20. Christopher Lasch, *The Agony of the American Left* (New York: Vintage, 1969), 78–94; Diggins, *Up from Communism*, 326–30; Victor S. Navasky, *Naming Names* (New York: Viking, 1980), 55–56; Diana Trilling, *We Must March My Darlings* (New York: Harcourt Brace Jovanovich, 1977), 60–63.

21. Macdonald to Mary McCarthy, 18 March 1952, in box 31, folder 779, Macdonald Papers; O'Neill, *Better World*, 297–98, 300–4.

22. Macdonald to Norman Birnbaum, 8 January 1959, in box 15, folder 377, Macdonald Papers.

23. Dwight Macdonald, "America! America!," *Discriminations*, 44–56.

24. Ibid., 57; Irving Kristol to Macdonald, 15 May 1958; Macdonald to Kristol, 21 May 1958; Michael Josselson to Macdonald, 28 April 1958, in box 15, folder 376, Macdonald Papers.

25. Macdonald, *Discriminations*, 57–59; Lasch, *Agony of the American Left*, 75; Macdonald to Michael Josselson, 30 March 1967, in box 12, folder 276, Macdonald Papers.

26. Peter Steinfels, *The Neoconservatives: The Men Who Are Changing*

America's Politics (New York: Simon and Schuster, 1979), 84–87; Lasch, *Agony of the American Left*, 72–75.

27. Lewis Coser to Macdonald, 16 November 1953; 25 February 1957; and 15 January 1957, in box 12, folder 288, Macdonald Papers; Macdonald, "Trotsky, Orwell, and Socialism," *Discriminations*, 344.

28. Nathan Glazer, *Remembering the Answers: Essays on the American Student Revolt* (New York: Basic Books, 1970), 3–4; interview with Sacks, 8 May 1970; Howe, *Decline of the New*, 219.

10. The New Left's Ancestral Voice

1. Macdonald, preface to *Politics*, n.p.; Paul Jacobs and Saul Landau, *The New Radicals: A Report with Documents* (New York: Vintage, 1966), 101.

2. Howard Zinn, *SNCC: The New Abolitionists* (Boston: Beacon, 1965), 273, 274; Jack Newfield, *A Prophetic Minority* (New York: Signet, 1967), 132.

3. Tom Hayden in "Confrontation: The Old Left and the New," *American Scholar* 36 (Autumn 1967), 577.

4. Macklin, "Please, high culture," 33; Glazer, "From the Old Left to the New," 601–3.

5. Marvin Meyers, *The Jacksonian Persuasion: Politics and Belief* (Stanford: Stanford University Press, 1960), vii.

6. Staughton Lynd, "Towards a History of the New Left," in Priscilla Long, ed., *The New Left: A Collection of Documents* (Boston: Porter Sargent, 1969), 6.

7. Dwight Macdonald, "Too Big," *Memoirs*, 373, 374; "The Port Huron Statement," in Jacobs and Landau, *New Radicals*, 154, 159.

8. Hayden quoted in Jacobs and Landau, *New Radicals*, 35.

9. Mario Savio, "An End to History," ibid., 234; Savio quoted in ibid., 61.

10. Carl Oglesby, "Liberalism and the Corporate State," ibid., 258.

11. Ibid., 261.

12. Ibid., 261; Hayden quoted in Jacobs and Landau, *New Radicals*, 34.

13. Theodore Draper, *The Rediscovery of Black Nationalism* (New York: Viking, 1970), 103n; John P. Diggins, *The American Left in the Twentieth Century* (New York: Harcourt Brace Jovanovich, 1973), 160.

14. Ibid., 164; H. Stuart Hughes, "On Being a Candidate," *Commentary* 35 (February 1963), 125.

15. Anthony Scaduto, *Bob Dylan: An Intimate Biography* (New York: Signet, 1973), 158–66, 171–72, 179–80.

16. Richard Flacks, "Some Problems, Issues, Proposals," in Jacobs and Landau, *New Radicals*, 164.

17. Quoted in Robert Penn Warren, *Who Speaks for the Negro?* (New York: Vintage, 1966), 95.

18. Quoted in ibid., 397–98.

19. Robert Scheer, ed., *Eldridge Cleaver: Post-Prison Writings and Speeches* (New York: Vintage, 1968), 54; Macdonald, "A New Theory of Totalitarianism," 18n; Carmichael quoted in Bernard Weinraub, "The Brilliancy of Black," in Harold Hayes, ed., *Smiling Through the Apocalypse: Esquire's History of the Sixties* (New York: McCall, 1969), 683.

20. Kenneth Keniston, *Young Radicals: Notes on Committed Youth* (New York: Harcourt, Brace and World, 1968), 17–18, 43, 112–17, 131–32, 282.

21. Ibid., 248–50.

22. Howe, *Steady Work*, 246; Ralph Miliband, "Mills and Politics," in Irving Louis Horowitz, ed., *The New Sociology: Essays in Social Science and Social Theory in Honor of C. Wright Mills* (New York: Oxford University Press, 1964), 78, 81, 82, 83, 86.

23. Irving Louis Horowitz, *C. Wright Mills: An American Utopian* (New York: Free Press, 1983), 76; Dwight Macdonald, "The Mills Method," *Discriminations*, 294–300; Macdonald to C. Wright Mills, 1952, box 34, folder 855; and Mills to Macdonald, 18 March 1952, in box 34, folder 855, Macdonald Papers.

24. Macdonald, *Discriminations*, 299; Macdonald to Richard Gillam, 23 November 1970, in box 18, folder 458; and Macdonald to C. Wright Mills, 28 May 1949, in box 34, folder 855, Macdonald Papers; Horowitz, *C. Wright Mills*, 77, 249–50.

25. Theodore Roszak, *The Making of a Counter-Culture: Reflections on the Technocratic Society and Its Youthful Opposition* (Garden City, N.Y.: Doubleday, 1969), 25; Carl Oglesby, ed., introduction to *The New Left Reader* (New York: Grove Press, 1969), 23.

26. C. Wright Mills, "On the New Left," in Jacobs and Landau, *New Radicals*, 108–14.

27. Paul Goodman, "The New Reformation," in Irving Howe, ed., *Beyond the New Left* (New York: McCall, 1970), 88–89; King, *Party of Eros*, 78–88, 96–97; Michael Ferber and Staughton Lynd, *The Resistance* (Boston: Beacon, 1971), 267–68.

28. Dwight Macdonald, review of *Art and Social Nature*, *Politics* 3 (November 1946), 362; and Macdonald to Raymond Rosenthal, 18 September 1973, in box 43, folder 1073; Macdonald to Guggenheim Foundation, 1974 [?], in box 20, folder 509, Macdonald Papers.

29. Paul Goodman, *Growing Up Absurd* (New York: Random House, 1960), 241; Robert Mazzocco, "Good Man," *New York Review of Books* 14 (21 May 1970), 3.

30. Goodman, "New Reformation," 92, 95.

31. Paul Goodman, *People or Personnel and Like a Conquered Province* (New York: Vintage, 1968), 188–89.

32. Oglesby, ed., *New Left Reader*, 32; Herbert Marcuse quoted in "Rebellion," *Saturday Review* 103 (25 April 1970), 36; Diggins, *American Left in the Twentieth Century*, 188–94.

33. I. F. Stone, *In a Time of Torment* (New York: Vintage, 1968), 262.

34. Jacobs and Landau, *New Radicals* 320.

35. I. F. Stone, "Henry Wallace—a Great American," *Nation* 159 (22 July 1944), 92; Stone, *The Truman Era* (New York: Monthly Review Press, 1953), 67–68.

36. Stone, *Time of Torment*, 2.

37. Dwight Macdonald to author, 20 December 1970.

38. Noam Chomsky to author, 13 May 1970; Chomsky, "Nationalism and Conflict in Palestine," *Columbia Forum* 13 (Winter 1969), 16.

39. Chomsky to author, 13 May 1970; Chomsky, *American Power and the New Mandarins* (New York: Vintage, 1969), 19; Chomsky to Macdonald, 14 June 1970, in box 10, folder 246, Macdonald Papers.

40. Chomsky, *American Power*, 16, 323–24, 358–59.

41. Dwight Macdonald, "The Responsibility of Intellectuals," *Memoirs*, 100–2.

42. Chomsky, *American Power*, 299–301, 307.

43. Macdonald, "The Bomb," 171, 173; Chomsky, *American Power*, 298–300, 371.

44. Macdonald, preface to *Politics*, n.p.

45. Chomsky, *American Power*, 216–217n.

46. Staughton Lynd quoted in John Corry, "Spokesman for the New Left," *New York Times Magazine*, 23 January 1966, 12.

47. Finn, *Protest: Pacifism and Politics*, 226; Staughton Lynd, "Socialism, the Forbidden Word," *Studies on the Left* 3 (Summer 1963), 18.

48. Newfield, *Prophetic Minority*, 145; Staughton Lynd to author, n.d. [1970]; interview with Dan Lourie, 30 March 1970.

49. Lynd to author, n.d. [1970]; Lynd, "'Again—Don't Tread on Me,'" *Newsweek* 76 (6 July 1970), 30; and Lynd, "The Prospects of the New Left," in John H. M. Laslett and Seymour Martin Lipset, eds., *Failure of a Dream?: Essays in the History of American Socialism* (Garden City, New York: Doubleday, 1974), 713–14.

50. Lynd quoted in Corry, "Spokesman for the New Left," 35.

51. Newfield, *Prophetic Minority*, 145; Staughton Lynd, "Coalition Politics or Nonviolent Revolution?", *Liberation* 10 (June–July 1965), 21.

52. Finn, *Protest: Pacifism and Politics*, 231, 239; Lynd, "Coalition Politics or Nonviolent Revolution?", 18.

53. Finn, *Protest: Pacifism and Politics*, 225.

54. Macdonald, "The Bomb," 170.

55. McGeorge Bundy, "A Letter to Twelve College Presidents," *Atlantic Monthly* 175 (May 1945), 52–54.

56. Memorandum from Dwight D. Eisenhower, 29 April 1946, in Henry L. Stimson Papers, Yale University, quoted in Seymour Melman, *Pentagon Capitalism: The Political Economy of War* (New York: McGraw-Hill, 1970), 231, 234.

57. Dwight Macdonald, "Comment: The Wilson Speech," *Politics* 1 (March 1944), 36.

58. Dwight Macdonald, "Wallace and the Labor Draft," *Politics* 2 (February 1945), 34.

59. Robert Heilbroner, "Military America," *New York Review of Books* 15 (23 July 1970), 5.

11. A Critical American

1. Quoted in Israel Shenker, "Ideological Labels Changing Along with the Label-Makers," *New York Times*, 12 November 1970, 41.

2. Dwight Macdonald in "Confrontation: The Old Left and the New," *American Scholar*, 575–76.

3. Ibid.

4. Louis Kampf, "The Trouble with Literature . . . ," *Change* 2 (May-June 1970), 30; Frederick Crews, *Out of My System: Psychoanalysis, Ideology, and Critical Method* (New York: Oxford University, 1975), 135.

5. Macdonald in "Confrontation: The Old Left and the New," *American Scholar*, 575–76.

6. Quoted in Diggins, *American Left in the Twentieth Century*, 165.

7. Dwight Macdonald, "An Exchange on the Columbia Student Strike of 1968," *Discriminations*, 450–52, 455–58, 463; Macdonald to Joel Carmichael, 17 March 1970, in box 10, folder 225, Macdonald Papers.

8. Macdonald, "Columbia Student Strike," 462–64; Macdonald to Louis Kronenberger, 5 June 1968, in box 26, folder 692; and Macdonald to Charles Abrams, 7 June 1968, in box 5, folder 57, Macdonald Papers.

9. Macdonald to Joel Carmichael, 17 March 1970, in box 10, folder 225; and Macdonald to E. S. Wells Kerr, 4 November 1968, in box 25, folder 663, Macdonald Papers.

10. Dwight Macdonald, "Our Invisible Poor," *Discriminations*, 97–98; and "An Open Letter to Michael Harrington," *New York Review of Books* 11, (5 December 1968), 48; Harrington, *Fragments of the Century*, 172–73.

11. Arthur Schlesinger, Jr., *A Thousand Days: John F. Kennedy in the White House* (New York: Fawcett Crest, 1967), 921–22; Macdonald to author, 20 December 1970.

12. Daniel Patrick Moynihan, "One-Third of a Nation," *New Republic* 186 (9 June 1982), 18–19.

13. Norman Podhoretz, *Breaking Ranks: A Political Memoir* (New York: Harper & Row, 1979), 181–82, 183, 186; Dwight Macdonald, "A General View of the Ruins," and "My Kind of Anticommunism," *Discriminations*, 403, 425.

14. Susan Sontag, *Styles of Radical Will* (New York: Delta, 1969), 217.

15. Macdonald to Nicola Chiaromonte, 21 March 1966, in box 10,

folder 244; and Macdonald to David McReynolds, 24 June 1968, in box 55, folder 1338, Macdonald Papers; Macdonald, *Discriminations*, 406, 424.

16. Dwight Macdonald, "Politics," *Esquire* 70 (July 1968), 10.

17. Macdonald to Nicola Chiaromonte, 5 July 1967, in box 10, folder 244; Macdonald to Mary McCarthy, 11 April 1966, and 17 May 1967, in box 31, folder 780, Macdonald Papers; Macdonald, *Discriminations*, 404–21.

18. Kadushin, *American Intellectual Elite*, 131–33.

19. Walter Johnson, ed., *The Papers of Adlai E. Stevenson*, vol. 8 (Boston: Little, Brown, 1979), 804–5, 806, 808; Richard J. Walton, *The Remnants of Power: The Tragic Last Years of Adlai Stevenson* (New York: Coward-McCann, 1968), 149, 172–86; Macdonald to Arthur M. Schlesinger, Jr., 16 November 1952, in box 45, folder 1109; and Macdonald to Nicola Chiaromonte, 6 July 1965, in box 10, folder 244, Macdonald Papers.

20. Dwight Macdonald, "A Day at the White House," *Discriminations*, 140–42, 153–54; Eric F. Goldman, *The Tragedy of Lyndon Johnson* (New York: Dell, 1969), 471–72.

21. Macdonald, "A Day at the White House," 145, 154; Goldman, *Tragedy of Lyndon Johnson*, 472.

22. Norman Mailer, *The Armies of the Night* (New York: Signet, 1968), 37, 55.

23. Norman Mailer to Macdonald, 13 February 1958, Macdonald to Mailer, 11 November 1964, and Mailer to Macdonald, 24 November 1964, in box 32, folder 804, Macdonald Papers.

24. Mailer, *Armies of the Night*, 38–39, 55; "The Banners of Dissent," *Time* 90 (27 October 1967), 25; Hilary Mills, *Mailer: A Biography* (New York: Empire Books, 1982), 314–16.

25. Mailer, *Armies of the Night*, 204–11; Dwight Macdonald, "*Armies of the Night*, or Bad Man Makes Good," *Discriminations*, 210–16; Mailer to Macdonald, 20 May 1968, in box 32, folder 804, Macdonald Papers.

26. Dwight Macdonald, "Will They Ever Get 'Getting Straight' Straight?," *New York Times* sec. 2, 12 July 1970, 11.

27. Ibid.; Jessica Mitford, *The Trial of Dr. Spock* (New York: Vintage, 1970), 32.

28. Dwight Macdonald, "Civil Disobedience," *Discriminations*, 441–47; Macdonald to Mary McCarthy, 27 March 1967, in box 31, folder 780, Macdonald Papers; Macdonald, "The Neo-Non-Conservatism," *Memoirs of a Revolutionist*, 333–43.

29. Macdonald, "Civil Disobedience," 447–48; Macdonald, Noam Chomsky, and Alexander Calder for Resist, 1 May 1970, copy in author's possession; "An Appeal for Nationwide Tax Resistance," n.d., copy in author's possession.

30. Herbert Marcuse to Macdonald, 16 May 1973, in box 55, folder 1340; and Hannah Arendt to Macdonald, 1 May 1973, in box 6, folder 98, Macdonald Papers.

31. Macdonald, *Discriminations*, 414; Macdonald to editor of New York

Post, 19 June 1967, in box 9, folder 202; and Macdonald to Nicola Chiaromonte, 21 June 1967, in box 10, folder 244, Macdonald Papers.

32. Macdonald to Hannah Arendt, 30 August 1967, in box 6, folder 98, Macdonald Papers; Arendt, "He's All Dwight," 31–33; Macklin, "Please, high culture," 33, 34.

33. *New York Times*, 20 December 1982, sec. D, p. 14.

Bibliography

MANUSCRIPT COLLECTIONS

Dwight Macdonald, Papers. Yale University Library.

WORKS BY DWIGHT MACDONALD

Books

Macdonald, Dwight. *Henry Wallace: The Man and the Myth* (New York: Vanguard, 1948).
_____. *Memoirs of a Revolutionist: Essays in Political Criticism* (Cleveland: Meridian, 1958).
_____. *Against the American Grain* (New York: Random House, 1962).
_____. *On Movies* (New York: Berkley Medallion, 1971).
_____. *Discriminations: Essays and Afterthoughts, 1938–1974* (New York: Grossman, 1974).

Articles

_____. "'Time' and Henry Luce," *Nation* 144 (1 May, 1937).
_____. "'Fortune' Magazine," *Nation* 144 (8 May 1937).
_____. Letter to the editor, *New Republic* 90 (19 May 1937).
_____. "Time, Fortune, Life," *Nation* 144 (22 May 1937).
_____. Letter to the editor, *Nation* 144 (19 June 1937).
_____. "Laugh and Lie Down," *Partisan Review* 4 (December 1937).

———. "Cross Country," *Partisan Review* 4 (February 1938).

Macdonald, Dwight and editors. "Discussion: Once More Kronstadt," *New International* 4 (July 1938).

———. "Reading from Left to Right," *New International* 4 (July 1938).

———. "War and the Intellectuals: Act II," *Partisan Review* 6 (Spring 1939).

———. "Reading from Left to Right," *New International* 5 (July 1939).

———. "Notes on a War," *New International* 5 (November 1939).

———. "Socialist Stomatology," *New International* 5 (November 1939).

———. "The United States at War," *New International* 6 (June 1940).

———. "Notes on a Strange War," *Partisan Review* 7 (May-June 1940).

———. "Reading from Left to Right," *New International* 6 (June 1940).

———. "National Defense: The Case for Socialism" *Partisan Review* 7 (July-August 1940).

———. "Trotsky is Dead," *Partisan Review* 7 (September-October 1940).

———. "Fascism: A New Social Order," *New International* 7 (May 1941).

Greenberg, Clement and Dwight Macdonald. "Ten Propositions on the War," *Partisan Review* 8 (July-August 1941).

———. "Reply by Greenberg and Macdonald," *Partisan Review* 8 (November-December 1941).

Macdonald, Dwight. "The Burnhamian Revolution," *Partisan Review* 9 (January-February 1942).

———. "The (American) People's Century," *Partisan Review* 9 (July-August 1942).

———. "Roosevelt's Conservative War," *Partisan Review* 9 (November-December 1942).

Letters from Dwight Macdonald and editors. *Partisan Review* 10 (July-August 1943).

Macdonald, Dwight. "The Future of Democratic Values," *Partisan Review* 10 (July-August 1943).

———. "Why Politics?," *Politics* 1 (February 1944).

———. "A Theory of 'Popular Culture,'" *Politics* 1 (February 1944).

———. "Comment: The Wilson Speech," *Politics* 1 (March 1944).

———. "On the Conduct of the Lynn Case," *Politics* 1 (April 1944).

———. "The Supreme Court's Moot Suit," *Politics* 1 (June 1944).

———. "How 'Practical' is a Radically Segregated Army?," *Politics* 1 (July 1944).

———. "By Way of Rejoinder," *Politics* 1 (July 1944).

———. "'Here Lies Our Road!' said Writer to Reader," *Politics* 1 (September 1944).

———. "Thomas for President?," *Politics* 1 (October 1944).

———. "Comment: Russomania in England," *Politics* 1 (November 1944).

———. "Wallace and the Labor Draft," *Politics* 2 (February 1945).

———. "'Why?'—Underside View," *Politics* 2 (April 1945).

———. "Conscription and Conscientious Objection," *Politics* 2 (June 1945).

———. "Politicking," *Politics* 3 (January 1946).

———. "The Root Is Man," part one, *Politics* 3 (April 1946).

———. Reply by the editor, *Politics* 3 (May 1946).

———. "The Root Is Man," part two, *Politics* 3 (July 1946).

Peck, James and Dwight Macdonald. "Atomic Bombs, Union Made," *Politics* 3 (August 1946).

Macdonald, Dwight. Editor's reply, *Politics* 3 (November 1946).

———. Review of *Art and Social Nature*, *Politics* 3 (November 1946).

———. "'Partisan Review' and 'Politics,'" *Politics* 3 (December 1946).

———. Comment on Simone Weil, "Factory Work," *Politics* 3 (December 1946).

———. "Why Destroy Draft Cards?," *Politics* 4 (March-April 1947).

———. "Peacemakers," *Politics* 5 (Spring 1948).

———. "On the Elections," *Politics* 5 (Summer 1948).

———. "A Personal Letter to 2500 People," *Politics* 5 (Winter 1948).

———. "The Uncommon People," *Politics* 6 (Winter 1949).

———. Editor's reply, *Politics* 6 (Winter 1949).

———. "The Waldorf Conference," special insert, *Politics* 6 (Winter 1949).

———. "A New Theory of Totalitarianism," *New Leader* 34 (14 May 1951).

———. "Why I Am No Longer a Socialist," *Liberation* 3 (May 1958).

———. "Parajournalism II: *The New Yorker* and Tom Wolfe," *New York Review of Books* 6 (3 February 1966).

———. Preface to *Politics* 1 (New York: Greenwood Reprint Corporation, 1968).

———. "Politics," *Esquire* 70 (July 1968).

———. "An Open Letter to Michael Harrington," *New York Review of Books* 11 (5 December 1968).

_____. "Will They Ever Get 'Getting Straight' Straight?," *New York Times*, sec. 2, 12 July 1970.

BOOKS AND ARTICLES

Aaron, Daniel. *Writers on the Left* (New York: Avon, 1965).

Allen, Woody. *Without Feathers* (New York: Warner Books, 1976).

American Committee to Defend Leon Trotsky. *News Bulletin*, no. 6 (3 May 1937).

Arendt, Hannah. *Eichmann in Jerusalem: A Report on the Banality of Evil* (New York: Viking, 1963).

_____. "He's All Dwight," *New York Review of Books* 11 (1 August 1968).

_____. *The Jew as Pariah: Jewish Identity and Politics in the Modern Age*, ed. Ron H. Feldman (New York: Grove Press, 1978).

_____. *The Origins of Totalitarianism* (Cleveland: World, 1958).

"As to Facts and Values: An Exchange," *Partisan Review* 9 (May-June 1942).

Atlas, James. *Delmore Schwartz: The Life of an American Poet* (New York: Farrar, Straus and Giroux, 1977).

"The Banners of Dissent," *Time* 90 (27 October 1967).

Barnes, Jack. Introduction to James P. Cannon, *Letters from Prison* (New York: Merit, 1968).

Barrett, William. "The Resistance," *Partisan Review* 13 (September-October 1946).

_____. *The Truants: Adventures Among the Intellectuals* (Garden City, N.Y.: Doubleday, 1982).

Bell, Daniel. *The End of Ideology: On the Exhaustion of Political Ideas in the Fifties* (New York: Free Press, 1962).

_____. *Marxian Socialism in the United States* (Princeton: Princeton University Press, 1967).

_____. "The Strange Tale of Bruno R.," *New Leader* 42 (28 September 1959).

_____. *The Winding Passage: Essays and Sociological Journeys, 1960–1980* (Cambridge, Mass.: Abt, 1980).

Bourne, Randolph. *War and the Intellectuals: Collected Essays, 1915–1919*, ed. Carl Resek (New York: Harper & Row, 1964).

Bundy, McGeorge. "A Letter to Twelve College Presidents," *Atlantic Monthly* 175 (May 1945).

Burnham, James. "Politics for the Nursery Set," *Partisan Review* 12 (Spring 1945).

Carr, E. H. *The Bolshevik Revolution*, vol. 1 (London: Macmillan, 1966).

Chambers, Whittaker. *Witness* (Chicago: Henry Regnery, 1952).

Chiaromonte, Nicola. *The Worm of Consciousness and Other Essays* (New York: Harcourt Brace Jovanovich, 1976).

Chomsky, Noam. *American Power and the New Mandarins* (New York: Vintage, 1969).

_____. "Nationalism and Conflict in Palestine," *Columbia Forum* 13 (Winter 1969).

"Confrontation: The Old Left and the New," *American Scholar* 36 (Autumn 1967).

Corry, John. "Spokesman for the New Left," *New York Times Magazine* (23 January 1966).

Cowley, Malcolm. *The Dream of the Golden Mountains* (New York: Viking, 1980).

_____. —*And I Worked at the Writer's Trade: Chapters of Literary History, 1918–1978* (New York: Viking, 1978).

_____. "Partisan Review," *New Republic* 90 (19 October 1938).

_____. "The Record of a Trial," *New Republic* 90 (7 April 1937).

_____. "Ten Little Magazines," *New Republic* 116 (31 March 1947).

Crews, Frederick. *Out of My System: Psychoanalysis, Ideology, and Critical Method* (New York: Oxford University Press, 1975).

Dellinger, David. Letter to the editor, *Politics* 3 (November 1946).

Deutscher, Isaac. *The Prophet Outcast: Trotsky 1929–1940* (New York: Vintage, 1965).

_____. *Stalin: A Political Biography* (New York: Oxford University Press, 1949).

Dickstein, Morris. *Gates of Eden: American Culture in the Sixties* (New York: Basic Books, 1977).

Diggins, John P. *The American Left in the Twentieth Century* (New York: Harcourt Brace Jovanovich, 1973).

_____. *Up from Communism: Conservative Odysseys in American Intellectual History* (New York: Harper & Row, 1975).

Draper, Theodore. *The Rediscovery of Black Nationalism* (New York: Viking, 1970).

Dunne, Finley Peter. *Mr. Dooley: Now and Forever* (Stanford: Stanford University Press, 1954).

"Editorial Comment," *New Masses* 16 (26 February 1935).

Editorial. *Fourth International* 1 (May 1940).

Editor's reply. *Partisan Review* 20 (November-December 1953).

Elson, Robert T. *Time Inc.: The Intimate History of a Publishing Enterprise, 1923–1941* (New York: Atheneum, 1968).

Epernay, Mark. *The McLandress Dimension* (Boston: Houghton Mifflin, 1963).

Farrell, James T. *The League of Frightened Philistines* (New York: Vanguard, 1945).

Ferber, Michael and Staughton Lynd. *The Resistance* (Boston: Beacon, 1971).

Fiedler, Leslie. "*Partisan Review*: Phoenix or Dodo?," *Perspectives USA* 16 (Spring 1956).

Finn, James. *Protest: Pacifism and Politics* (New York: Vintage, 1968).

Forgue, Guy J., ed. *Letters of H. L. Mencken* (Boston: Northeastern University Press, 1981).

Gates, Albert. "In Reply," *New International* 8 (April 1942).

Gilbert, James B. *Designing the Industrial State: The Intellectual Pursuit of Collectivism in America, 1880–1940* (Chicago: Quadrangle, 1972).

———. *Writers and Partisans: A History of Literary Radicalism in America* (New York: John Wiley and Sons, 1968).

Gill, Brendan. "Happy Times," *Yale Alumni Magazine* (October 1973).

Ginsberg, Allen. "America," in *Howl and Other Poems* (San Francisco: City Lights, 1959).

"Glamour Pusses," *Time* 44 (9 September 1946).

Glazer, Nathan. *Remembering the Answers: Essays on the American Student Revolt* (New York: Basic Books, 1970).

Glazer, Penina M. "From the Old Left to the New: Radical Criticism in the 1940s," *American Quarterly* 24 (December 1972).

Goldman, Eric F. *The Crucial Decade—and After: America 1945–1960* (New York: Vintage, 1960).

———. *Rendezvous With Destiny* (New York: Vintage, 1956).

_____. *The Tragedy of Lyndon Johnson* (New York: Dell, 1969).

Goodman, Paul. *Growing Up Absurd* (New York: Random House, 1960).

_____. "The New Reformation," in Irving Howe, ed., *Beyond the New Left* (New York: McCall, 1970).

_____. "Our Best Journalist," *Dissent* 5 (Winter 1958).

_____. *People or Personnel and Like a Conquered Province* (New York: Vintage, 1968).

Greenberg, Clement and Dwight Macdonald. "Ten Propositions on the War," *Partisan Review* 8 (July-August 1941).

Grumbach, Doris. *The Company She Kept* (London: Bodley Head, 1967).

Harrington, Michael. *Fragments of the Century: A Social Autobiography* (New York: Saturday Review Press, 1973).

Hart, Henry. Letter to the editor, *Nation* 144 (26 June 1937).

_____, ed. *The Writer in a Changing World* (New York: Equinox Cooperative Press, 1937).

Hays, Arthur Garfield. Letter to the editor, *Politics* 1 (April 1944).

Heilbroner, Robert. "Military America," *New York Review of Books* 15 (23 July 1970).

Hentoff, Nat. *Peace Agitator: The Story of A. J. Muste* (New York: Macmillan, 1963).

Hicks, Granville. "A 'Nation' Divided," *New Masses* 35 (7 December 1937).

_____. *Part of the Truth* (New York: Harcourt, Brace and World, 1965).

_____. *Where We Came Out* (New York: Viking, 1954).

_____. "The Writers' Congress," *New Masses* 23 (15 June 1937).

Hook, Sidney. "Failure of the Left," *Partisan Review* 10 (March-April 1943).

_____. *Political Power and Personal Freedom* (New York: Criterion, 1959).

_____. Horowitz, Irving Louis. C. *Wright Mills: An American Utopian* (New York: Free Press, 1983).

Howe, Irving. *Decline of the New* (New York: Horizon Press, 1970).

_____. "The Dilemma of Partisan Review," *New International* 8 (February 1942).

_____. *Leon Trotsky* (New York: Penguin, 1979).

_____. *A Margin of Hope: An Intellectual Autobiography* (New York: Harcourt Brace Jovanovich, 1982).

_____. *Steady Work: Essays in the Politics of Democratic Radicalism* (New York: Harcout, Brace and World, 1966).

Hughes, H. Stuart. *An Approach to Peace* (New York: Atheneum, 1966).

_____. "On Being a Candidate," *Commentary* 35 (February 1963).

Jacobs, Paul and Saul Landau. *The New Radicals: A Report with Documents* (New York: Vintage, 1966).

Jerome, V. J. *Intellectuals and the War* (New York: Workers Library, 1940).

Jezer, Marty. *The Dark Ages: Life in the United States, 1945–1960* (Boston: South End Press, 1982).

Johnson, Walter, ed. *The Papers of Adlai E. Stevenson*, vol. 8 (Boston: Little, Brown, 1979).

Kadushin, Charles. *The American Intellectual Elite* (Boston: Little, Brown, 1974).

Kampf, Louis. "The Trouble With Literature . . . ," *Change* 2 (May-June 1970).

Kazin, Alfred. *New York Jew* (New York: Knopf, 1978).

_____. *Starting Out in the Thirties* (Boston: Atlantic-Little, Brown, 1965).

Kemler, Edgar. *The Irreverent Mr. Mencken* (Boston: Little, Brown, 1950).

Keniston, Kenneth. *Young Radicals: Notes on Committed Youth* (New York: Harcourt, Brace and World, 1968).

King, Richard. *The Party of Eros: Radical Social Thought and the Realm of Freedom* (Chapel Hill: University of North Carolina Press, 1972).

Koestler, Arthur. *The Trail of the Dinosaur and other Essays* (New York: Macmillan, 1956).

_____. *The Yogi and the Commissar* (New York: Macmillan, 1945).

Kostelanetz, Richard. *Master Minds: Portraits of Contemporary American Artists and Intellectuals* (New York: Macmillan, 1969).

Kristol, Irving. "'Civil Liberties,' 1952—A Study in Confusion," *Commentary* 13 (March 1952).

Kunitz, Stanley J., ed. *Twentieth Century Authors*, first supplement (New York: H. H. Wilson, 1955).

Lasch, Christopher. *The Agony of the American Left* (New York: Vintage, 1969).

_____. *The New Radicalism in America 1889–1963: The Intellectual as a Social Type* (New York: Knopf, 1965).

Lelchuk, Alan. "Philip Rahv: The Last Years," in Arthur Edelstein, ed. *Images and Ideas in American Culture: The Functions of Criticism* (Hanover, N.H.: University Press of New England, 1979).

Lenin, Vladimir. *State and Revolution* (New York: International Publishers, 1932).

Lerner, Max. *Actions and Passions: Notes on the Multiple Revolution of Our Time* (New York: Simon and Schuster, 1949).

Letter from David Dellinger, Donald Harrington, et al. *Politics* 4 (January 1947).

Letter to the editor. *Nation* 149 (26 August 1939).

Lottman, Herbert R. *Albert Camus: A Biography* (Garden City, N.Y.: Doubleday, 1979).

Lynd, Staughton. "'Again—Don't Tread on Me,'" *Newsweek* 76 (6 July 1970).

_____. "Coalition Politics or Nonviolent Revolution?," *Liberation* 10 (June-July 1965).

_____, ed. *Nonviolence in America: A Documentary History* (Indianapolis: Bobbs-Merrill, 1966).

_____. "The Prospects of the New Left," in John H. M. Laslett and Seymour Martin Lipset, eds. *Failure of a Dream?: Essays in the History of American Socialism* (Garden City, New York: Doubleday, 1974).

_____. "Socialism, the Forbidden Word," *Studies on the Left* 3 (Summer 1963).

_____. "Towards a History of the New Left," in Priscilla Long, ed. *The New Left: A Collection of Documents* (Boston: Porter Sargent, 1969).

McCarthy, Mary. *On the Contrary* (New York: Farrar, Straus and Giroux, 1961).

McKenzie, Barbara. *Mary McCarthy* (New York: Twayne, 1966).

MacIver, Robert and Reinhold Niebuhr. Letters to the editor, *Politics* 2 (May 1945).

Macklin, F. Anthony. "Please, high culture: An interview with critic Dwight Macdonald," *Film Heritage* 8 (Spring 1972).

MacLeish, Archibald. "Post-war Writers and Pre-war Readers," *New Republic* 102 (10 June 1940).

Mailer, Norman. *Advertisements for Myself* (New York: G. P. Putnam's Sons, 1959).

———. *The Armies of the Night* (New York: Signet, 1968).

Malaquais, Jean. Letter to the editor, *Politics* 2 (September 1945).

Markowitz, Norman D. *The Rise and Fall of the People's Century: Henry A. Wallace and American Liberalism, 1941–1948* (New York: Free Press, 1973).

Mazzocco, Robert. "Good Man," *New York Review of Books* 14 (21 May 1970).

Melman, Seymour. *Pentagon Capitalism: The Political Economy of War* (New York: McGraw-Hill, 1970).

Meyers, Marvin. *The Jacksonian Persuasion: Politics and Belief* (Stanford: Stanford University Press, 1960).

Miliband, Ralph. "Mills and Politics," in Irving Louis Horowitz, ed. *The New Sociology: Essays in Social Science and Social Theory in Honor of C. Wright Mills* (New York: Oxford University Press, 1964).

Mills, Hilary. *Mailer: A Biography* (New York: Empire Books, 1982).

Mitford, Jessica. *The Trial of Dr. Spock* (New York: Vintage, 1970).

Moynihan, Daniel Patrick. "One-Third of a Nation," *New Republic* 186 (9 June 1982).

Muggeridge, Malcolm. *The Most of Malcolm Muggeridge* (New York: Simon and Schuster, 1966).

Myers, Constance Ashton. *The Prophet's Army: Trotskyists in America, 1928–1941* (Westport, Conn.: Greenwood, 1977).

Nathan, Otto and Heinz Norden, eds. *Einstein on Peace* (New York: Schocken, 1960).

Navasky, Victor S. *Naming Names* (New York: Viking, 1980).

Newfield, Jack. *A Prophetic Minority* (New York: Signet, 1967).

Nomad, Max. *Aspects of Revolt* (New York: Bookman Associates, 1959).

Oglesby, Carl, ed. Introduction to *The New Left Reader* (New York: Grove Press, 1969).

"Old Left, New Broom," *Time* 108 (6 December 1976).

O'Neill, William L. *A Better World: The Great Schism: Stalinism and the American Intellectuals* (New York: Simon and Schuster, 1982).

"On the 'Brooks-MacLeish' Thesis," *Partisan Review* 9 (January-February 1942).

Orwell, Sonia and Ian Angus, eds. *The Collected Essays, Journalism and*

Letters of George Orwell, vol. 3 (New York: Harcourt Brace Jovanovich, 1968).

"Our Country and Our Culture: A Symposium," *Partisan Review* 19 (May-June 1952).

"Partisan Review Controversy," *New International* 8 (April 1942).

Paul, Sherman. *Edmund Wilson: A Study of Literary Vocation in Our Time* (Urbana: University of Illinois Press, 1965).

Peck, James. *Underdogs and Upperdogs* (Canterbury, N.H.: Greenleaf, 1969).

Phillips, William. "Fashions of Revolt," *Commentary* 40 (October 1965).

_____. "The Lions and the Foxes," *Partisan Review* 12 (Spring 1945).

_____ and Philip Rahv. "The Fugitives from Politics: Dwight Macdonald," *Partisan Review* 13 (November-December 1946).

Podhoretz, Norman. *Breaking Ranks: A Political Memoir* (New York: Harper & Row, 1979).

_____. *Doings and Undoings: The Fifties and After in American Writing* (New York: Farrar, Straus, 1964).

_____. *Making It* (New York: Random House, 1967).

Potter, David M. *People of Plenty: Economic Abundance and the American Character* (Chicago: University of Chicago Press, 1958).

"Professor Out of Step," *Time* 101 (1 January 1973).

Rahv, Philip. "Disillusionment and Partial Answers," *Partisan Review* 15 (May 1948).

_____. "Ten Propositions and Eight Errors," *Partisan Review* 8 (November-December 1941).

"Rebellion," *Saturday Review* 103 (25 April 1970).

Rideout, Walter B. *The Radical Novel in the United States, 1900–1954* (Cambridge: Harvard University Press, 1956).

Roskolenko, Harry. *When I Was Last on Cherry Street* (New York: Stein and Day, 1965).

Roszak, Theodore. *The Making of a Counter-Culture: Reflections on the Technocratic Society and Its Youthful Opposition* (Garden City, N.Y.: Doubleday, 1969).

Rustin, Byard. *Down the Line* (Chicago: Quadrangle, 1971).

Safire, William. *Safire's Political Dictionary* (New York: Random House, 1978).

Scheer, Robert, ed. *Eldridge Cleaver: Post-Prison Writings and Speeches* (New York: Vintage, 1968).

Schlesinger, Arthur M., Jr. *A Thousand Days: John F. Kennedy in the White House* (New York: Fawcett Crest, 1967).

————. *The Vital Center* (Boston: Houghton Mifflin, 1962).

Serge, Victor. *Memoirs of a Revolutionary, 1901–1944* (New York: Oxford University Press, 1963).

Shachtman, Max. "Radicalism in the Thirties: The Trotskyist View," in Rita James Simon, ed. *As We Saw the Thirties* (Urbana: University of Illinois Press, 1967).

Shanker, Albert. Letter to the editor, *Politics* 5 (Summer 1948).

Shapiro, Karl. Letter to the editor, *Partisan Review* 8 (September-October 1941).

Shenker, Israel. "Ideological Labels Changing Along With the Label-Makers," *New York Times* (12 November 1970).

Simpson, Eileen. *Poets in Their Youth: A Memoir* (New York: Random House, 1982).

Sontag, Susan. *Styles of Radical Will* (New York: Delta, 1969).

Speer, Albert. *Inside the Third Reich: Memoirs* (New York: Macmillan, 1970).

Spender, Stephen. "Defense of Britain," *Partisan Review* 7 (September-October 1940).

"A Statement by the Editors," *Partisan Review* 9 (January-February 1942).

"Statement of the L.C.F.S.," *Partisan Review* 6 (Summer 1939).

Steinfels, Peter. *The Neoconservatives: The Men Who Are Changing America's Politics* (New York: Simon and Schuster, 1979).

Stone, I. F. "Henry Wallace—a Great American," *Nation* 159 (22 July 1944).

————. *In a Time of Torment* (New York: Vintage, 1968).

————. *The Truman Era* (New York: Monthly Review Press, 1953).

Swanberg, W. A. *Norman Thomas: The Last Idealist* (New York: Charles Scribner's Sons, 1976).

"Symposium: Thirty Years Later: Memories of the First American Writers' Congress," *American Scholar* 35 (Summer 1966).

"Symposium: What Will I Do When America Goes to War?," *Modern Monthly* 9 (June 1935).

Trilling, Diana. *We Must March My Darlings* (New York: Harcourt Brace Jovanovich, 1977).

Trotsky, Leon. *In Defense of Marxism: Against the Petty-Bourgeois Opposition* (New York: Merit, 1965).

————. *My Life* (New York: Charles Scribner's Sons, 1930).

————. "The U.S.S.R. in War," *New International* 5 (November 1939).

Utley, Freda. *Odyssey of a Liberal: Memoir* (Washington, D.C.: Washington National Press, 1970).

Wallace, Henry. *Soviet Asia Mission* (New York: Reynal and Hitchcock, 1946).

Walton, Richard J. *The Remnants of Power: The Tragic Last Years of Adlai Stevenson* (New York: Coward-McCann, 1968).

Walzer, Michael. *Just and Unjust Wars* (New York: Basic Books, 1977).

Warren, Robert Penn. *Who Speaks for the Negro?* (New York: Vintage, 1966).

Weinraub, Bernard. "The Brilliancy of Black," in Harold Hayes ed. *Smiling Through the Apocalypse: Esquire's History of the Sixties* (New York: McCall, 1969).

"What is Henry Wallace?," *Time* 51 (15 March 1948).

Whitfield, Stephen J. "The Holocaust and the American Jewish Intellectual," *Judaism* (Fall 1979).

Wilson, Edmund. *Classics and Commercials: A Literary Chronicle of the 1940's* (New York: Farrar, Straus and Giroux, 1950).

Wistrich, Robert. *Trotsky: Fate of a Revolutionary* (London: Robson, . 1979).

Wittner, Lawrence S. *Rebels Against War: The American Peace Movement 1941–1960* (New York: Columbia University Press, 1969).

Young-Bruehl, Elizabeth. *Hannah Arendt: For Love of the World* (New Haven, Conn.: Yale University Press, 1982).

Zinn, Howard. *SNCC: The New Abolitionists* (Boston: Beacon, 1965).

UNPUBLISHED MATERIAL

Kirby, Linda Kaye. "Communism, the Discovery of Totalitarianism, and the Cold War: *Partisan Review*, 1934 to 1948" (Ph.D. diss., University of Colorado, 1970).

Index

Macdonald, Dwight
American Committee for Cul-
    tural Freedom and, 93, 94
armaments and, 54
attack on Finland and, 22
Brooks and, 33
bureaucratic collectivism and,
    26, 67
Cannon and, 28–30
capitalism and, 55
civil disobedience and, 130–31
death of, 133
difference between progressives
    and radicals according to,
    67–68
Dissent and, 96
elections and, 80
Encounter and, 94, 95
formation of *Politics* and, 43
Fortune and, 7, 8, 9
genocide and, 59–61
Goodman and, 110–11
Hiroshima and, 63–64, 68
Howe and, 31
joins the Socialist Workers
    party, 17
League of Cultural Freedom and
    Socialism and, 16
MacLeish and, 33
Mailer and, 129–30
marriage and, 9, 96
Marxism and, 24–25, 41, 53,
    66, 69, 100
Mills and, 108–9
New Deal and, 35, 53, 58
New International and, 19, 23,
    27
New Left and, 104–5, 122–23
New Yorker and, 90, 122
pacifism and, 70, 73–88, 126
Partisan Review and, 12, 41–42
picketing and, 75
racism and, 57–58, 76
reasons for being a Trotskyist,
    24, 27
Resist and, 130

at the Second American Writers'
    Congress, 12–13
socialism and, 35–36, 67
Students for a Democratic
    Society and, 123–24
Trotsky and, 11, 20
Vietnam and, 3, 125–27
views on Roosevelt, 24, 40
views on the Soviet Union, 22,
    84, 86
views on war, 31–32, 35, 38,
    43–44, 46–47, 131–32
at the Waldorf Conference,
    81–83
Wallace and, 77–80
at the White House Festival of
    the Arts, 128
Workers party and, 27–28
Macdonald, Nancy, 43, 96
McGovern, George, 3
Machajski, Waclaw, 25
MacIver, Robert, 63
MacLeish, Archibald, 3, 7, 12,
    32–33, 54
McLuhan, Marshall, 45
McNamara, Robert S., 104
McReynolds, David, 127
Mailer, Norman, 83, 89–90, 129–30
Malaquais, Jean, 61
Malcolm X, 119
Managerial Revolution, The (Burn-
    ham), 26
Mansfield, Mike, 115
Marching Song (Lawson), 13
Marcuse, Herbert, 111–12, 132
Markowitz, Norman D., 79
Marquart, Frank, 96
Marshall Plan, 84
Marx, Karl, 7, 68
Marxism, Macdonald and, 24–25,
    41, 53, 66, 69, 100
Matthiessen, F. O., 81, 82
Mayer, Milton, 45, 76
Memoirs of a Revolutionist, 132
Memoirs of Hecate County (Wilson),
    34